Bookkeeping for Small Businesses

Andy Lymer

First published in Great Britain in 1984 by Hodder Headline. An Hachette UK company.

This edition published in 2015 by John Murray Learning

Copyright © 1984, 1993, 2003, 2010 A.G. Piper, A.M. Lymer and N. Rowbottom

Copyright © 2015 Andy Lymer

The right of Andy Lymer to be identified as the Author of the Work has been asserted by him in accordance with the Copyright, Designs and Patents Act 1988.

Database right Hodder & Stoughton (makers)

The *Teach Yourself* name is a registered trademark of Hachette UK.

British Library Cataloguing in Publication Data: a catalogue record for this title is available from the British Library.

ISBN 9781473609143

eISBN 9781473609150

1

The publisher has used its best endeavours to ensure that any website addresses referred to in this book are correct and active at the time of going to press. However, the publisher and the author have no responsibility for the websites and can make no guarantee that a site will remain live or that the content will remain relevant, decent or appropriate.

The publisher has made every effort to mark as such all words which it believes to be trademarks. The publisher should also like to make it clear that the presence of a word in the book, whether marked or unmarked, in no way affects its legal status as a trademark.

Every reasonable effort has been made by the publisher to trace the copyright holders of material in this book. Any errors or omissions should be notified in writing to the publisher, who will endeavour to rectify the situation for any reprints and future editions.

Cover image © iStock

Typeset by Cenveo® Publisher Services.

Printed and bound in Great Britain by CPI Group (UK) Ltd., Croydon, CR0 4YY.

John Murray Learning policy is to use papers that are natural, renewable and recyclable products and made from wood grown in sustainable forests. The logging and manufacturing processes are expected to conform to the environmental regulations of the country of origin.

Carmelite House
50 Victoria Embankment
London EC4Y 0DZ
www.hodder.co.uk

Also available
in ebook

Contents

Advantages of using a computer in bookkeeping
Management of information technology in bookkeeping
Further information

18 Partnership

UK Partnership Act 1890
Creating or changing a partnership

19 Limited companies

Public and private companies
The Memorandum and Articles of Association
Share capital
Debentures
Unsecured loan stock
Books of account
Accounts and audit

20 The analysis and interpretation of accounts

Analysis of the Final Accounts
The Profit and Loss Account
The Statement of Financial Position

Taking it further

General bookkeeping help
Other business advice and help
Courses and qualifications
Bookkeeping software

Introduction

The aim of this book is to provide a concise introductory text which is both readable and interesting, and clearly relevant to the routine recording of business transactions, while at the same time covering the main syllabus requirements of elementary examinations in bookkeeping.

There is a difference between bookkeeping and accountancy. Bookkeeping is concerned with the initial recording of financial transactions rather than their detailed interpretation or use as a decision-making aid. It is on the process of bookkeeping, rather than the use of its output, that this book focuses. The second chapter introduces some common business documents. These often provide the basic raw material from which the subsequent bookkeeping entries and financial statements are prepared. The use of computers in keeping business books may lead to the elimination of some of these documents, but the accurate recording of each business transaction remains essential. These records provide an important part of the material which is used and interpreted by the accountant and the manager.

This edition includes an introductory chapter on the use of computers in support of the bookkeeping activity. Information technology is playing an increasing role in the collection, recording and processing of accounting data and therefore some appreciation of its impact is necessary. However, the basic principles of bookkeeping remain unchanged and it continues to be important that bookkeepers understand these principles.

In this text the style which has proved so successful in earlier editions has been retained where appropriate, and the guidance provided by previous authors is gratefully acknowledged.

This edition also includes 'Objectives' at the beginning and 'Focus Points' at the end of each chapter. The 'Objectives' provide an overview of each chapter and after completion you should review the 'Focus Points' before going on to the next chapter. The 'Taking it further' section offers various suggestions for further improvement of your bookkeeping skills after you have worked through this guide. It also suggests ways for you to gain qualifications in this area to illustrate your skills.

Bookkeeping is not mysterious: indeed its 'rules' are logical and straightforward, and readily mastered with practice. Thus the text includes many worked examples, carefully graded questions and three complete examination papers with fully worked solutions. To gain the most from this support you should always prepare your own solutions to each question and then compare them with the ones provided in the text.

The permanent VAT rate at the time of writing of 20% has been used in some examples but the principles of recording VAT remain the same whatever its rate.

A. Lymer May 2015

Acknowledgements

The authors and publishers are grateful to the Royal Society of Arts Examinations Board (now OCR), for permission to reproduce the complete examination papers at the end of this book. Answers have been amended to take into account changes in accounting rules and terminology. Any errors in these questions are therefore those of the author, not of the examination board.

What is bookkeeping?

In this chapter you will learn:

▶ *About Books of Prime Entry*
▶ *About double entry bookkeeping*
▶ *That detailed records are essential*

Question What is bookkeeping?

Answer The process of correctly recording in **Books of Account** cash, credit and other transactions.

Question What are Books of Account?

Answer The primary Book of Account is called the **Ledger,** so called because all transactions, after first being recorded in subsidiary books, are afterwards grouped or summarized in Accounts in the Ledger.

Question Why should goods or services be bought or sold on 'credit'?

Answer Almost all business dealings are conducted on a credit basis to avoid the inconvenience and danger of carrying large amounts of cash. The supplier of goods or services is usually content to accept payment at some future date. The main exception is the retail trade for a private individual.

Question Why is it necessary to record these transactions?

Answer Even in the smallest business the proprietor or manager will want to have accurate and up-to-date information about how much has been bought and sold, how much money has been received for sales, how much has been paid away for purchases, etc. Private individuals often find it convenient to have the same information for their cash receipts and payments. You can imagine that with a very large business, chaos would quickly result without this information.

Question So bookkeeping really involves analysing in some way or another these various transactions?

Answer You could say it involves recording these transactions so as to permit analysis in a systematic fashion, in a way that can be applied to all businesses of whatever kind, and that is intelligible not only now but at any future time.

Question Do you mean by this 'the Double Entry System of bookkeeping'?

Answer Yes.

Question Why is it called 'Double Entry'.

Answer Every transaction has at least two effects, or aspects. We describe one aspect as a debit and one aspect as a credit.

Question So it does not mean recording the same transaction twice?

Answer No, not at all. If I have bought goods worth £100 from Smith which are payable in 30 days' time, the first part of the transaction is that my business has received goods which it hopes to resell at a profit; the second part of the transaction is that Smith, my supplier, has become my creditor, and has a claim on me for £100.

Question Would it be the same if you had bought the goods and paid for them at once, instead of getting them on credit?

Answer Yes, that would be a cash purchase. But instead of Smith becoming my creditor, I would have to record the £100 reduction in cash held by the business.

Question What is the real advantage of the Double Entry System?

Answer For the reason that every transaction can be looked at from its twofold aspect; the record made is complete instead of being only partial.

The practical advantage is that you put the whole of the facts on record. These are:

▶ The business has gained £100 worth of goods (this is described as a debit).

▶ Smith has a claim on you for £100 (this is described as a credit).

Obviously, to know these facts is of importance in any business.

Question Well, does this hold good with situations other than buying transactions? Would the same state of affairs exist with the selling of goods?

Answer In exactly the same way. The first aspect in the selling transaction is that your business has given up £100 worth of goods as an ordinary sale. The second is that the person who has received them has become your debtor, i.e. they are indebted to you, on the assumption that you, in this case, are giving credit, because you are the supplier.

Question Does the Double Entry System stop at this?

Answer No. It goes much further. Because of this twofold aspect I have been talking about, it enables you to compare the proceeds of the sales you have made with the cost to you of the goods you have bought, and so obtain your profit or loss on trading.

Similarly, as it shows the claims other people have on you (your creditors or accounts payable), and the claims you have on other people (your debtors or accounts receivable) you can tell very quickly what is the position of affairs of your business at any particular date so far as these people are concerned.

Question Is this important?

Answer Yes. If the amount of accounts payable of the business exceed its accounts receivable, any goods which it hopes to sell and the 'ready' money it has available, it may be insolvent, that is to say, it cannot pay its debts as they become due.

Question When we began talking, you said the Ledger was the Book of Account, and that all transactions were first recorded in what you called 'Subsidiary Books'. What are these Subsidiary Books, and why are they kept in addition to the Ledger?

Answer The Subsidiary Books are termed **Journals** or **Day Books** because, very much like a journal or diary, they are completed daily (or should be).

They are designed to relieve the various accounts in the Ledger of a great amount of detail which, while indispensable to the business, can better be given in a subsidiary book than in the Ledger itself.

If you take, for example, the purchasing side of a business, a very great amount of detail may have to be recorded as to the supplier, the quantity, quality and price per unit of the goods, total amount payable and so on.

But, so far as the double entry or twofold aspect of all the buying transactions is concerned, they are all in the first place purchases of goods for the business. In the second place, credit must be given to all the various suppliers from whom the purchases have been made. Thus there will be one account in the Ledger for incoming goods, or purchases, and other accounts, also in the Ledger, for the individual suppliers.

Question So the Journals or Day Books do not form part of the Double Entry System at all?

Answer Correct. These Subsidiary Books are outside the Double Entry System. Their function is to provide the information from which the Ledger Accounts are written up.

That is why they are often referred to as Books of **Prime** or **First Entry**. With very few exceptions it is a well-recognized rule in bookkeeping that no transaction should be recorded in a Ledger Account unless it has first been recorded in a subsidiary book, or a book of first entry or a computer-based substitute.

Focus points

You should now appreciate some of the basic facts about Double Entry bookkeeping as a process.

* All transactions are fully recorded in a Book of Prime Entry.
* Two entries in the Ledger, one debit and one credit, are needed in respect of each transaction.
* Detailed records are essential to enable you to manage a business.

Testing Yourself

1 Explain briefly the theory of 'Double Entry', and of 'debit and credit'.

2 What do you understand by the term Double Entry, as applied to a system of account keeping? Give examples to illustrate.

3 'Bookkeeping by Double Entry means recording the same transaction twice.' Is this correct?

4 What are the advantages to be derived from keeping a set of books using the Double Entry System?

Business documents

In this chapter you will learn:

- ▶ *About common business documents*
- ▶ *How to recognize each document and what should be in it*
- ▶ *How to complete these documents*

Financial documents

An **invoice** is the primary document which records details of a sale to a customer or the purchase from a supplier. An example follows, and in many systems the advice and delivery notes are produced at the same time. The data on them is very similar and provision is made for appropriate signatures to verify the details shown on each particular document.

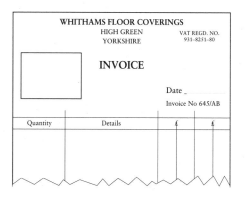

► **Example 2.1**

E Whitham sells floor covering at discount prices. On 1 May xxx1, M Lowbridge was supplied with one piece of brown kitchen floor covering measuring 6 metres long by 2 metres wide, with a recommended retail price of £10 per square metre.

E Whitham gives M Lowbridge a discount of 25%, and makes a standard delivery charge of £5. Delivery to 69 Markbrook Drive, Marktown, Yorkshire. All transactions are subject to Value Added Tax of 10%.

A completed invoice would look something like this.

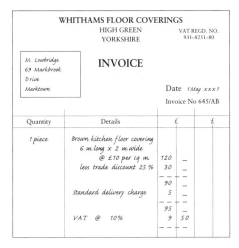

WHITHAMS FLOOR COVERINGS
HIGH GREEN
YORKSHIRE

VAT REGD. NO.
931–8251–80

M. Lowbridge
69 Markbrook
Drive
Marktown

INVOICE

Date 1 May xxx1

Invoice No 645/AB

Quantity	Details	£	£
1 piece	Brown kitchen floor covering 6 m long x 2 m wide		
	@ £10 per sq m	120 _	
	less trade discount 25 %	30 _	
		90 _	
	Standard delivery charge	5 _	
		95 _	
	VAT @ 10%	9	50

![brain icon] **Remember this**

Note the inclusion of VAT in the example above. Value added tax is something you will have to pay on many things you buy as a business – and you may even have to charge it. We will not include VAT in the first part of this book as you learn the basics of bookkeeping, but will bring this back into our accounts later to show you how to account for it if this applies to you.

A **statement** in the accounting context refers to the summary of the purchase or creditor ledger account that is sent to a customer, or by a supplier to your business, at regular intervals, usually monthly, requesting payment of the amount due. Some businesses produce it at the same time as the ledger account is updated. In a very simple bookkeeping system it may have to be copied from the personal ledger.

When a statement is received it should be compared with the records kept by the recipient. Sometimes the amount requested by the statement will agree with your own records, sometimes there will be a difference. This can arise for a number of reasons; for example, clerical errors, goods or services invoiced but not yet received, cheques paid, items in dispute, goods returned and credit notes not yet issued, and discounts or other allowances not recorded. After the necessary adjustments have been made the two balances should reconcile, i.e. show the same amount. The statement can then be signed by the person who has been authorized to certify the amount that can be paid.

The statement sent by the bank is known as a Bank Statement and the reconciliation process is described in Chapter 6.

A **cheque** is a common way in which payment is made to a supplier. The cheques used by small businesses are like personal ones and are illustrated below.

The counterfoil or 'stub' (not shown here) and the cheque are pre-numbered, e.g. 397. The other numbers are used by the bank. Generally, pre-printed cheques will also show the number of the bank account and the name of the business or person who will be writing the cheque.

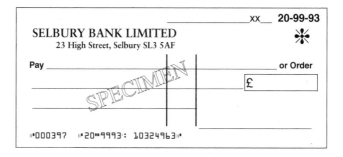

▶ **Example 2.2**

Mary Smith has received goods to the total net value of £346 for her flower shop from Growmore Nurseries Ltd. Complete the cheque for full settlement of this amount on 31 July xxx1.

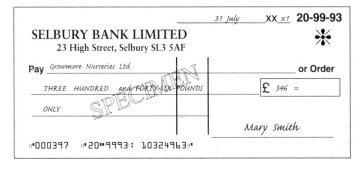

The size of the counterfoil or stub restricts the amount of information that can be recorded. Therefore, when paying a supplier, an account reference could be included and will be adequate. When paying other, sundry items it would be appropriate to include a reference to the invoice or other document supporting the payment. Any cash discount allowed by the supplier should also be recorded here so that a record is available to ensure that the double entry record is written up correctly.

Many organizations now use a computer to print cheques and a copy can be used as the cheque payments record, called a cheque list or sheet. This list, or the counterfoil if cheques are written by hand, is then used to write up the Cash Book.

An alternative form of payment is the **Bank-giro system** or other forms of **electronic funds transfer** (**EFT**) which allows payment to be made directly from your bank to any other bank. Service utilities such as gas, electricity, etc, send a prepared form with the invoice for this purpose. When regular payments of the same amount will be due the **standing order** (STO or S/O) can be used. This is an instruction by the debtor to their bank to make a transfer to the creditor. It is also possible for the debtor, or potential debtor, to authorize the creditor to initiate the transfer; this is known as a **direct debit** (DD or D/D).

Credit cards are also very commonly used by businesses. These are very like payment by cheque in that the receiver gets their money almost straight away. However, as the payer, you get 'credit' for these sums until you choose to settle the bill with your credit card provider. To track what is owed they will send you a monthly **statement** (or give you access to one online) and you can choose when to settle this bill (within certain limits).

For small transactions businesses can also use bank debit cards. These are like instant cheques in effect and money leaves your account, as the payer, and enters the recipient's account almost instantaneously.

A **'banker's draft'** is similar to a cheque but is issued by the bank at the request of the debtor and as it is guaranteed by the bank it is accepted immediately as cash.

These are rarely used in paper form these days however, and larger transactions for which drafts would have been used are usually transferred electronically now.

The **Paying-in Book** provides details of items paid into the bank. The form used for personal accounts and small business transactions is shown below and space for recording details of the separate cheques is on the reverse.

The form is perforated and the bank will retain the larger right-hand portion and leave the left-hand portion in the book after stamping it to acknowledge receipt of the amount paid in.

DATE				**SELBURY** **CREDIT**		Notes £50			
CREDIT THE						£20			
ACCOUNT OF						£10			
				SELBURY BANK LIMITED		£5			
Notes £50				DATE _____		Coins £1			
£20						Other coins			
£10						TOTAL CASH £			
£5						CHEQUES, etc.			
Coins £1									
Other coins				ACCOUNT	ACCOUNT NUMBER	£			
TOTAL CASH £									
CHEQUES, etc.				Paid in by_____	Customers are advised that the Bank reserves the right at its discretion to postpone payment of cheques drawn against uncleared effects which may have been credited to the account.				
£									

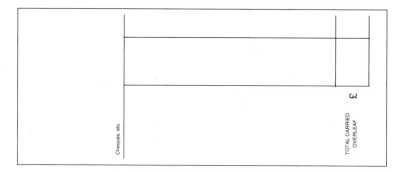

▶ **Example 2.3**

You are employed by Benyon and Walkley Ltd as a cashier. Your employers keep a current account (16271763) at Selbury Bank. On 1 April xxx1, you pay the following items into the bank on behalf of your employer:

19	£20 notes
33	£5 notes
128	£1 coins
1	50p coin
3	20p coins
17	bags of £5 in each bag

plus cheques payable to Benyon and Walkley Ltd from:

C Tootill	£189.56
S Fowler	£165.45

You are required to complete all parts of the paying-in slip shown above. (Make your own entries before comparing with the solution.)

This example asks you to enter several items which in practice might be pre-printed on the paying-in slip, and if they are there will be no need to enter them by hand.

The counterfoil may be used as a prime document to write up the cash received sheet, and used to check the receipts shown on the bank statement.

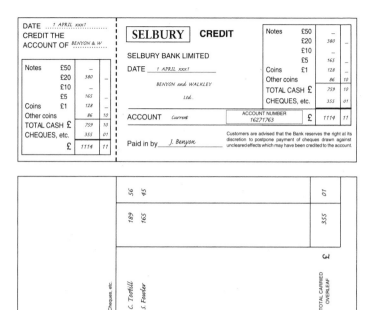

The **Receipt Book** is a memorandum book, usually in duplicate or triplicate, which is used to provide a record of money (cash or cheques) received. They are usually pre-printed and pre-numbered and will show the date, amount received, person/company it is received from, nature of payments, i.e. cash or cheque, any discount allowed and the signature of the person who made out the receipt.

▶ Example 2.4

Micklethwaite Electrics keep a cash receipt book and retain two copies of each receipt issued. Prepare the document that you would issue to Keith Miller acknowledging receipt of his cheque payment.

On 23 February xxx1 you received a cheque on behalf of Micklethwaite Electrics, 85 Leeds Road, Ripon from Keith Miller, 10 Halstead Road, Pannal Ash in full settlement of Sales Invoice No B 973 dated 6 February xxx1. The amount of the invoice was £230. Keith Miller is entitled to a cash discount of 5% if settlement is made during February.

```
RECEIVED WITH THANKS      Date  23-2-x1
From KEITH MILLER
Cash
Cheque                                       218.50
Discount                                      11.50
Total                                       £230.00

Signed   G  N  Other
For MICKLETHWAITE ELECTRICS
                                               1436
```

Some systems might require the full description of the
debtor and if Keith Miller is not sufficient to ensure correct
identification then his address could be included, as could the
invoice number and description of the items involved.

Nowadays it is less common to issue receipts for payments
made by cheque or transfers through the banking system.

The **Bank Cash Book** is a book or sheet in which payments into
the bank and withdrawals from the bank are recorded.

BANK CASH BOOK
RECEIPTS   PAYMENTS

Date	Particulars	Discount Allowed	Details	Bank	Date	Particulars	Discount Received	Details	Bank

▶ **Example 2.5**

Pauline Weldon operated a small mail-order company. All her receipts were paid immediately into the bank and all her payments were made by cheque. Her Cash Book showed a balance in hand of £748.24 on 1 October xxx1.

You are provided with the above proforma and are required to enter the following transactions and balance.

During October she made the following deposits into the bank:

Paying-in Book counterfoils:

Dated	In respect of cheque from	Cheque £	Discount £
Oct 7	A Abram	74.82	5.18
Oct 7	B Barrett	137.80	12.20
Oct 18	C Cook	58.75	–
Oct 18	D Dennison	24.30	–
Oct 28	B Barrett	37.18	2.82
Oct 28	C Cook	42.43	–

Her payments for October showed the following details:

Cheque Book counterfoils:

Date	Payable to	Cheque No	Cheque £	Discount £
Oct 5	D Dunn	342	82.00	–
7	Autos Ltd	343	189.25	10.75
9	Wages/salaries	344	237.87	–
14	E Evans	345	17.22	–
22	Brown & Co	346	98.79	–
29	Francis & Co	347	132.80	2.20

Prepare your own Bank Cash Book and enter the transactions, then check with the following solution. **Note:** Receipts are entered on the left-hand side and payments on the right.

There may also be a 'folio', or reference, column for the cheque numbers.

BANK CASH BOOK

RECEIPTS   PAYMENTS

Date	Particulars	Discount Allowed	Details	Bank	Date	Particulars	Discount Received	Details	Bank
xxx1					xxx1				
Oct 1	Balance			748.24	Oct 5	D. Dunn	–	342	82.00
7	A. Abram	5.18	74.82		7	Autos Ltd	10.75	343	189.25
7	B. Barrett	12.20	137.80	212.62	9	Wages/			
			———			Salaries	–	344	237.87
18	C. Cook	–	58.75		14	E. Evans	–	345	17.22
18	D. Dennison	–	24.30	83.05					
			———		22	Brown & Co.	–	346	98.79
28	B. Barrett	2.82	37.18						
28	C. Cook	–	42.43	79.61	29	Francis & Co.	2.20	347	132.80
					31	Balance			365.59
		20.20		1123.52					
		———		———					———
Nov 1	Balance			365.59			12.95		1123.52

The **Cash Book** will usually record both bank and cash transactions as described in Chapter 5, but there may be separate cash sheets and/or a **Petty Cash Book** as described in Chapter 7.

Wages documents

A **clock card** is the original document on which employees record the date and the time at which they arrive and leave work or when they start and finish particular jobs. A typical example of a clock card is given below.

Name ....
Department ....

	MON.	TUE.	WED.	THU.	FRI.	SAT.	SUN.
H O U R S							
NORMAL	1.1	1.2	1.5	2.0		SPLIT SH.	

A **piece-work card** is the original document on which the employee records the amount or the number of units produced. It is used when payment is 'per unit'.

The time at work, and the work produced, multiplied by the appropriate rates will enable the gross wages to be calculated.

There are usually deductions to be made from this gross amount, for example tax, national insurance and other compulsory items. There may also be voluntary deductions, such as trade union subscriptions, Save As You Earn, etc., to complete the calculation of the net amount which will be paid to the employee.

▶ **Example 2.6**

Jenny Stone works in the goods inwards department of Fenwold Electrical. Her clock card number is 100. She is paid £5.20 per hour for a 35-hour week. She is paid time and a quarter for any weekday overtime and time and a half for overtime worked on a Saturday.

Hours worked week ending 27 February:

Monday	8 hours	Tuesday	9 hours	Wednesday	9 hours
Thursday	8 hours	Friday	6 hours	Saturday	3 hours

Deductions for the week:

National Insurance contributions	13.8% of gross wage over £111 per week
Income Tax	20% of all earnings over £192 per week
Save As You Earn Scheme	£5.00 per week
Trade Union Subscriptions	£1.00 per week

Note: Employers' National insurance contribution is the same amount as the employee's contribution in this example, although this is not usually the case in reality.

You are required to calculate Jenny Stone's net pay for the week ending 27 February xxx1.

Name: Jenny Stone   Clock Card No: 100
Department: Goods inwards   Week beginning: 27 February xxx1

GROSS PAY
Hours worked: 40 hours 0 minutes during normal working hours

Basic	35	@ £6.50	£227.50
Overtime	5	6.50 × 1.25	40.63
		3 hours on Saturday	
Overtime	3	6.50 × 1.50	29.25
Total gross pay			£297.38

DEDUCTIONS

National Insurance (13.8% of gross >£111/ week)	£25.72	
Income Tax (20% over £192/week)	21.08	
SAYE	5.00	
TU subscription	1.00	
Total deductions		£52.80
NET PAY		£244.58

These calculations for all employees should be entered into a **Wages Book,** or more likely onto a **Payroll Sheet,** for the week. In a computer system the details for each employee could automatically be added to their records and be used to provide the equivalent of the Payroll Sheet. A typical Wages Book (Payroll Sheet) is shown below.

PAYROLL

Department ....   Week Ending...

CLOCK NO	NAME	HOURS		RATE	GROSS PAY	DEDUCTIONS					NET PAY	EMPLOYERS' NI
		Basic	OT			Tax	NI	Pensn	Vol	Total		

This data for Jenny Stone, calculated above, would be entered as shown below.

PAYROLL

Department ... *Goods inwards* ...   Week Ending ... *27 Feb xxx1* ...

CLOCK NO	NAME	HOURS		RATE	GROSS PAY	DEDUCTIONS					NET PAY	EMPLOYERS' NI
		Basic	OT			Tax	NI	Pensn	Vol	Total		
100	Jenny Stone	43	5 3	6.50 18.13 9.75	297.38	21.08	25.72	-	6.00	52.80	244.58	25.72

This particular payroll requires the total hours paid at basic rate (43) and the premium overtime hours 5 at time and a quarter (1.25) plus 3 at time and a half (1.5), a total of 2.75 hours, to be shown. Note the column for Employers' National Insurance.

There are rules and regulations governing the calculation of this amount in practice but at this stage of your studies a simple rule was provided. That said, treat this as the same as the employee's NI.

NOTE AND COIN ANALYSIS

When employees are paid in cash it is essential that the exact amount of their net pay can be put into individual pay packets to ensure rapid payment at the appropriate time. This requires the analysis of each net amount into the notes and coins required. It is usual to use the minimum number but sometimes it has been agreed that there will always be, say, at least four one pound coins in a packet. In this situation the usual analysis, shown below, would have to be modified to reflect the particular constraint.

| Net wages | £20 | £10 | £5 | £1 | 20p | 10p | 5p | 2p | 1p |

using the 'maximum' rule £20 divides into the wage six times, so 6; etc.

etc.

	£20	£10	£5	£1	20p	10p	5p	2p	1p
£127.57	6	–	1	2	2	1	1	1	–
£143.68	7	–	–	3	3	–	1	1	1
£271.25	13	–	1	5	5	1	2	2	1

When obtaining the money for the pay it will be provided by the bank (or sometimes by the cashier) in accordance with this analysis.

£20	@	13	260.00
10		0	0.00
5		1	5.00
1		5	5.00
20p		5	1.00
10p		1	.10
5p		2	.10
2p		2	.04
1p		1	.01
			271.25

Naturally, computer programs are available to provide this analysis as a by-product from the payroll work. Sometimes the net wage or salary will be rounded up to the nearest pound each week and the difference carried forward to be adjusted the next week or month. There has also been some pressure from employers for employees to have a bank account into which direct payments could be made and this is now common in most businesses. One obvious reason for this is the avoidance of large cash amounts in transit or being held at the point of payment; also less likelihood of paying the wrong person. The process of operating the payroll remains the same however, and payslips are still issued (usually still in paper form).

Inventory records

Inventory (sometimes called stock) is defined as those goods which the business intends to resell, perhaps after conversion or assembly. It is often a significant asset of an enterprise and records should be kept showing receipts, issues and the amount of inventory. Some bookkeeping systems will also record orders and although some records will show the quantity others may show the value as well. The procedures may be integrated into an overall system that provides the justification for paying purchase invoices, issuing sales invoices and means of controlling the amount of stock being held.

An **advice note** from a supplier is notification that goods will be delivered in response to an order. It may be used as confirmation that their request for supplies has been processed.

The **delivery note** (sometimes the advice note) from a supplier comes with the goods when they are delivered to your business. It may be used for subsequent processing, e.g. recording the receipt of the goods, or to compare with a goods received note made by your business when the goods were received.

A **stores requisition note** is, as its name suggests, a request to issue goods from inventory, authorized by an agreed procedure. It is used to record the issue of inventory on the bin card or stores record and for crediting the stock account and debiting the recipient if the system has been designed for that purpose, usually in manufacturing enterprises.

Stock cards are records of a particular item in inventory. If held in bins/racks/trays they may be called **bin/rack/tray cards.** In principle it is a record kept with the physical inventory and updated at the time of any physical movement. Usually only quantity is recorded. Inventory ledger records are kept in a stores office and/ or the accounts department and may record quantity and value.

This record uses the 'running balance' format rather than a 'two-sided' one, and has the advantage of always showing the up-to-date balance. From time to time the physical inventory should be counted and the amount compared with the bin card and the inventory ledger card. There may be some differences due to transactions not yet recorded but any differences remaining should be investigated, if material, and all records amended to show the actual quantity. Other causes of a difference may be clerical error, unrecorded issue to cover scrap, theft or items stored somewhere else.

Using the form below, write up an inventory record card for Jigsaws, ref no 1610:

Balance in hand on 1 February xxx1		*50*
2 February	*issues req. no. 220*	*25*
7 February	*issues req. no. 231*	*10*
15 February	*receipts order no. 126*	*100*
18 February	*issues req. no. 261*	*50*

INVENTORY RECORD				
DATE	REF	IN	OUT	BALANCE

Solution

INVENTORY RECORD				
JIGSAWS			Part No.	1610
DATE	REF	IN	OUT	BALANCE
xxx1 Feb 1	Balance			50
2	Req . 220		25	25
7	Req . 231		10	15
15	Order 126	100		115
18	Req . 261		50	65

This illustration only uses quantities. Some systems also record the value of receipts, issues and the balance. Purchases are usually valued at actual cost, issues at the average cost of the balance immediately before the issue. There are other bases of valuation which are acceptable.

Testing Yourself

1 Knox Sawmills have a current account (no 16760272) at Selbury Bank Ltd. On 2 March xx1x the business pays in the following items at the local branch:

3	£20 notes
7	£10 notes
12	£5 notes
74	£1 coins
35	50p coins
16	20p coins
200	2p coins

and cheques made payable to Knox Sawmills from

F Rigton	£108.25
A C Killinghall	£365.12
Duck and Drake	£49.96

You are required to:

a complete all parts of the paying-in slip given below.

b describe two possible uses of the counterfoil slip retained in the bank paying-in book.

<table>
<tr><td>
DATE ....
CREDIT THE
ACCOUNT OF ....

Notes	£50	
	£20	
	£10	
	£5	
Coins	£1	
Other coins		
TOTAL CASH £		
CHEQUES, etc.		
	£	
</td>
<td>
SELBURY   **CREDIT**

SELBURY BANK LIMITED

DATE _____

_____

ACCOUNT

ACCOUNT NUMBER

Paid in by_____

Customers are advised that the Bank reserves the right at its discretion to postpone payment of cheques drawn against uncleared effects which may have been credited to the account.
</td>
<td>

Notes	£50	
	£20	
	£10	
	£5	
Coins	£1	
Other coins		
TOTAL CASH £		
CHEQUES, etc.		
	£	
</td></tr>
</table>

Cheques, etc.			£
			TOTAL CARRIED OVERLEAF

2 Josephine Swift makes all payments over £15 by cheque and pays all receipts into the bank at the end of each day. On Monday 27 February her Bank Cash Book showed a balance of £4960 Dr.

The following information is available for the next week:

Cheques drawn:

27 Feb	R Loftus (creditor) £300	Cheque No 1610
27 Feb	Stock £600	Cheque No 1611
28 Feb	Advertising £150	Cheque No 1612
1 March	Electricity Board £125	Cheque No 1613
2 March	Petrol account £65	Cheque No 1614
3 March	Rover and Waters Garages(deposit on car) £1000	Cheque No 1615

Bank Lodgements:

28 Feb	Cash takings			£250
28 Feb	Cheques:	B Blue	£25.25	
		T Roe	£70.00	
		R Lamb	£82.91	
1 March	Cash takings			£325
	Cheques:	T Williams	£600	
	R Potter		£350 (in settlement of account of £375.00)	
3 March	Cheques:	R Lowther	£275 (debtor)	
		XY Equipment Ltd	£100 (sale of old typewriter)	

On 5 March she received her bank statement which revealed the following information:

Date	Details	Debit	Credit	Balance
27 Feb	Brought forward			4960.00
28 Feb	Bank charges	40.00		4920.00
1 March	Cash and cheques		428.16	5348.16
1 March	1611	600.00		4748.16
2 March	1610	300.00		4448.16
2 March	1612	150.00		4298.16
2 March	Sundry		1275.00	5573.16
2 March	Standing Order (XY Insurance Company)	100.00		5473.16
3 March	1613	125.00		5348.16

You are required to:

a write up and balance the Bank Cash Book for the week beginning 27 February xxx1 (after receipt of the Bank Statement), using the format given below

b prepare a Bank Reconciliation Statement on 5 March xx1x (after completing Chapter 6).

BANK CASH BOOK

Date	Particulars	Discount Allowed £	Details £	Bank £	Date	Particulars	Discount Received £	Details £	Bank £

3 C Ponsford manages a small firm employing four workers. During the week ending 31 December xxx1 each worker earned take-home pay as follows:

L Jennett	£160.56
J Smith	£90.75
J Grala	£100.20
G Thomas	£136.40

C Ponsford pays wages at the end of each week in cash using notes and coins of £10, £5, £1, 50p, 20p, 10p, 5p, 2p and 1p. C Ponsford insists that each worker receives at least one £1 coin.

You are required to:

a rule up and complete a note and coin analysis in table form using the least number of notes and coins permissible
b reconcile the value of the total notes and coins with the total pay bill.

4 D Swift maintains manually prepared inventory record cards for the recording of the receipts and issues of various items of stock held in the stores.

You are required to:

a draw up an inventory record card showing the following rulings and headings:

Item		INVENTORY CARD					
Date	Details	Receipts		Issues		Balance	
		Units	£	Units	£	Units	£
Sep 1	Balance					12	144

b record the following movements of the item of inventory reference number DW/04 for the month of September xxx1. The cost price of each item is £12 and there were 12 items in inventory at 1 September xxx1.

Receipts
September	8	Invoice No 784	20 units
September	15	Invoice No 847	48 units
September	22	Invoice No 984	20 units

Issues
September	6	Issue Note No A237	8 units
September	17	Issue Note No D534	18 units
September	24	Issue Note No B631	64 units

c On making a physical inventory check on 30 September xxx1, Swift discovered that there were eight units in inventory. Adjust the inventory record card for this difference and give some possible explanation.

The business transaction, purchases and sales

In this chapter you will learn:

► *About purchase and sales journals*
► *About purchase and sales returns*
► *That complete accuracy is required*

Objective

This chapter describes the process for recording the purchases and sales of a business.

The business transaction

We are familiar in our daily life with buying articles we want and paying cash for them. But unless we are in business the idea of selling goods is not so familiar, nor is the process of receiving payment for what we have sold. And yet every business is concerned with buying and selling goods or services, usually on a credit basis, so that at some later date it pays for what it has bought and is in turn paid for what it has sold.

These are recurrent transactions in particular goods which the business buys, sells or manufactures.

Merchanted goods are those which it resells in the same condition as when purchased. *Manufactured goods* are the finished article which, with the assistance of employees, are worked up from the raw materials.

Therefore, from the purely trading standpoint, a kind of trade cycle can be recognized. Goods are bought first of all in sufficient quantity to meet customers' requirements, either as the finished article or as raw material. They are what is called the **Stock, Stock in Trade** or, now most commonly, **Inventory** of the business.

When the goods are sold in the finished state to customers at the selling price, and on credit terms, these customers become the **debtors** (now more commonly called accounts receivable) of the business; that is, they are indebted to it, and when they in turn make payment the **Cash in Hand** or **Cash at Bank** of the business is replenished. From these increased cash resources, the business can buy more goods, and so the cycle repeats itself.

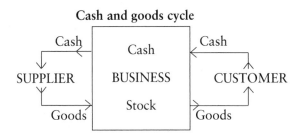

Cash and goods cycle

At any given time a business will possess:

► Inventory

► claims on customers, which may be described as Debtors, or Accounts Receivable

► Cash in Hand and/or Cash at Bank

These forms of property represent the trading resources of the business, which we describe as **Assets**.

Assets are defined as anything controlled by the business which, it is hoped, will provide some future benefit. For example, we hope to benefit from holding stocks by selling them for a profit at a later date. We hope to benefit from a motor vehicle as it can be used to deliver our goods and services, or transport our employees and assist them in generating orders for our business.

Assets are classified into **Non-current (sometimes called Fixed) Assets** and **Current Assets**. Non-current assets, such as an office, factory or warehouse and motor vehicles are expected to generate some benefit for the business beyond one year. Current assets, such as stock, debtors and money in the bank, are expected to provide benefits which will be consumed within the coming year. For example, debtors are generally current assets because the business expects to receive payment from customers (the benefit) within a year.

The distinction between these two kinds of assets is important because our non-current assets have been bought to be retained, while our current assets, as we have seen, are an essential result of the business's everyday transactions. Indeed, they enter into and form part of these transactions.

In addition to assets, we must also record any resources which we owe to other parties outside the business. We describe these obligations as **Liabilities**. Those amounts which are due to external parties after more than one year, such as bank loans, are described as **Non-current (sometimes called Long-term) Liabilities**. Those amounts due within one year, such as creditors or accounts payable to our suppliers, are described as **Current Liabilities**.

The amount by which the assets of the business are greater than its liabilities is the **Capital** or **Equity** of the business. The Capital reflects the resources that have been invested into the business by its proprietor(s) or owner(s) plus any profits that have been generated on that investment over the life of the business to date (but not yet withdrawn by the owners). We can think of capital as a liability to the proprietor(s) – the proprietor invests resources into a business and expects them to be used to generate a **Profit** thereby providing some return on their investment. The equity capital is the amount of investment and any subsequent profits that are owed to the proprietor by the business.

We measure it by recording what assets have been bought or generated from the proprietors' investment less any liabilities the business owes to outside parties.

An example will help to make this clear:

▶ Example 3.1

Brown begins business on 1 January xxx1, by investing £10 000 in cash. He leases office premises for five years at a cost of £6000, obtains goods on credit from Smith costing £2000, and gets a £5000 three-year loan from the bank. The total assets of his business are:

Office lease, cost	*£6000*
Inventory, cost	*2000*
Cash in bank (10k – 6k +5k)	*9000*
	£17 000

but this is not the amount of Brown's Capital invested in the business because £2000 of these assets have been supplied on credit by Smith and £5000 have been supplied by the bank, for which the business is liable. What is owed is, therefore, a liability of the business to outside parties and does not represent what is owed to Brown, as proprietor. We therefore define Capital as corresponding to 'the excess of the Assets over the Liabilities of a business': Brown's Capital = Total Assets £17 000, *less* Liabilities £7000 = £10 000, or put in another way, Brown's capital of £10 000 is represented by:

Fixed assets	*£6000*
Current assets	*£11000*
Less Current liabilities	*£(2000)*
Less Long-term liabilities	*£(5000)*
	£10 000

Remember this

In the Books of Account, the use of brackets or parentheses such as £(2000) generally signifies a negative or minus.

We have seen that from its start the business must be provided with a certain minimum amount of investment, or Capital.

One purpose of bookkeeping is to enable the business, at any time, to prepare a statement of its position (a Balance Sheet) to show how it has dealt with the Capital invested, that is to say, in what types of assets and liabilities the Capital is now represented.

Remember this

Capital doesn't necessarily represent cash. Whilst cash is often invested by the proprietor to start the business, this will be used to buy other assets, borrow money and generate profits from trading. Therefore, capital shows how the proprietor's investment is represented by different types of assets less any liabilities.

SOURCES OF FUNDS

We classify three sources of funds in bookkeeping:

1 Equity Capital (E): the proprietor invests their own resources into the business.

2 Liabilities (L): the business borrows money from someone outside the business.

3 Revenues (R): the business generates funds from trading.

APPLICATIONS OF FUNDS

We classify two uses of funds in bookkeeping:

1 Assets (A): we use funds to purchase items which provide benefits for the business both now and in the future.

2 Expenses (X): we use funds to gain benefits which are used up by the business.

APPLICATIONS OF FUNDS = SOURCES OF FUNDS

Assets + Expenses = Equity Capital + Liabilities + Revenues

$$A \quad + X \quad = E \quad\quad\quad + L \quad\quad + R$$

Debits $\quad\quad$ *= Credits*

Debits = Increases in the Applications of Funds (A + X) or Decreases in the Sources of Funds (E+L+R)

Credits = Increases in the Sources of Funds (E+L+R) or Decreases in the Applications of Funds (A+X).

The Purchase and Sales Journals in the bookkeeping system

As you know, we use a diary to make daily notes of things that happen to us. We enter into it brief but sufficient details of what has taken place. Diaries very often form a useful reference for the future if we want to look back and remember what we did or felt at a particular point in time.

In the early stages of business development it is not difficult for us to imagine the proprietor of the business making a similar record of transactions with people who had become suppliers and customers, narrating what they had bought, and from whom; what they had sold, and to whom. Just as a diary is a daily record, so also is a **Journal**. It is prepared as soon as possible after the transaction has taken place. It is essentially a *primary* record, and hence we derive the meaning of the term 'Journal' in bookkeeping as a **Book of Prime Entry** (or first entry). No matter what subsequent use we make of the particulars recorded in it, the desirability of a primary record is obvious as it captures details of what has occurred at, or close to, the point of the transaction, before details are lost or forgotten.

To the extent that the transactions of the business are recurrent, even in the smallest undertaking we should expect to see a record of:

▶ purchases

▶ sales

▶ payments to suppliers

▶ receipts from customers.

As soon as the transactions entered into became more numerous, some kind of analysis of the Journal would be imperative if the proprietor at any time wished to know:

▶ how much they had purchased

▶ how much they had sold

▶ the total of the cash payments

▶ the total of the cash receipts.

With numerous daily transactions, putting on record the fact that £100 worth of goods had been purchased on credit from Jones, and £100 worth of goods had been sold on credit to Smith, the Journal entries might take the following form:

> *Business chargeable with incoming goods at cost £100.*
> *Jones to be credited with £100.*

Smith chargeable with goods £100. Business to be credited with issue of goods at selling price £100.

If, however, we took matters a step further, and used the symbols **Dr** (debit) instead of 'chargeable with' and **Cr** (credit) instead of 'to be credited', the entries could easily be stated in the following way:

Business	*Dr £100.00*	
Jones		*Cr 100.00*

and

Smith	*Dr £100.00*	
Business		*Cr 100.00*

This would be a much simpler and more concise way of putting the transaction on record, but the repetition of the recurrent entries over a period of time would make detailed analysis always essential to arrive at, for example:

▶ our total purchases, and

▶ our total sales for that period

as well as the need for similar analysis for cash paid and cash received.

For that reason, the first form of Journal was modified to comply with these requirements of the proprietor; in one section of it were recorded **purchases**, in another **sales** and in yet another **cash**, either in total, or as in many cases today:

▶ **Cash received**, and

▶ **Cash paid.**

To the first of these subsections of the Journal was given the title **Purchase Journal** (or Purchase Day Book); to the second **Sales Journal** (or Sales Day Book); and to the third **Cash Book** or **Cash Journal,** with the result that in them we now find:

- our total purchases

- our total sales and

- our purely cash transactions in as great a detail as we desire, or the requirements of the business demand.

Certain transactions take place which it would not be appropriate to record in the three subdivisions of the Journal described above. These comparatively infrequent transactions are considered in Chapter 8.

Note that some small organizations with very few transactions may not use these journals. They will attach a slip to a batch of invoices and other documents, summarize the slips as appropriate and use the summaries to produce accounts. This is known as a **slip system**. It can be sufficient as a record of prime entry if transaction numbers are low.

Supposing we begin with the **Purchase Journal** or **Day Book**:

▶ **Example 3.2**

Enter the following purchases in the Purchase Day Book of H Yates, a cycle dealer, total the Day Book, but do not post the entries to the Ledger.

xxx1

Feb	2	Received invoice from the Speedy Cycle Co Ltd for:
		2 Gents' Roadsters, model A625 at £125, less 20% trade discount.
		2 Ladies' Roadsters, model A725 at £110, less 20% trade discount.
		2 Crates at £5.00 each.
	15	The Drake Cycle Co Ltd, invoiced:
		3 Gents' Special Club models B21 at £140, less 15% trade discount.
		3 Ladies' Special Club models B20 at £120, less 15% trade discount.
		2 Crates at £6.00 each.

27 Received invoice from the Victoria Manufacturing Co Ltd:

2 Racing models A16 at £170, less 15% trade discount.

1 Crate at £5.00.

In these three purchase transactions, we notice that:

▶ The goods purchased are exclusively for resale, i.e. they are goods in which Yates is dealing

▶ A deduction is made on account of **trade discount**. This is a common allowance made by a supplier to a retailer with whom there are regular dealings and may represent:

  ▷ a margin of profit for the retailer, who sells the goods at the advertised list price

  ▷ an inducement to the retailer to continue to trade with the supplier.

▶ Prior to entry in the last four columns of the Day Book, it is seen that the trade discount has been deducted in the 'details' column, and we must always be careful to follow this procedure.

▶ All that concerns Yates is the net cost of the cycles which have been bought.

▶ The suppliers have in each case included in their invoice price the cost of packing crates. These clearly do not refer to the cost of the goods dealt in, and are therefore entered in a separate column. Moreover, it is usual for the suppliers to issue credit notes as and when the crates are later returned to them in good condition. There may in consequence be a recovery of all or the greater part of the total purchase cost under this heading.

Purchase Day Book

Date	Supplier	Description	Details £	Goods Total £	Gents' Models £	Ladies' Models £	Crates and Packing £
xxx1							
Feb 2	Speedy Cycle Co Ltd	2 Gents' Roadsters, Model A625, at £125.00	250.00				
		2 Ladies' Roadsters, Model A725, at £110.00	220.00				
			470.00				
		Less 20% Trade discount	94.00				
			376.00	386.00	200.00	176.00	10.00
		2 Crates at £5.00	10.00				
15	Drake Cycle Co Ltd	3 Gents' Special Club models, B21, at £140.00	420.00				
		3 Ladies' Special Club models, B20, at £120.00	360.00				
			780.00				
		Less 15% Trade discount	117.00				
			663.00	675.00	357.00	306.00	12.00
		2 Crates at £6.00	12.00				
27	Victoria Manufacturing Co Ltd	2 Racing models, A16, at £170.00	340.00				
		Less 15% Trade discount	51.00				
			289.00	294.00	289.00		5.00
		1 Crate at £5.00	5.00				
				£1355.00	£846.00	£482.00	£27.00

The solution to the example, as shown, enables Yates to see at a glance:

- from whom goods have been purchased
- what has been purchased
- the total cost of the purchases, suitably analysed, including
- the cost of crates, packing, etc.

If, as in the first transaction, trade discount of 20% is allowed by the supplier then a very simple trading account to reflect the sale of one Gents' Roadster would show Sales £125, Cost of sales £100. The difference is called **gross profit** and is £25, or 20% of the sales, which is the amount of the trade discount. If the cycle is sold for less than the expected price then the gross profit will be less than expected, and vice versa.

The gross profit expressed as a percentage of the selling price, or sales, was 20%. It may also be expressed as a percentage of the cost of sales, in this case £25 as a percentage of £100, or 25%. Always be very careful to remember whether you are referring to sales or cost of sales. When based on cost of sales it is sometimes called the mark-up, i.e. the percentage added to cost to give estimated selling price.

What about Value Added Tax (VAT)? More about VAT is provided at the end of Chapter 4 and at this stage it is only necessary to say that an extra column would be required in the Purchase and Sales Day Books. This is illustrated in the next example, where VAT at the rate of 20% is assumed in respect of all sales and purchases.

Example 3.3

From the following particulars compile the Purchase Day Book, Sales Day Book and Returns Book of D Morris.

Full details must be shown in the Day Books. No posting to the Ledger is required.

March 10 Sold to W Humphrey, Lincoln, 200 metres floral cotton cloth at £2 per metre; 100 metres of best blue cotton cloth at £2.40 per metre. Whole invoice less 10% trade discount.

12 Received invoice from R Ridgwell, Bolton, for 50 sheets at £3.50 each; 40 tee-shirts £2.80 each.

15 Sent a debit note to W Hunt for £12, being an overcharge on cotton supplied to D Morris on February 5.

18 Sent an invoice to S Bonham, Coventry, for 100 metres of linen at £5.00 per metre, less 5% trade discount; 300 metres of floral cotton at £2 per metre; trimmings £15.

20 Bought goods from B Davis, Ely, 500 metres of floral cotton at £1.00 per metre; 400 tee-shirts at £2 each; sundry remnants £15.

22 W Humphrey, Lincoln, returned 50 metres of the floral cotton supplied on March 10, as being of inferior quality.

23 Received a debit note from A Jenkinson, Wolverhampton, for 20 metres of linen returned to D Morris at £7 per metre less 20% trade discount.

24 Sent an invoice to T Butterworth, Norwich, for 300 metres of linen at £7.00 per metre less 5% trade discount; 150 metres of best blue cotton at £2.40 per metre less 10% trade discount; assorted buttons £10.

27 Received a credit note from V Luxton, for 30 metres of white cotton returned by D Morris at £1.00 per metre.

29 Bought from General Supplies Ltd, London, showcases and fittings £1000 net.

You are required to calculate the appropriate trade discount and VAT. The actual invoice from your supplier and your own sales invoices would include these amounts.

Remember this

Great care must be exercised in setting out the Day Books. It may be a useful exercise for you to prepare your day books, and then compare them with the entries which follow rather than merely reading the entries. You may be wondering why time is spent recording data from an invoice into a journal; why not file the invoice or summarize several invoices together, or enter details directly into a computer? Any of these methods, or other similar ones, may be used according to the wishes and objectives of the owner or manager depending upon the availability of computing resources and staff.

Different systems will do it differently, but using day books, as shown here, is arguably the best, at least once your business processes more than a few transactions each day.

What is essential is that the basic data is accurately recorded, in a permanent form, to which access can be obtained rapidly whenever required. The latter two objectives have already been illustrated by the use of separate Purchase and Sales Journals. This system will be useful should the financial information need to be checked by an auditor or bank. The Purchase and Sales Journals can easily become separate files of Purchase invoices received and copies of our own Sales invoices. However, to encourage you to appreciate the system of the recording cycle a Journal approach is used.

Computer software is readily available that will provide an integrated system of Journals (see Chapter 17); but the basic principles of Journals, as described in this chapter, and the Ledger, as described in Chapter 4, will continue to be observed because of their importance as permanent records of transactions. They can also provide a useful source of management information by telling us what we are selling, to what type of customers, in what combinations and in what markets or geographical areas.

Before beginning to record these transactions in the Purchase and Sales Journals, it is essential for us to realize that they are being stated from the point of view of the business of which D Morris is the proprietor.

The first process is to classify each of them as being:

▶ a purchase transaction

▶ a sales transaction

▶ the return of goods to a **supplier,** or the obtaining of an allowance *from* them

▶ the return of goods by a **customer,** or the granting of an allowance *to* them.

They can then be recorded in the appropriate Journal. In the latter two cases the result will be that the amount of the original purchases and sales will be reduced accordingly, but instead of altering the entries in the Purchase and Sales Journals, we shall make use of **Purchase Returns Journals** and **Sales Returns Journals** (see below).

Let us now summarize the points arising in this and Example 3.2.

In the first place, the **analysis columns** which follow the total column enable us to analyse as fully as we may wish the details of our purchases and sales.

Purchase Day Book

March xxx1

Date	Supplier	Description	Invoice No	Details £	Total £	VAT £	Cotton £	Linen £	Sheets £	Tee-shirts £	Sundries £	Special Items £
xxx1												
March 12	R Ridgwell, Bolton	50 sheets at £3.50 each		175.00					175.00			
		40 tee-shirts at £2.80		112.00						112.00		
				287.00								
		VAT 20%		57.40		57.40						
			1		344.40							
20	B Davis, Ely	500 metres floral cotton at £1.00 per metre		500.00			500.00					
		400 tee-shirts at £2.00 each		800.00						800.00		
		Remnants		15.00							15.00	
				1315.00								
		VAT 20%		263.00		263.00						
			2		1578.00							
29	General Supplies Ltd, London	Showcases and fittings		1000.00								1000.00
		VAT 20%		200.00		200.00						
			3		1200.00							
					£3122.40	£520.40	£500.00		£175.00	£912.00	£15.00	£1000.00

46

D. MORRIS

Sales Day Book

Fo 2

Date	Customer	Description	Inv.No	Details £	Total £	VAT £	Cotton £	Linen £	Sheets £	Tee-shirts £	Sundries £
xxx1											
March 10	W Humphrey, Lincoln	200 m Floral cotton @ £2 per m		400.00							
		100m best Blue Cotton @ £2.40 per m		240.00							
				640.00							
		Less 10% Trade discount		64.00							
				576.00			576.00				
		Add VAT 20%		115.20		115.20					
			4		691.20						
18	S Bonham, Coventry	100m Linen @ £5 per m		500.00							
		Less 5% Trade discount		25.00							
				475.00				475.00			
		300m Floral cotton @ £2 per m		600.00			600.00				
		Trimmings		15.00							15.00
				1090.00							
		Add VAT 20%		218.00		218.00					

March xxx1

(*Continued*)

23	T Butterworth, Norwich							
	300m Linen @ £7 per m	5	2100.00			1308.00		
	Less 5% Trade discount		105.00					
			1995.00		1995.00			
	150m best Blue cotton @ £2.40 per m		360.00					
	Less 10% Trade discount		36.00					
			324.00	324.00				
	Assorted buttons		10.00					10.00
			2329.00					
	Add VAT 20%	6	465.80			465.80		
						2794.80		
			£4794.00	£799.00	£1500.00	£2470.00		£25.00

D. MORRIS

Fo 1

Purchases Returns and Allowances Book

March xxx1

Date	Supplier	Description	Debit Note No	Details £	Total £	VAT £	Cotton £	Linen £	Sheets £	Tee-shirts £	Special Items £
xxx1											
March 15	W Hunt	Overcharge goods supplied Feb 5		12.00			12.00				
		Add VAT 20%		2.40		2.40					
			7		14.40						
27	V Luxton	30 metres White cotton returned at £1.00 per metre		30.00			30.00				
		(Their credit note)									
		Add VAT 20%		6.00		6.00					
			8		36.00						
					£50.40	£8.40	£42.00				

D. MORRIS

Sales Returns and Allowances Book

Date	Supplier	Description	Credit Note No	Details £	Total £	VAT £	Cotton £	Linen £	Sheets £	Tee-shirts £	Special Items £
xxx1											
March 22	W Humphrey	50 metres floral cotton, invoice Mar 10, inferior at									
		£2.00 per metre		100.00							
		Less 10% Trade discount		10.00							
				90.00			90.00				
		Add VAT 20%		18.00		18.00					
			9		108.00						
23	A Jenkinson, Wolverhampton	20 metres Linen at £7.00 per metre		140.00							
		Less 20% Trade discount		28.00							
				112.00				112.00			
		(Their debit note)									
		Add VAT 20%		22.40		22.40					
			10		134.40						
					£242.40	£40.40	£90.00	£112.00			

Secondly, we see that an *Invoice No* column is provided. In this is entered the reference number *given by the business* to its suppliers' invoices, as well as to its own invoices to customers. If for any reason the original purchase invoice or copy sales invoice has to be consulted, it can quickly be referred to in the purchase or sales invoice files.

Thirdly, Returns and Allowances Books, whether for purchases or sales, are ruled in almost exactly the same way as the Purchase and Sales Journal themselves, the difference being that the heading 'Invoice No' is replaced by 'Debit Note No' and 'Credit Note No' respectively, thus facilitating reference to these documents.

Fourthly, it is apparent that a check can be placed on the arithmetical accuracy of the bookkeeping work by agreeing periodically, often at the end of each month, the 'cross' cast or 'cross addition' of the Analysis Columns with the cast or addition of the Total Column in each of the subsidiary books.

Finally, we have an example of the purchase by the business of Fixed Assets, the showcases and fittings. As these have been bought for retention and not for resale, it is essential to provide an additional analysis column, in this case headed 'Special Items'. The provision of this column enables us to see at a glance the total value of such special purchases during the period.

As VAT (Value Added Tax) was applicable to these transactions we required an additional analysis column in which to record the VAT. On the purchase from R Ridgwell, which totalled £287.00, there would be VAT; at 20% this is £57.40 and would be added to the invoice to give a total of £344.40. Similarly with the invoice from B Davis, VAT of £263.00 is added, giving a total of £1578.00, and with that from General Supplies VAT is £200, making a total of £1200.00. These will be recorded in the Purchase Day Book and the VAT analysed into the extra column that has been added.

Exactly the same procedure takes place with the Sales. The VAT must be added to each invoice. This will increase each one by 20%, e.g. invoice number 4 to W Humphrey for goods costing £576.00 will have VAT of £115.20 added and the invoice total will be £691.20; and similarly for the other sales, and purchases and sales returns.

Remember this

For many businesses in the services industry, there will be very few purchases of stock and therefore little need for a Purchases Journal. Focus will instead be on measuring and recording the amount of labour time expended upon each sale.

Focus points

On completion of this chapter you should be:

* familiar with the Purchase and Sales Journals, their structure, purpose and how invoices should be recorded in them
* able to recognize that purchase and sale returns follow a similar pattern
* aware that complete accuracy is essential at this initial stage. Any error made will be processed throughout the bookkeeping system.

Testing Yourself

1 In the context of an accounting system for a manufacturing company, what would be your recommendations for dealing with purchase invoices? Show how to design the book (or spreadsheet) in which you suggest they should be entered.

2 What are the functions of the Purchase Analysis Journal? Give a specimen layout and make six entries in it. Total all columns and check the cross cast.

3 Goods purchased by a business may comprise either goods for resale at a profit, or goods for retention and use. Give two examples of each, and explain how such purchases are recorded in the Books of Account.

4 'The Books of Prime Entry are developments from the ordinary Journal.' Is this a correct statement? Draw out the design for a Purchase Day Book and a Sales Day Book in a business having three main departments.

5 PQ & Co, Merchants, have three departments, A, B and C. You want to keep separate trading accounts for each. With this end in view, design the Sales Day Book, making four specimen entries, and explain how the book would function.

6 A trader wishes to ascertain separately the gross profit earned by each of the two departments which comprise his business.

   Show how the columnar system of bookkeeping would allow him to do this without opening any additional books or accounts. Give any designs for necessary day books and explain how the system works.

7 What are the Returns Inwards and Outwards? Where should these items be entered in the books of a trader? What effect has each upon the profits of a business?

8 On 1 February, B Grey owed A White £16 for goods supplied.

   On 13 February he bought from White on credit three shirts at £8 each, six pairs of socks for £7 and a pair of jeans for £17.

   Set out in full the invoice made out by White relating to the purchases on 13 February. Include VAT at 20%.

9 XY is a manufacturer of electrical appliances. Give the ruling for a Purchase Book which you would recommend he should keep. Enter the following invoices received. Ignore VAT.

Feb 2 AB, £250 for goods.
 4 PQ, £120 for repairs to machinery.
 5 CD, £70 for advertising.
 6 AB, £575 for goods.
 8 X City Council, £1240 for general rates. PO telephones, £84.
 12 GH, £100 for goods.
 14 Overnite, £30 for carriage.
 15 AB, £2250 for new plant.

10 On 1 February xxx1, you supplied to T Thomas, 200 grey pullovers at £7 each, less a trade discount of 7½%. Thomas returned 50 pullovers as not up to sample and you agreed to credit him with their value.

Enter the items in the Returns Book concerned and draw up the credit note to Thomas, including VAT at 20%.

11 G Bath, a retailer, purchased two items for resale in his shop, one of Product A and one of Product B. The following figures relate to these two items.

	Product A	Product B
Manufacturer's Recommended Retail Price	£1500	£4000
Trade Discount allowed to retailers	20%	25%

It is G Bath's intention to sell these two products at the recommended retail price.

You are required to:

a calculate the price which G Bath will pay for each product;
b calculate the gross profit as a percentage of selling price on each product, if the products are sold at the recommended retail price;

   c calculate the gross profit as a percentage of cost price for each product.

Ignore VAT.

12 Enter the following transactions of Milner & Co Ltd in the appropriate Books of Prime Entry; rule off at 28 February xxx1, and post as necessary to the Impersonal and Private Ledgers.

Note: Special care should be taken in drafting the form of the Books of Prime Entry. **Read Chapter 4 before posting to the ledgers.**

Feb	4	Bought from T Lloyd, Lincoln, 500 metres of baize at £2.35 per metre, 2000 metres of satin at £5.60 per metre, less 10% trade discount in each case.
	10	Sold to T Williams, York, 400 metres curtain material at £6.50 per metre, and sundry fittings £8. Box charged £10.
	11	Bought showcase and counter for showroom from Universal Supplies Ltd, London, £750.00.
	12	Returned to T Lloyd, Lincoln, 200 metres of satin as invoiced on 4 February.
Feb	18	Bought from J Grey, Taunton, 300 metres linen at £7.25 per metre, less 5% trade discount and 250 metres baize at £2.35 per metre net.
	20	Received debit note from T Williams, York, for box invoiced on 10 February.
	24	Sold to D Wilson, Coventry, 300 metres baize at £4.00 per metre net, and 600 metres satin at £7.00 per metre less 10% trade discount.

Ignore VAT.

Purchase and sales transactions and ledger accounts

In this chapter you will learn:

▶ *About debiting and crediting accounts*
▶ *About VAT*
▶ *About debtors and creditors control accounts*

This chapter includes details of how the Ledger is made up and how information is entered into it. The important distinction is also drawn between Personal and Impersonal Ledgers and some details of their interactions are given. The section concludes with a brief comment on VAT.

Question As I see it, the Purchase and Sales Day Books are written up from the original purchase invoices, and the copies of the sales invoices to customers?

Answer Yes, that is right, but it is of the utmost importance that every purchase invoice, whether for goods or services, should be certified correct by the responsible officials of the business before being entered in the Purchase Journal.

Question The final column in the first example's Purchase Journal was headed 'Crates and Packing', but there was no similar column in the second one. Why is this?

Answer This depends upon the business. Suppliers may or may not charge for any crates and packing material that are used. If they do so, a record must clearly be made of the expense. It is a cost which we should record separately because it may be recoverable if and when such items as crates are returned to the suppliers; otherwise the cost must be borne by the business.

Question With both the Purchase and the Sales Journals there is then no one particular form of ruling?

Answer No. There cannot be. The system of bookkeeping aims to provide the information in the form in which it is required, or which is of the greatest use. For this reason care must be exercised in the choice of the analysis columns. These may represent the principal materials dealt in, or the departments responsible for their production and sale, and so on.

Question If goods are bought and sold on credit, I should have thought it was also very important to know:

▶ how much the business has purchased *from any one supplier,*

and

▶ how much it has sold *to any one customer.*

But as there are numerous transactions with different suppliers and customers, how could this be done from the Journals alone?

Answer By using the Ledger, or principal book of account, we are able to discover very quickly not only what has been purchased from or sold to any particular person, *but how that person stands in relation to the business at any particular time*, that is, whether they are its accounts payable or receivable. Put in another way, we want to know how much we have sold to each customer period by period because if possible we hope to increase our sales to them, and we also want to know how much that customer owes us for goods delivered, since their payments to us provide the monies out of which we have to pay our suppliers.

Question So the Ledger Account records not only the trading aspect of our transactions, but also the *cash aspect*?

Answer Yes. Both aspects must be recorded as affecting suppliers and customers, but at the moment we are only concerned with the *trading aspect*.

The Ledger

PERSONAL ACCOUNTS

We have spoken of Ledger Accounts as playing an essential part in summarizing the transactions of the business so far as they concern those with whom it deals.

It is now necessary to describe the Ledger Account rather more precisely, and to consider its other functions.

Its usual format is as follows:

JONES

Dr					Cr
Date	Details	Amount	Date	Details	Amount
		£			£

In the format we notice:

▶ Name of Account. This may be the name of the person, in this case Jones, who is either a supplier or a customer of the business. In other cases it may also represent the impersonal subject matter with which the account deals such as the name of a particular expense or asset of the business.

▶ The vertical double line in the centre divides the account into two equal parts. That on the left we term the **Debit** side, denoted by the symbol **Dr**, and that on the right the **Credit** side, with the symbol **Cr**. *On both sides* of the account, it will be observed, there are three columns headed respectively: Date, Details and Amount.

In the ordinary way, a separate page, or folio, of the Ledger is used for each account opened, and the Ledger itself may be a bound book; a loose-leaf book; in the form of cards, with a separate card for each account; or a series of files in a computer-based system.

If we assume that Jones is a supplier of goods to the business, the structure of the account enables us to put to his credit, i.e. on the right-hand, or *credit*, side, the value of the goods supplied by him. The right-hand side may also be regarded generally as that on which we enter increases in sources of finance. That may be credit given by suppliers, amounts invested into the business by the proprietor or revenues gained from trading. We therefore make a credit (Cr) entry on the right-hand side of the account showing the amount of credit he has granted us, i.e. the value of goods or services supplied by him.

Let us suppose Jones has supplied goods to the value of £10. This being an ordinary purchase transaction, the first record will be made in the Purchase Journal, as we have seen. It will ultimately be put (or 'posted' as this action is usually called) to the credit of Jones's account, as follows:

JONES

Dr							Cr
Date	Details	PRJ Fo	Amount	Date	Details	PJ Fo	Amount
				xxx1			£
				Jan 1	Goods	2	10.00

At this point we must remember:

▶ It is not necessary, but in appropriate circumstances it might be helpful, to repeat here the full description of the goods. By inserting a column for the Purchase Journal folio (PJ Fo) we can readily turn back to the initial entry in the Purchase Journal and, if we wish, to the original document, on which it was based, i.e. in this case the supplier's invoice.

▶ The purpose of our Ledger Account with Jones is to summarize or assemble within it *all our transactions* with him; otherwise it would be impossible to determine the position of the business in relation to him.

Because we are now thinking of Jones as a *supplier*, it is logical to assume, in the first instance, that any items on the left-hand or *debit* side will be in respect of payments made to him, reducing the amounts owed to him (decreasing the liability).

If, however, the business has had occasion to return goods to him because of unsatisfactory quality, or error in price, and a *credit note* is received signifying his acceptance of them, this also is a matter which must be recorded on the *debit* side. The effect of the return of the goods is *to reduce the liability of the business* to Jones as its creditor. In this case, the initial entry will have been made in the **Purchase Returns or Allowances**

Book, and from that we shall post to the *debit* of Jones's Ledger Account, as under:

JONES

Dr								Cr
Date	Details	PRJ	Amount	Date	Details	PJ	Amount
		Fo				Fo	
xxx1	Returns or			xxx1			
Jan 6	allowances	3	£1.50	Jan 1	Goods	2	£10.00

Should Jones, on the other hand, be a *customer* of the business a Ledger Account will be opened in identical form, but if goods to the value of £10 are *sold* to him, his account will be debited, that is the entry will be made on the *left-hand* side:

JONES

Dr							Cr
Date	Details	SJ	Amount	Date	Details	SRJ	Amount
		Fo				Fo	
xxx1			£				
Jan 1	Goods	2	10.00				

He now appears as a *debtor* (i.e. account receivable) to the business, as indeed he is, the details of the original sale being found on Folio 2 of the **Sales Journal.**

He is *indebted* to the business, and therefore the entry appears on the left-hand, debit side. The left-hand side may be regarded generally as that on which we enter increases in assets (future benefits) and expenses (where the business has consumed some benefit). Jones, as a debtor, is an asset of the business – we expect a future benefit when he settles his debt. We therefore make a debit (Dr) entry on the left-hand side of the account showing that the assets of the business have increased.

Finally, should goods be returned by him, or the business make him any kind of allowance, the amount, as posted from the **Sales Returns and Allowances Book,** will be put to his credit.

The result will be, as we should expect:

▶ to offset by that amount his original indebtedness of £10

▶ to indicate that the business, having delivered defective goods, or made an overcharge, now proceeds to give Jones the necessary *credit*.

The Ledger Account would then appear:

JONES

Dr							Cr
Date	Details	SJ Fo	Amount	Date	Details	SRJ Fo	Amount
xxx1			£	xxx1			£
Jan 1	Goods	2	10.00	Jan 16	Returns or allowances	3	1.50

When the *cash* as well as the *trading aspect* of these transactions has been dealt with, we shall be in a position to determine, at any time and irrespective of the number of items, the balance of indebtedness due either *to* or *by* the business.

So far as we have been dealing with persons *external* to the business, the *personal* aspect of the sales and purchase transactions has now been recorded.

By that we mean *the effect upon the people* with whom the transactions have been entered into, resulting in their becoming the creditors or debtors of the business.

If we have carefully followed the construction of the Ledger Account as shown, it is apparent that the entries are postings from the various books of first entry – from the Journals. That is to say, the Journals provide the basis for the writing up of all Ledger Accounts.

We may even lay it down as a rule with very few exceptions that: *No entry shall be made in a Ledger Account, unless it has first appeared in the Journal.*

We should remember that the Journal will not necessarily be a bound book. It may consist of a spreadsheet or word-processed document prepared by a computer or a file of invoices.

Remember this

Increases in A + X = debit, Increases in E + L + R = credit

IMPERSONAL ACCOUNTS

We stated at the beginning of the previous section that the name of the account might be that of the person with whom the business dealt, or of the impersonal subject-matter referred to in it.

The former we have now called a **Personal Account**, and the latter is called an **Impersonal** or **Nominal Account**.

Jones's account, whether he be a supplier or a customer, is a *Personal Account*. His position, as someone external to the business, has been looked at from the *personal* aspect.

There is, however, another aspect to be considered, and that is *the effect upon the business* as an impersonal unit, of the transactions with Jones and any other suppliers and customers.

When in the first place we regarded Jones as a *supplier* his account was credited with £10, but at the same time we must remember that the business then came into possession of £10 worth of *goods*, which we hope to sell to our benefit in the future. We therefore have an increase in an asset, an *impersonal account*, normally described as 'Goods purchased', 'stocks', 'inventory' or, more usually, **Purchases**.

We must remember:

▶ The essence of the Double Entry System is to record the dual aspect of each transaction *within the Ledger*, or book of account.
In the event of no 'Purchases' Account being opened we should have recorded in the Ledger *one aspect of the transaction only* – the personal aspect.

▶ The business, or its proprietor, desires to know, period by period, how much has been *purchased* of the various kinds of goods dealt in.

The opening of the Ledger Account for 'purchases' permits the periodic totals of the Purchase Journal to be posted to it on the chargeable, or *debit*, side.

Sometimes it is contended, and truthfully, that the total cost of purchases, suitably analysed, can be seen at a glance in the Purchase Journal.

This, however, is no reason for eliminating the Ledger Account for 'purchases', because, as stated above, we desire to complete the *double entry within the Ledger*, and also obtain, in the summarized form which the Ledger account gives, the total amount of goods received by it month by month during the trading year.

As, in practice, the various subdivisions of the Journal are ruled off at monthly intervals, a note of the monthly totals in summarized form is clearly very helpful and this role is performed by the **Purchases** Account in the Ledger.

The following illustrates in another way what has been described above:

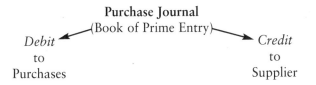

Purchase Journal
(Book of Prime Entry)
Debit ← → *Credit*
to   to
Purchases   Supplier

or, in account form, assuming the total purchases for the month were £1410:

Nominal Ledger Account

PURCHASES

Dr								Cr
Date	Details	PJ Fo	Amount	Date	Details	Fo	Amount	
xxx1			£					
Jan 31	Total purchases for month	2	1410.00					

We may also add that, from the point of view of the business, the charge or *debit* to the 'Purchases' Account may be made by taking the *total* only of the appropriate column in the Purchase Journal.

This is in striking contrast to the necessity for giving *credit* to each separate supplier in *their own personal account*. We cannot avoid this latter step because we must know at any time *how the business stands in relation to each supplier*.

Purchase returns and allowances

We saw earlier that Jones, as a supplier, was charged or *debited* with the goods returned to him, as we then owed him less money. This debit entry reflects a decrease in the liabilities of the business. We also need to reduce the amount of purchases we had entered (as we no longer have those goods that have been returned). As we are decreasing an asset of the business, we make a credit entry:

Purchase Returns and Allowances Book

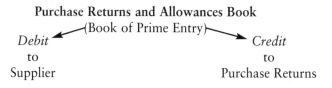

(Book of Prime Entry)

Debit	*Credit*
to	to
Supplier	Purchase Returns

or, in account form, assuming total purchase returns for the month were £71.50:

Nominal Ledger Account

PURCHASE RETURNS AND ALLOWANCES

Dr								Cr
Date	*Details*	*PJ*	*Amount*	*Date*	*Details*	*PRJ*	*Amount*
		Fo				*Fo*	
xxx1			£	xxx1			£
Jan 31	Total purchases for month	2	1410.00	Jan 31	Total returns and allowances for month	3	71.50

Purchases of a capital nature

In Example 3.3 we saw that the purchase by D Morris of showcases and fittings was recorded, together with his other purchases, in the Purchase Journal kept by him.

The personal aspect of this transaction is a credit to the suppliers in the Ledger Account opened in their name, i.e. a *personal account*.

But, as with the receipt of goods which we intend to resell, we have similarly to put on record somewhere the purchase of these capital goods, or as they are usually called, *fixed assets*.

We don't however charge them to the purchases since they are not goods in which the business is dealing.

Remember this

The classification of Fixed Assets will depend upon your type of business. For example, IT equipment is normally considered a Fixed Asset as it is intended to be used in the business. However, for a computing retailer or wholesaler, this could be classed as stock, a current asset, where they intend to resell it.

But, nevertheless, an account must be opened for them in the Ledger, in order to complete the double entry *in the Ledger*, and so we should open an account under the general heading of 'Fixtures and Fittings'.

In this case the business has acquired a fixed asset, which we hope will provide benefits both now and in the future, and it is right that it should be charged or, as we say, *debited* with the purchase cost of £1000.

The question now arises: in which *section* of the Ledger shall the account be opened?

What we have already done is to describe:

▸ **Personal Accounts**, e.g. Jones

▸ **Impersonal Accounts**, e.g. Purchases,

the latter being the counterpart, in summarized form, of the former, so far as the effect upon the business is concerned.

Because of the existence of these two types of account, it is customary, in practice, to use two entirely separate Ledgers, known respectively as the **Personal Ledger** and the **Impersonal** or **Nominal Ledger**.

It is also usual to keep separate personal ledgers, one for customers, usually called the **Sales Ledger**, and the other for suppliers, the **Purchase Ledger**.

If it would be useful to divide either of these ledgers there is no reason why not, and for a larger business this may be useful in practice. The usual basis is by alphabet – to spread the work amongst different operators; by area so that different salesmen can be provided with relevant information; and sometimes by particular categories of sales.

By contrast, the accounts in the Impersonal Ledger are unlikely to be very numerous, and in the main they relate to those matters which affect the business in its *ordinary trading activities*, such as purchases, sales, wages, etc.

We could, of course, from the standpoint of the effect upon the business, open the 'Fixtures and Fittings' Account in the Impersonal Ledger, and in that account record all dealings in that particular type of property. But, because the fixtures and fittings have no direct relation to the day-to-day trading activities, a further section of the Ledger is provided for the accounts of this and similar types of fixed asset.

This further section is termed the **Private Ledger**, and represents the third and final division of the Ledger as a book of account. It was called the **Private Ledger** from the days when only the owner or a director would have access to these '**private accounts**'. It is merely another illustration of the division of the Ledger into whatever sections the owners or managers think will be useful.

One again, we post the *total* of the 'special items' or 'capital items' column in the Purchase Journal, so that the Fixtures and Fittings Account appears as follows:

FIXTURES AND FITTINGS

Dr							Cr
Date	Details	PJ Fo	Amount	Date	Details	Fo	Amount
xxx1			£				
March 31	Showcases and fittings	1	1000.00				

or in diagram form:

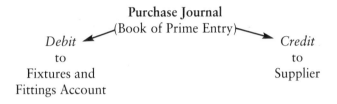

Purchase Journal
(Book of Prime Entry)

Debit
to
Fixtures and
Fittings Account

Credit
to
Supplier

Sales

Much of what we have said regarding the completion of the double entry under the heading of purchases will apply in the case of sales, although in the reverse direction.

We are still dealing with the *impersonal aspect or the effect upon the business* of the delivery of goods or services to the customer.

If goods or services are sold on credit to Brown, for example, in her capacity as a *customer,* from the *personal aspect*, Brown becomes our debtor and must be charged or *debited* with what she has received at *selling price*. In other words, we have an increase in an asset as the business will receive a future benefit when Brown repays us.

Impersonally the business is entitled to credit an impersonal account, which may be headed 'Goods sold', or more usually, **Sales**. This credit entry recognizes that the business has an increase in funds, sales revenue.

Our reasons for so doing are:

- As in the case of purchases, the double entry must be completed *within the Ledgers*.

- The business, or its proprietor, desires to know, period by period, how much has been sold of the various kinds of goods we deal in.

Therefore, we will open an account in the Impersonal Ledger, headed 'Sales', the periodic totals of the Sales Journal will be posted to it on the *credit* side, and, as with purchases, the Sales Journal will usually be ruled off and posted at monthly intervals.

At any time, therefore, we may obtain a comparison of the *cost of purchases*, with the *proceeds of sales*, by examining these two accounts in the Impersonal Ledger.

Stated in another way, we have:

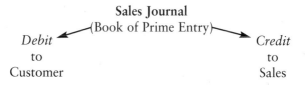

Sales Journal

Debit ◀─(Book of Prime Entry)─▶ Credit
to | to
Customer | Sales

or, in account form, assuming the sales value for the month to be £2000.00:

SALES

Dr							Cr
Date	Details	Fo	Amount	Date	Details	SJ Fo	Amount
				xxx1			£
				Jan 31	Total sales for month	2	2000.00

At this stage we record the total sales as shown in the Sales Journal (a more detailed analysis is given later in the chapter).

This is because, irrespective of the *kind* of goods sold, they may all be regarded as *sales*, and dealt with in the Ledger as one item.

In recording the *personal aspect*, however, a separate debit to each customer in their own *personal account* is essential if we are to know precisely:

▶ how much has been sold to them

▶ the amount of their indebtedness to the business at any particular time.

SALES RETURNS AND ALLOWANCES

Should Brown, to whom £2000 worth of goods have been sold, return any part of the goods, or make a claim on the business for an allowance in respect of the invoice price to her, the effect upon the business will be to reduce the initial *credit* to the 'Sales' Account. In other words, the latter account will be *debited*:

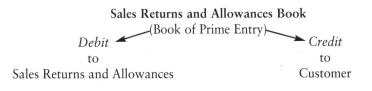

Sales Returns and Allowances Book

(Book of Prime Entry)

Debit
to
Sales Returns and Allowances

Credit
to
Customer

or, in account form, assuming the total amount of the sales returns and allowances for the month to be £50:

Nominal Ledger Account

SALES RETURNS AND ALLOWANCES

Date	Details	SRJ Fo	Amount	Date	Details	SJ Fo	Amount
		Dr					Cr
xxx1			£	xxx1			£
Jan 31	Total returns and allowances for month	5	50.00				

SALES OF A CAPITAL NATURE

These are far less frequently encountered than purchases of other classes of goods. However, the need for a systematic approach to data processing means that all transactions will be processed in accordance with pre-planned procedures, so all transactions are captured in our journals (and then accounts).

It is possible to record such sales by inserting a 'Special Items' column in the Sales Journal, but in practice use is almost always made of the earliest form of Journal, or the General Journal (without analysis columns) as illustrated in Chapter 8.

Examples that may be cited of this type of 'sale' are the disposal of a lorry, salesperson's car or machinery used in the business.

The Journal entry in this case provides the basic narrative of the transaction for entry in the Ledgers. This includes the personal (Sales) Ledger as relates to the person they are sold to, and the account of the particular asset in the Private Ledger to record the effect on the business. For example,

Journal

Date	Narrative	Dr	Cr
xxx	Person to whom sold	XX	
	Capital asset account being sale of lorry, car, etc, to AN Other		XX

Consider the following to illustrate this example.

▶ **Example 4.1**

On 1 January xxx1, D Morris had in his factory machinery with a book value of £5000 (i.e. cost in the accounts at the time). On 15 January a stitching machine was sold to a dealer, realizing £150.

Private Ledger Account

MACHINERY

Dr							Cr
Date	Details	Fo	Amount	Date	Details	Fo	Amount
xxx1			£	xxx1			£
Jan 1	Balance		5000.00	Jan 15	A Dealer, Stitching machine		150.00

An important point in connection with this transaction would be the loss or profit on sale, i.e. the proceeds of sale of £150 would have to be compared with that proportion of the opening balance of £5000 which represented the actual machine sold. The principles describing how this comparison will be made are described in more detail in Chapter 15. The important fact to note at this point however is that 'sales' of a capital asset are not recorded in the 'Sales Account' in the Ledger (that is just used for sales of what we normally produce to sell – not for ad hoc sales of capital items) but simply credited to the Asset's Impersonal account or to a Disposal account to record the effect on the business.

Sales Journal
or
General Journal
(Book of Prime Entry)

Debit ← → *Credit*
to — to
Customer — Machinery Account
or
Machinery Disposal Account

Impersonal, or Nominal, and Private Ledgers

While the Personal Ledger is restricted to the accounts of suppliers and customers in its purchase and sales sections respectively, the following examples are typical of the accounts appearing in the Impersonal Ledger and the Private Ledger:

Impersonal Ledger (Also called the **Nominal Ledger**)	**Private Ledger**
Purchases	Capital (of Proprietor)
Sales	Factory, warehouse or office
Purchase returns	premises
Sales returns	Machinery
Wages	Tools
Carriage	Fixtures and fittings
Salaries	Motor vehicles
Cash discounts allowed	Patents
Cash discounts received	Trade marks
Bad debts	Inventory
Travelling expenses	Investments
Packing expenses	Loans
Repairs	
Interest paid	
Interest received	
Rent	
Rates	
Commission	

In general, those items appearing above under the heading 'Impersonal Ledger' relate to accounts in which we find details of the *income statement*, or *revenue position* of the business. For example, we compare the revenue accounts such as sales against the expense accounts such as purchases, wages and salaries.

Those, on the other hand, under the heading of 'Private Ledger' relate to the **assets**, **liabilities** and **equity capital** of the business.

Several of the accounts in the Private Ledger are sometimes called **Real** accounts, in particular office premises, plant and machinery, etc., as they refer to assets that are 'real' in the physical sense. Clearly the Private Ledger, particularly in the case of a sole trade or partnership, relates to matters of a more private nature and may be more closely controlled by the proprietor rather than being part of the routine bookkeeping.

Ledger Accounts

Now that we have become familiar with the general application of Double Entry principles to the recording of Purchases and Sales transactions *within the Ledgers*, let us carry Example 3.3 a stage further and *post to the Ledger Accounts* from the various Books of Prime Entry which we have already written up.

1 PURCHASES

In the Purchase Day Book of D Morris earlier we saw it is necessary to give **credit** to each one of the three suppliers who have supplied goods. Such credit will clearly be given in the Personal (Purchase) Ledger, and the three accounts required will be opened as follows:

D MORRIS

Purchase Ledger

R RIDGWELL, BOLTON

Dr							Cr
Date	Details	Fo	Amount	Date	Details	PJ Fo	Amount
				xxx1			£
				March 12	Goods & VAT	1	344.40

B DAVIS, ELY

Dr							Cr
Date	Details	Fo	Amount	Date	Details	PJ Fo	Amount
				xxx1			£
				March 20	Goods & VAT	1	1578.00

GENERAL SUPPLIES LTD, LONDON

Dr							Cr
Date	Details	Fo	Amount	Date	Details	PJ Fo	Amount
				xxx1			£
				March 29	Goods &		
					VAT	1	1200.00

In each case the entries appear on the *credit side* since, until payment is made to them, the suppliers are creditors of the business.

The use of the words 'Goods and VAT' in the 'Details' column is all that is necessary, as full particulars of the goods can quickly be found on Folio 1 of the Purchase Journal itself.

We must now consider the *impersonal aspect*, which records the assets we have gained as 'Goods Purchased' or 'Purchases'. It is necessary, too, for us to remember that by this is meant 'goods purchased for resale', so that we must in any event exclude the item of Showcases and Fittings.

Our Impersonal Ledger Account for Purchases will then be:

PURCHASES

Dr							Cr
Date	Details	PJ Fo	Amount	Date	Details	Fo	Amount
xxx1			£				
March 31	Total for month:						
	Cotton		500.00				
	Sheets		175.00				
	Tee-shirts		912.00				
	Sundries		15.00				
		1	1602.00				

It is unlikely that we will be happy with the form of this account, because month by month new totals will appear in it, and the subsequent addition of the 'Amount' column will be somewhat complicated. This makes it harder to understand the information this account contains than is strictly necessary.

For this reason, it may be preferred to open a separate Purchase Account *for each class of goods*, or to enter them in one account, but in *columnar* form.

If the first method is chosen we will have four separate purchase accounts:

Nominal Ledger

PURCHASES – COTTON

Dr							Cr
Date	Details	PJ Fo	Amount	Date	Details	Fo	Amount
xxx1			£				
March 31	Total for month	1	500.00				

PURCHASES – SHEETS

Dr							Cr
Date	Details	PJ Fo	Amount	Date	Details	Fo	Amount
xxx1			£				
March 31	Total for month	1	175.00				

PURCHASES – TEE-SHIRTS

Dr							Cr
Date	Details	PJ Fo	Amount	Date	Details	Fo	Amount
xxx1			£				
March 31	Total for month	1	912.00				

PURCHASES – SUNDRIES

Date	Details	PJ Fo	Amount	Date	Details	Fo	Amount
xxx1			£				
March 31	Total for month	1	15.00				

Dr / Cr

For the showcases and fittings purchased, an account in the Private Ledger will be opened, as below:

FIXTURES AND FITTINGS

Date	Details	PJ Fo	Amount	Date	Details	Fo	Amount
xxx1			£				
March 31	Total for month	1	1000.00				

Dr / Cr

It must be noted that the charge to the business for *purchases* and *fixtures and fittings* is made on the *debit* side, the amount in each case being the *total* of the appropriate analysis column in the Purchase Journal.

We now see that:

▶ The Purchase Journal as a Book of Prime Entry provides a basis for the Double Entry.

▶ The dual aspect of the transactions has been recorded *within the Ledgers*.

▶ Arithmetical agreement has been obtained, in that the sum of the *credit* entries or postings in the Purchase Ledger is equal to the sum of the *debit* postings in the Impersonal and Private Ledgers.

▶ While the postings to the Impersonal and Private Ledger Accounts are made on 31 March and in *total* only, those to the Personal Ledger are made as soon as possible after the initial record in the Journal and use the dates of the original transactions. It is essential to have our Ledger Account with each supplier 'up to date'.

2 PURCHASE RETURNS AND ALLOWANCES

In the Purchase Returns Book we see there are two entries relating, in the first case, to an overcharge, and in the second, to the return of goods by the business to one of its suppliers.

In recording the *personal aspect* we must remember that the suppliers' accounts in the Purchase Ledger will be *debited* as we no longer owe them as much money.

This is a logical step to take because, had the overcharge not been detected, we should have *debited* Hunt with a payment *greater* than was actually due to him. The issue of a Debit Note now clearly reduces the amount of any subsequent payment to him by the business.

Further, the *receipt of a Credit Note* from Luxton enables the business to debit him with the cost of the goods returned for which, when purchased, it had originally given him credit.

The Purchase Ledger Accounts for the two suppliers will then appear as follows:

Purchase Ledger

W HUNT

Dr								Cr
Date	Details	PRJ Fo	Amount	Date	Details	PJ FO	Amount
xxx1			£				
March 15	Overcharge	1	14.40				

V LUXTON

Dr								Cr
Date	Details	PRJ Fo	Amount	Date	Details	PJ Fo	Amount
xxx1			£				
March 27	Returns	1	36.00				

As to the *impersonal* aspect, the stocks will need to be *credited*. Why? The purchases of stock have been decreased by the amount of goods returned and adjustments, in total, of £42.00.

The **Purchase Returns** or **Returns Outwards Accounts,** will then be credited on 31 March with the **total of** the appropriate analysis columns in the Purchase Returns Journal as below:

PURCHASE RETURNS – COTTON

Dr							Cr
Date	Details	PRJ Fo	Amount	Date	Details	PRJ Fo	Amount
				xxx1			£
				March 31	Total for month	1	42.00

You will have noticed that the suppliers of goods were credited with the total of 'Goods and VAT' and the purchases accounts debited with the cost of goods only from the analysis columns. To complete the double entry and record the position of the business in respect of VAT the appropriate entries must be made in the VAT account in the Nominal (Impersonal) Ledger, using the monthly totals from the analysis columns in the Books of Prime Entry.

When the Impersonal/Nominal Ledger account is written up, the balance will be the amount that is due to be paid to the relevant tax authorities (e.g. HMRC). Occasionally more may have been paid with purchases than has been charged on sales and a claim can be made for repayment if this occurs. This may happen in any period where sales are slow for example. It may also occur with sales of goods which are zero-rated for VAT (i.e. where VAT on purchases can be reclaimed, but no VAT is charged on sales). More details on VAT can be found at the end of the chapter.

Nominal Ledger Account

VAT

Dr							Cr
Date	Details	Fo	Amount	Date	Details	Fo	Amount
xxx1			£	xxx1			£
March 31	Total for purchases during month	1	520.40	March 31	Total for sales during month	2	799.00
	Total for sales returns and allowances for month	2	40.40		Total for purchase returns and allowances for month	1	8.40

These figures show that VAT of £799.00 has been charged to customers and will be collected from them, less £40.40 in

respect of returns and allowances,	i.e.	758.60
We have been charged, and will pay to the suppliers £520.40 less £8.40	i.e.	512.00
so the remaining balance of		£246.60

is due to the tax authorities. VAT is not a charge on the business: the business charges the customer and accounts for the total charge to the tax authorities after the appropriate allowance is made for the VAT that has been paid to suppliers.

Once more, it is seen that:

▶ the double entry is completed within the Ledgers, Personal and Nominal

▶ arithmetical agreement is maintained, the sum of the *debit* items being equal to the sum of the *credits,* and

▶ while the postings to the accounts of Hunt and Luxton are made on the dates of the transactions with them, those to the Purchase Returns Accounts are made in total on 31 March.

3 SALES

The Sales Journal gives us full particulars of the sales to the three customers for whom we shall open separate accounts in the Sales Ledger.

To record the personal aspect, we must show that they are debtors to the business (an asset), and therefore their accounts will be in *debit*, taking the following form:

W HUMPHREY, LINCOLN

Dr							Cr
Date	Details	SJ Fo	Amount	Date	Details	Fo	Amount
xxx1			£				
March 10	Goods and VAT	2	691.20				

S BONHAM, COVENTRY

Dr							Cr
Date	Details	SJ Fo	Amount	Date	Details	Fo	Amount
xxx1			£				
March 18	Goods and VAT	2	1308.00				

T BUTTERWORTH, NORWICH

Dr							Cr
Date	Details	SJ Fo	Amount	Date	Details	Fo	Amount
xxx1			£				
March 24	Goods and VAT	2	2794.80				

We should now be able to understand the meaning of what has been done in our bookkeeping work. If in the case of *personal* accounts, like those set out above, the entries appear on the debit side, or there is an excess in value of debit entries over credit entries, the person whose name appears at the head of the account is always a debtor to the business. They are an asset from which the business will gain a future benefit when they pay for the goods we have sold them (less any returns).

If the value of debits is greater than credits in an *impersonal* account, such as 'Purchases', it indicates that the business has stock or inventory assets that we hope to sell in the future and generate benefits for the business.

When dealing with *sales*, it is necessary to enter a *credit* showing that new funds have been generated by the business from trading.

Therefore, an account will be opened in the Impersonal Ledger for Sales, as follows:

SALES

Dr							Cr
Date	Details	Fo	Amount	Date	Details	SJ Fo	Amount
				xxx1			£
				March 31	Total for month		
					Cotton	2	1500.00
					Linen		2470.00
					Sundries		25.00
							3995.00

As explained earlier, when we discussed the analysis of purchases, we will, however, probably prefer to open separate Sales Accounts for the various kinds of goods to correspond with the columns in the Sales Journal.

The result will then be:

SALES – COTTON

Dr								Cr
Date	Details	Fo	Amount	Date	Details	SJ Fo	Amount	
				xxx1			£	
				March 31	Total for month	2	1500.00	

SALES – LINEN

Dr								Cr
Date	Details	Fo	Amount	Date	Details	SJ Fo	Amount	
				xxx1			£	
				March 31	Total for month	2	2470.00	

SALES – SUNDRIES

Dr								Cr
Date	Details	Fo	Amount	Date	Details	SJ Fo	Amount	
				xxx1			£	
				March 31	Total for month	2	25.00	

By means of these analysed Impersonal Accounts it is now possible for the proprietor of the business to easily compare, month by month, the **purchase cost** with the **proceeds of sale** of the various articles in which they are dealing.

Obviously, in the long run sales should exceed purchases or the business will not make profits, but from month to month there will be changes in the level of stocks owned by the business and the direct comparison of purchases and sales may therefore be inappropriate, as any single month where purchases exceed sales for that item may be explainable just by changes in inventory holdings.

4 SALES RETURNS AND ALLOWANCES

As with Purchases, we find in the Sales Daybook two entries which must be posted to the Ledger, involving the completion of the *personal aspect* as a separate posting to the account of each customer, and of the *impersonal aspect* at the end of the month (in total only).

We find, however, this difference from the Purchases process: the goods returned by Humphrey are part of those sold to him during the month under review; while both items come under the head of 'Returns', there being no question of an overcharge.

Let us try to visualize what these two entries mean. It may be simpler to deal first with the impersonal aspect.

The business has received the goods, increasing its inventory assets. It is, therefore, logical that we should charge or *debit* the business with the *total* value of the returned goods.

At the same time, the customers owe less money to the business (the accounts receivable asset has decreased). Therefore, we *credit* their accounts with the amount of the returned goods showing that they now owe less money. This credit, in the case of Humphrey, will cause his account to appear as follows:

W HUMPHREY, LINCOLN

Dr							Cr
Date	Details	SJ Fo	Amount	Date	Details	SRJ Fo	Amount
xxx1				xxx1			£
March 10	Goods and VAT	2	691.20	March 22	Returns	2	108.00

and from it we can see that his original indebtedness is now reduced, *which is in line with the facts.*

As for Jenkinson, he too will receive a *credit*, as follows:

A JENKINSON, WOLVERHAMPTON

Dr							Cr
Date	Details	Fo	Amount	Date	Details	SRJ Fo	Amount
				xxx1			£
				March 23	Returns	2	134.40

However, since we know nothing of his original indebtedness to the business (perhaps he bought goods in a previous period that these are returns of?), the position is that he appears as a creditor for the amount shown above. Payment may either be made to him in settlement, or more probably, the credit will be taken into account by him when he next pays for any further goods supplied.

Finally, to complete the double entry, we need to post the totals of the appropriate columns in the Sales Returns Journals to the Debit of the Impersonal Ledger Accounts for 'Sales Returns – Cotton' and 'Sales Returns – Linen', just as we did with Purchases.

In both cases, the business has received goods, either from a supplier, or from a customer.

SALES RETURNS – COTTON

Dr							Cr
Date	Details	Fo	Amount	Date	Details	Fo	Amount
xxx1			£				
March 31	Total for month	2	90.00				

SALES RETURNS – LINEN

Dr							Cr
Date	Details	Fo	Amount	Date	Details	Fo	Amount
xxx1			£				
March 31	Total for month	2	112.00				

Summary

With each of the Journals we have been careful to regard them as providing the basis for the completion of the double entry *within the Ledgers*. They have, therefore, served their purpose in enabling us to look at each one of the *purchasing* and *selling transactions* from their *dual aspect*, or the Personal and Impersonal aspect.

Irrespective of the *number* of these transactions during any particular period, we are now in a position to tabulate the information contained in the Ledger Accounts in the form of *balances* that now exist (i.e. compare any and all debit entries with any and all credit entries). These balances will be obtained by reviewing of each account. The total amount on the debit side is called a *debit balance*, and on the credit side a *credit balance*. Where entries appear on both debit and credit sides, the excess of the one side over the other will be the balance, but you will better understand the importance of this after we have dealt with Cash Receipts and Cash Payments in Chapter 5.

In this example there are only two accounts with both debit and credit entries: VAT, which was summarized earlier in the chapter, and W Humphrey, shown below. Here the debits are greater than the credits so the net balance will be a debit.

At the end of each month, or whenever a balance is needed, two entries are made. A balancing amount which ensures that the total credits equals the total debits is entered on the credit side (marked c/d for 'carried down'), the two columns total and the balancing amount brought down (marked b/d) as the new debit, completing the double entry.

W HUMPHREY, LINCOLN

Dr							Cr
Date	Details	SJ Fo	Amount	Date	Details	SRJ Fo	Amount
xxx1				xxx1			£
March 10	Goods and VAT	2	691.20	March 22	Returns	2	108.00
				31	Balance	c/d	583.20
			676.20				691.20
	31 Balance	b/d	583.20				

We can extract and list the balances as they now appear in the various Ledger Accounts as we have credited them in this chapter so far:

Page	Ledger	Name of Account	Dr	Cr
			£	£
58	Purchase	R Ridgwell		344.40
59		B Davis		1578.00
59		General Supplies Ltd		1200.00
61		W Hunt	14.40	
62		V Luxton	36.00	
64	Sales	*W Humphrey	583.20	
64		S Bonham	1308.00	
64		T Butterworth	2794.80	
66		A Jenkinson		134.40
60	Impersonal	Purchases – Cotton	500.00	
60		Sheets	175.00	
60		Tee-shirts	912.00	
60		Sundries	15.00	
62		Purchase returns – Cotton		42.00
65		Sales – Cotton		1500.00
65		Linen		2470.00
65		Sundries		25.00
67		Sales returns – Cotton	90.00	
67		Linen	112.00	
63		VAT		246.60
60	Private	Fixtures and fittings	1000.00	
			£7540.40	£7540.40

* Note that the Ledger account shown earlier (Nominal Ledger Account) with only the sale recorded has been subsequently updated to reflect the 'returns and allowances' as above.

It should be mentioned that in the average business by far the greater number of accounts will be found in the Personal Ledgers, and especially in that section of those Ledgers containing the accounts of customers (i.e. the Sales Ledger). As the business increases its sales it may become necessary to divide up this Ledger on an alphabetical or territorial basis if the Accounting Department is to do its work with speed and efficiency. Alternatively control accounts may be useful to remove detail from the Sales Ledger itself to secondary records. The next section reviews how this may work in practice.

Control accounts

Reference was made earlier (Chapter 1) to 'one account in the ledger for incoming goods or purchases and other accounts for the individual suppliers'. If these suppliers become numerous it may be simpler to have one account, called **Accounts Payable (or Creditors) Control Account**, for recording the totals of the transactions, and subsequently analysing these totals to the individual suppliers elsewhere. Similarly there would be an account for the customers, for which the control account would be called the **Accounts Receivable** (or **Debtors**) **Control Account**.

The illustration in this chapter for 'Purchases' showed first an account for total purchases which was subsequently replaced by separate accounts for different types of purchases. Use of the total purchases account provides one illustration of a control account – in this case a control account for purchases. The more usual control account is for the personal accounts, and it is preferable to have at least two, one for accounts receivable (as listed in the Sales Ledger) and the other for accounts payable (as listed in the Purchase Ledger).

If an Accounts Payable Control Account had been used, the entries made in it for the transactions in the recent example would have been:

Accounts Payable Control Account

Dr								Cr
Date	Details	PJ Fo	Amount	Date	Details	PRJ Fo	Amount	
xxx1			£	xxx1			£	
March 31	Purchases returns and allowances for the month	1	50.40	March 31	Goods supplied for the month, and VAT thereon	1	3122.40	

and separate *subsidiary* records would be kept to show the position of each individual supplier. The net balance on the accounts payable control account (£3122.40 minus £50.40, i.e. £3072.00) should equal the sum of the balances on the individual suppliers accounts.

			£
	R Ridgwell	Cr	344.40
	B Davis	Cr	1578.00
	General Supplies Ltd	Cr	1200.00
			3122.40
minus	W Hunt Dr 14.40		
	V Luxton Dr 36.00		
			50.40
			£3072.00

With opening balances and more entries, as is usual in practice, the benefits from the use of the control account become more apparent. Control Accounts may be used wherever it is considered useful to a particular situation; maybe merely to divide the Personal Ledger (sales) into alphabetical sections, or areas of the country, or the responsibility of particular sales staff.

Value Added Tax

Question What is VAT?

Answer Many countries have introduced a tax calculated as a percentage of the sales of the business. In the UK, this is known as the Value Added Tax (VAT) (and in other countries it may be called a Sales Tax) and the appropriate percentage (currently 20% for most goods and services) on the value of sales has to be accounted for to HMRC. As allowance is given for VAT paid on purchases, a business in effect pays over the VAT on the value added by the business and recovers it from the customer. The balance of VAT charged to customers over the VAT suffered on purchases must be handed over to HMRC. On the other hand, if the tax suffered by it exceeds that which has been charged, a repayment is due. Only registered businesses are affected by this tax. Any business may register, but registration is not compulsory unless turnover exceeds £81,000 per annum (for 2014/15). A business not registered cannot charge VAT nor can it recover VAT suffered on its purchases.

Question What extra records does the business have to keep?

Answer The business with proper records will require very little extra; another column in the Purchase and Sales Day Books and an additional nominal ledger account is all that is necessary. The example in this chapter illustrated the bookkeeping requirements.

Similarly, an extra column would be required in the cash book for the VAT on cash transactions when purchases and sales are not made with credit.

Question This seems to be a simple procedure. Why do some people complain about the complexity of VAT?

Answer The bookkeeping is straightforward. The difficulties arise because certain goods and services are exempt from VAT (i.e. have VAT charged at 0% but VAT on purchases can't be reclaimed), while others are zero-rated (i.e. VAT is again 0% but this time VAT on purchases can be reclaimed).

Question Where should a trader go for advice?

Answer The local officer of HMRC or an accounting adviser should be consulted for the precise details applicable to a particular enterprise (see also *Teach Yourself Small Business Taxation*).

EXEMPTION

Exemption for a transaction means that no liability to account for tax to the tax authorities arises when the transaction is performed. Equally, the trader undertaking the exempt transaction is given no credit by the tax authorities for any tax invoiced by suppliers on the goods and services used for the exempt business.

ZERO-RATING

Zero-rating a transaction means that it is brought within the scope of the tax, but the rate applied to output is zero. If the person carrying out the transaction is a taxable person they are accountable in the usual way, but the result is that their outputs carry no tax because a zero rate is applied to them, while they are allowed credit for or repayment of tax on their inputs. Exports are relieved from tax by means of this technique (i.e. all agents are zero-rated).

Focus points

On completion of this chapter you should be familiar with:

❋ The basic principles of Debiting and Crediting accounts and the nature, use and inter-relation of the following:

Day Books/Journals	Personal Accounts
Purchases	Purchase Ledger
Sales	Sales ledger
Purchase returns	Control Accounts
Sales returns	
The Ledger	Impersonal Accounts (or Nominal)
	Real Accounts
	Private Accounts

❋ The principle and use of Debtors and Creditors Control Accounts.

❋ The principles of VAT and the recording of the VAT aspects of purchases and sales.

Testing Yourself

1 Name the different Ledgers employed in the ordinary trading concern, and mention the classes of account you would expect to find in each.

2 Explain:

   a Nominal Accounts
   b Real Accounts
   c Personal Accounts.

3 On which side of the following Ledger Accounts would you expect to find the balance? Give reasons for your answer in each case:

   a Bad Debts Account
   b Plant and Machinery Account
   c Sales Account
   d VAT Account
   e Returns Outwards Account.

4 W Green has the following transactions with J Black:

xxx1		£
July	10 Goods sold to W Green	422.00
	15 Goods returned by W Green	20.00
Oct	10 Goods sold to W Green	392.00
	10 Goods returned by Green	10.00
	11 W Green charged extra due to pricing error	45.00

You are required to show how each of the above items would be recorded in the books of J Black.

5 During the month of October xxx9, Ian Webster's transactions on credit were as follows:

			£	
Oct	1	Purchases from D Hudson	180.00	subject to 20% trade discount
	4	Sales to M Whitehead	85.00	
	7	Sales to A Woods	115.00	
	10	M Whitehead returns goods	20.00	
	15	Purchases from M Douglas	420.00	subject to 25% trade discount
	23	Returned goods to M Douglas (part of stock purchased on October 15)	30.00	list price
	25	Sales to M Whitehead	170.00	
	28	Purchases from D Hudson	86.00	
	30	Received credit note from Hudson in respect of goods (which had been purchased on October 28) with a list price excluding VAT of	16.00	
	31	Whitehead returns goods	36.00	

(**Note**: All purchases, sales and returns are subject to Value Added Tax at 20%)

You are required to:

a write up Webster's sales, purchases, returns inwards and returns outwards day books for the month of October xxx9

b write up and balance the VAT account for the month of October xxx9, showing the amount due to/from the tax authorities.

6 The following sales have been made by Sevenoaks Trading during the month of July xxx1. The values represent the value of the goods, before adding VAT at 20%.

xxx1

July	1	to High Rise	£120
	5	to Brown & Co	£70
	10	to Carter Brothers	£240
	12	to Singh & Co	£160
	31	to Jones Ltd	£190

You are required to enter these transactions in the Sales Day Book, Sales Ledger and Nominal Ledger.

7 The credit sales and purchases for the month of October xxx1 for Teachers & Co are shown below exclusive of VAT.

xxx1

Oct	1	Bought from Kent Traders	£170
	3	Bought from Canterbury Ltd	£360
	5	Sold to Davenport & Co	£250
	10	Sold to East Ltd	£120
	12	Bought from Canterbury Ltd	£420
	31	Sold to Davenport & Co	£460

You are required to enter these transactions in the appropriate records of the company assuming that Teachers & Co are (a) not registered for VAT; (b) registered for VAT. Assume 20%.

8 The following transactions relate to November xxx1.

xxx1			£
Nov	1	Sales Ledger balances	3276
	30	Totals for the month:	4347
		Sales Day Book	
		Sales returns and allowances	265
		Cheques received from customers	1984
		Discounts allowed	29
	30	Total of individual Sales Ledger balances	5345

You are required to write up the Sales Ledger control account.

(Do not attempt this question until you have completed Chapter 5.)

Cash transactions

In this chapter you will learn:

▶ *About cash received and cash paid books*
▶ *How to use a three-column cash book*
▶ *How to post cash book entries to the ledger accounts*

Question From what you have been saying about the accounts in the various Ledgers, am I correct in thinking that all they show are balances of Trading Transactions?

Answer Yes, of Purchases and Sales on Credit Terms. We now consider the Receipt and Payment of *Cash* by the business. This usually occurs at the end of the period of credit allowed to or by it.

Question You said earlier that some portion of the Capital with which the business was begun must be in the form of Cash. That would be in order to pay its running expenses?

Answer Not only such expenses as Wages and Salaries, but also to pay suppliers who might initially be unwilling to give credit to a new business.

Question Would it be right to describe such Cash as the Working Capital employed?

Answer It forms a part, but by no means the whole, of the Working Capital. A better definition for Cash would be that it is a **Liquid Asset**, part of the Current Assets. Its subsequent use by the business may result in its remaining a **Current Asset**, as when goods are bought for stock, or becoming a **Fixed Asset**, when Plant, Fittings, etc., are purchased.

Some business transactions take place by the use of cash in the form of coin and notes. Others, including most larger transactions, use cheques, credit cards or electronic transfers. There are clearly differences in reality between cash and cheques or electronic transfers but there are similarities in the bookkeeping entries when purchases or sales are settled. Instead of using separate cash received and cheques received books and ledger accounts, one is used for all receipts (and one for all payments). The only exception is when a 'petty' cash fund is used for small payments under the control of a particular person.

A small business may use one cash book to record all receipts and payments whether cash, cheques or transfers. As it grows it will become more convenient to use separate books: one for small cash payments (petty cash see Chapter 7), another for larger payments and a third for receipts. The principles and procedures are similar in either case. We will explore these in the remainder of this chapter to show you how these books are kept.

Procedure on receipt of cash

When each day's incoming mail is opened, all remittances from customers will be passed on to whoever's job in the business is to deal with payments (i.e. the cashier). Payments received will usually be accompanied by the statements of accounts which the business has issued at monthly intervals to its customers. These statements are copies of the Personal Account in the Ledger and show the customer what should be paid. If it is up to date and the customer agrees that it records all the transactions accurately, the requested amount will be paid. Sometimes there are differences: perhaps cash or goods in transit over the time the statement was made, or queries over price or quality that have not yet been agreed. In this case a smaller amount will be paid and later effort must be made to identify and settle the disputed items that remain unpaid.

If these statements are not supplied with the payment (or an 'advice slip' you may have provided which summarizes the statement – many businesses provide these to be returned with payment to help with the accounting for payments), then the cashier must seek to match payment to the personal account of the debtor as best as he or she can.

On opening the mail the cashier will:

▶ compare the amount remitted with the total of the statement and

▶ check any **Cash Discount** which the customer may have deducted. A Cash Discount is an inducement offered by a business to its customers to ensure payment within the recognized period of credit – or shorter. As such it is an expense to the business, which must always be taken into account with the accompanying remittance. For example, if the terms upon which business is done are '2½% monthly account', and Mr Green's debt is £100, then *if he pays on or before the end of the month following delivery of the goods to him, he need pay £97.50* (i.e. £100–2½%) only. On the other hand, if he pays after the expiry of the credit period, the discount will not ordinarily be allowed.

Remember this

Where a Cash Discount relates to the customers of the business, it is termed **Discount Allowed**. It differs from *Trade Discount*, which we discussed earlier, in that it always relates to the cash or financial aspect of each transaction. Looked at in another way, it assists the business in collecting what is due from its customers by encouraging timely payments of money owing.

The cashier will also:

▶ enter the remittances in detail in either a rough cash diary or Journal, as a preliminary to entry in the Cash Book proper, or if few enough payments are received, enter them at once in the Cash Book. Whichever alternative is adopted, such initial entry is a **Prime** or **First** entry, and therefore corresponds in effect to the same process of recording of Purchases or Sales initially in the Purchase and Sales Journals/Day Books

▶ list the remittances on the counterfoil of the bank paying-in book, so that the total agrees with the total of the entries for the particular business day appearing in the Cash Book of the business. This ensures that the amount actually banked will agree with the business records

▶ create formal receipts in the name of each customer, which may be attached to the statements of account and then issued to the customers for their record of payment having been received. (In some businesses it is no longer usual to issue receipts for cheque payments and of course these receipts may often be issued by email.)

The Cash Book or Cash Journal will then be available for the ledger clerks (if these are separate staff), who will post the amount of each remittance *to the credit of the personal Ledger Account of the customer from whom it was received.*

The procedures described above are those that a very small business might use to ensure that there is a record of every stage in the process. Ensuring different people record remittances, to those who bank them, and to those who record the entries in journal and ledger accounts is best practice. This segregation of duties helps to minimize opportunities for fraud to occur. In practice, many small businesses would combine some of these activities and often have the same person do more than one of these stages. All the cheques may be listed by hand or by computer and the total entered in the bank account, and the same list used to support the paying-in slip.

Also, there may be notifications from customers that they have paid the account by credit transfer to your bank. These are treated in just the same way as for cheques received except of course there is nothing to bank.

Bookkeeping entries: Cash receipts

As we expect cash to bring benefits to the business in the future, such as interest earned on positive bank balances, it is classified as an asset. Therefore, increases in cash are recorded as debits and decreases in cash are recorded as credits.

We commence our records by opening a **Cash Received Journal** or **Cash Received Book** (same thing, just different title), in which all money received from customers, whether in the form of cheques, notes, coin, etc., will be entered. Bearing in mind the fact that in many cases Cash Discount has been allowed to the customers, it will be helpful to show the amount of the discount *by the side of* the item to which it relates so that a record is kept of how each discount is applied to each transaction. The entry for the payment of cash received from G Green would therefore be recorded as follows:

Cash Received Journal

Date	Customer	Total	Discount	Cash
xxx1		£	£	£
Feb 20	G Green	100.00	2.50	97.50

From this it is apparent that G Green has now settled the debt of £100, and in collecting what was due, the business has incurred an expense of £2.50 which, clearly, will reduce the figure of profit the business expects to make.

Like the Purchase and Sales Journals, the Cash Book will probably be ruled off and totalled at the end of each month, so that, as with our Purchase and Sales transactions, we can then:

▶ *give credit* to each customer immediately on receipt of the separate remittance; and

▶ *debit* or charge the cash account in total with the cash receipts, irrespective of the individual details making up the total.

The Cash Received Journal enables us to do this, and at the same time to comply with *double entry principles*, as the following diagram shows:

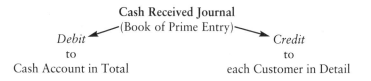

Cash Received Journal
(Book of Prime Entry)

Debit ← → *Credit*

to — to

Cash Account in Total — each Customer in Detail

or in account form which also records £50 received from B Brown (with no discount this time):

Cash Received Journal

Date	Customer	Total	Discount	Cash
xxx1		£	£	£
Feb 20	G Green	100.00	2.50	97.50
22	B Brown	50.00	–	50.00
		£150.00	£2.50	£147.50

Sales Ledger

G GREEN

Dr							Cr
Date	Details	Fo	Amount	Date	Details	CRJ Fo	Amount
xxx1			£	xxx1	Cash		£
Feb 1	Sales	1	100.00	Feb 20	Discount	1	97.50
						1	2.50
			£100.00				£100.00

P BROWN

Dr							Cr
Date	Details	Fo	Amount	Date	Details	CRJ Fo	Amount
xxx1	Sales		£	xxx1			£
Feb 1			50.00	Feb 22	Cash	1	50.00

Private Ledger

CASH

Dr				Cr			
Date	Details	CRJ Fo	Amount	Date	Details	Fo	Amount
xxx1			£				
Feb 28	Total cash received	1	147.50				

From the above example, note firstly that the *Cash Account* appears in the *Private Ledger*. This is as we should expect because the Private Ledger is concerned with Assets and Liabilities, and Cash Received is an Asset.

Secondly, note that, while our aim is to complete the double entry *within the Ledgers*, the sum of the two credit balances on the accounts of Green and Brown is £150, whereas we have a debit balance on Cash Account of £147.50 only.

So far as *discount allowed* is concerned, we have given credit to G Green personally *in the Ledger* for that amount, but we have not impersonally noted its effect upon the business. The business must be charged with that amount as an expense or loss resulting from its dealings with Green, and it is therefore necessary to open in the Nominal Ledger an account for discounts allowed.

DISCOUNT ALLOWED

Dr							Cr
Date	Details	CPJ Fo	Amount	Date	Details	Fo	Amount
xxx1			£				
Feb 28	Total discount	1	2.50				

From this you should be able to see that:

▸ the double entry is completed within the Ledgers (i.e. the total of the debit entries equates to the total of the credit entries).

▸ a Debit Balance created in an Impersonal Ledger Account, e.g. Discount Allowed, is a business expense. Also, a debit balance created on a Private Ledger Account (Cash) showing we have gained an asset of the business.

▸ the Debit Balances formerly appearing on the accounts of Green (£100) and Brown (£50) in the Sales Ledger will have been settled by the posting to their credit of the cash received and discount allowed.

Procedure on payment of cash

Periodically, the business will pay its *suppliers* for what has been purchased from them. At the end of each month a statement of account will usually have been received from them setting out the balance owed to them. This should be compared with the total in the various Purchase Ledger Accounts. Care should be taken to deduct the value of any goods returned to them by the business, if omitted in the statement, and similarly a deduction will be made for Cash Discount which, from our point of view, is called **discount received** or **receivable** if given to us by our suppliers. If the statement then does not match the Ledger accounts you will need to investigate the difference.

While payments can be made at any time, many businesses will look to settle bills once a month on or before the end of the month following delivery of the goods. A list can therefore be prepared for all *accounts payable*, setting out:

▶ the folio of the supplier's account in the Purchase Ledger

▶ the name of the supplier

▶ the total amount due

▶ the amount of the discount, and

▶ the sum now payable.

This list, together with the Statement of Account received from the suppliers, can be submitted to the proprietor or to whoever they have designated can do this task on their behalf, who will sign the cheques to be issued in settlement of each sum now due.

Some businesses pay in accordance with their own records of what is due rather than using a statement from the supplier (in case no statement is issued for example that prompts payment). This is a simpler process but eventually the two records must be reconciled (see Chaper 6, Customer/supplier statements).

Bookkeeping entries: Cash payments

When the business bought goods from suppliers on credit the *selling price* would have been recorded as a credit in the supplier's personal account.

When we pay these bills as they become due, we shall *debit* the amount from each of the *suppliers*, offsetting the amounts for which they appear as *creditors*, and indicating that the liability of the business to them has decreased. For the second aspect of the transaction, we must *credit* the payment from the cash account, showing that the amount of cash held by the business has decreased.

For this purpose, a *Cash Paid Journal*, or sometimes called a *Cash Paid Book*, may be opened, as a Book of Prime Entry, ruled with columns for discount and the actual cash paid. An example is given below.

Cash Paid Journal

Date	Supplier	Total	Discount	Cash
xxx1		£	£	£
Feb 23	L Lindsay	30.00	0.75	29.25

The record shown above indicates that a liability to L Lindsay of £30 has been satisfied by a cash payment of £29.25 and that a **gain** in the form of a £0.75 discount has been 'earned' (most likely for timely payment).

The Cash Paid Journal enables us to:

▶ charge (debit) each supplier on payments of money

▶ credit the cash account in total with the total cash payments irrespective of the individual details.

This may be put in another way:

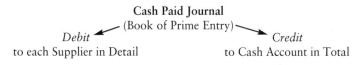

Cash Paid Journal
(Book of Prime Entry)

Debit ← → *Credit*
to each Supplier in Detail   to Cash Account in Total

or in account form which also records £58.50 paid to M Morris and £1.50 discount received.

Cash Paid Journal

Date	Customer	Total	Discount	Cash
xxx1		£	£	£
Feb 23	L Lindsay	30.00	0.75	29.25
26	M Morris	60.00	1.50	58.50
		£90.00	£2.25	£87.75

Purchase Ledger

L LINDSAY

Dr							Cr
Date	Details	CRJ Fo	Amount	Date	Details	Fo	Amount
xxx1			£	xxx1			£
Feb 23	Cash	2	29.25	Feb 1	Purchase		30.00
	Discount	2	0.75				
			£30.00				£30.00

M MORRIS

Dr							Cr
Date	Details	CRJ Fo	Amount	Date	Details	Fo	Amount £
xxx1			£	xxx1			
Feb 26	Cash	2	58.50	Feb 1	Purchase		60.00
	Discount	2	1.50				
			£60.00				£60.00

Private Ledger

CASH

Dr							Cr
Date	Details	Fo	Amount	Date	Details	CPJ Fo	Amount
				xxx1			£
				Feb 28	Total cash paid	2	87.75

As the counterpart of cash received, but in the reverse direction, the Cash Account in the Private Ledger has a credit balance, which here denotes a *liability*. Instead of having cash into the business to use to generate benefits in the future (a debit balance), the business actually owes money, a liability, to the bank (a credit balance).

As to the balances on the Ledger Accounts, the sum of the *debits* in the Purchase Ledger is £90, while the *credit* on the Cash Account is £87.75.

The impersonal aspect of discount received (sometimes called discount earned) is that a gain of £2.25 has been made for which credit may be taken. We may therefore open the following account in the Impersonal Ledger:

DISCOUNT RECEIVED

| Dr | | | | | | | Cr |
Date	Details	Fo	Amount	Date	Details	CPJ Fo	Amount
				xxx1			£
				Feb 28	Total		
					discount	2	2.25

As before, this completes the double entry *within the Ledgers*, and we see that a credit balance on an Impersonal Ledger Account is a business *gain*, while a similar balance on a Private Ledger Account is a *liability* of the business.

Remember this

Remember that credit entries record increases in the sources of funds such as revenues (discount received), liabilities and equity capital.

Goods and cash compared

This section compares and contrasts how we account for receiving goods (on credit) and how we account for payment of that debt when it falls due. It describes why we use separate accounts for goods received and sold but only one account for payments made (in and out).

1 When *goods* are bought, the Purchase Account is debited and the individual suppliers' accounts are credited; when goods are sold, the individual customers' accounts are debited, and the Sales Account is credited. In the Impersonal Ledger there are therefore two accounts used for the trading transactions: purchases and sales (i.e. we don't combine purchase and sale entries into one account). But in our *cash* dealings, recorded in total in the Private Ledger, we have *only one cash account*, debited for cash received and credited with cash paid.

2 Goods purchased will be valued at *cost price* per unit, but goods sold are valued at *selling price*. As such profit is included in the latter account but not the former.

3 Further, in a manufacturing business at least, goods purchased may largely consist of raw materials, while goods sold will be the finished product – an essentially different article more than just the total of each of its parts now. With cash, however, whether it is cash received or cash paid, the value per unit is the same.

For these reasons, even though we need to keep purchases and sales records separately, we are able to **merge** our cash received and our cash paid in one account only. We can illustrate this by using the figures given above:

CASH

| Dr | | | | | | | Cr |
Date	Details	CRJ Fo	Amount	Date	Details	CPJ Fo	Amount
xxx1			£	xxx1			£
Feb 28	Total cash received	2	147.50	Feb 28	Total cash paid	2	87.25

It is clear that the excess of the debit side, or £60.25, represents an *asset* of the business. If the larger amount appeared on the credit side, it would be a *liability*.

From this we may draw three conclusions:

► That instead of having two Books of Prime Entry – a Cash Received Journal and a Cash Paid Journal – *one book* will usually suffice, and we may call it the Cash Journal or, as is more usual, the **Cash Book**.

► Because it contains all our cash receipts and payments, the Cash Book is not only a Book of Prime Entry.

► It is also a Ledger Account, in that, *the position of the business in relation to cash held by the business* can quickly be seen from the Cash Book.

On the basis that incoming cash remittances are banked intact on the day of receipt, and all payments are made by cheque or electronic payments, writing up the Cash Book daily as Book of Prime Entry is equivalent to writing up the Ledger Account with the bank.

If, however, a minimum amount of cash must be retained by the business in order to pay petty expenses, and if, also, wages and salaries have to be paid in cash and not by cheque, it is necessary to provide *additional columns* in the Cash Book to record purely cash, as distinct from banking transactions or to use a separate petty cash book (see Chapter 7 for how this separate cash record is created if needed).

We will now work through an example to show you how this is all brought together in practice (a separate petty cash book example can be found in Chapter 7 if that approach is used instead).

► **Example 5.1**

From the following particulars, draw up the three-column Cash Book of V Treat. No posting to the Ledger is required and no money is to be paid into the bank unless and until instructions are given.

xxx1

Jan	1	Commenced business with cash in hand £60 and a balance at the bank of £325.
	3	Cash sales £336.
	4	Drew cheque £70 for private use; paid wages by cash £260.
	5	Paid rent by cheque £220.
	6	Paid into bank additional capital £1000.
	8	Received a cheque from Light Bros £240 in settlement of their account of £250 allowing cash discount of £10.
	9	Paid Brown & Sons cheque for £480, receiving discount £20.
	10	Received a cheque from Bilton Ltd, value £140, in settlement of their account £145 after cash discount of £5.
	11	Drew cheque £120 for cash for office use.
	12	Paid into bank the two cheques received from Light Bros and Bilton Ltd.
	13	Paid Jennens Ltd cheque £190, having deducted discount 5% from their account.
	16	Light Bros' cheque was returned by the bank marked R/D. This means 'Refer to drawer', in this case the person – Light Bros – who signed the cheque. This usually occurs as they have insufficient funds to pay the sums owed (i.e. the cheque has 'bounced').
	18	Paid wages by cash £230.
	31	Paid bank charges for the month £15.

Balance off the Cash Book and bring down the balances as on 31 January xxx1.

Note: The three columns of a three-column Cash Book refer to Discount, Cash and Bank. There are also three columns for receipts and three for payments (i.e. three debit-side columns and three credit-side columns). There is also usually space left to record the reference for the posting of the personal aspect of the transactions to the appropriate supplier or customer account.

If we look more closely at this example, we will see that provision is made in the columns headed 'Cash' and 'Bank' respectively for a statement at any time of the position of the business of its levels of cash in hand, and its cash at bank.

At the beginning of the month the proprietor introduced £385 as Cash Capital, divided as shown over the page, and the description of the item 'Capital A/c' indicates that that is the Account in the Ledger which is to be credited.

In our wording of the items in the Cash Book, we must be careful to choose words which will indicate *where the corresponding (debit or credit) entry is to be found*. This makes tracing entries in future easier to do if it is ever necessary and an auditor will need this if and when your accounts are checked.

Remember this

As it is an asset, increases in cash are recorded on the left-hand, debit side. Decreases in cash are recorded on the right-hand, credit side.

When a cheque received from a customer is returned by the bank marked R/D (refer to drawer) we must bring the Cash Book into line with the bank's own view of our position; we see how this is done in this example in the case of the cheque received from Light Bros. Having *debited* the bank account with £240 on 12 January we must now *credit* the account on 16 January. We therefore cancel the original charge to the bank with a *credit* entry and, to complete the double entry *within the Ledgers*, post the amount to the *debit* of Light Bros' account, reviving the original debt due from them. Their position is now the same as it was before the worthless cheque was received (and of course we now need to chase this sum owed again).

In this example you can see that columns are provided in which to record cash discount *allowed* and *received*. When the cheque from Light Bros was first received on 8 January, £10 was allowed to them as discount, the *total* due by them being £250. But as their cheque is returned on 16 January it is not enough merely to credit the bank with the amount of the *cheque*; we must in addition write back to Light Bros's account the discount which was, of course, only allowed by the business in the belief that the cheque was good. It is this third column for discount which led to the use of the phrase 'three-column cash book'.

A credit is given in the bank account for charges made by the bank for the month. The bank will, *in their own books,* have debited the business with this sum and, in order that the two sets of records shall agree, this entry must be made.

On 31 January balances can be inserted on the *credit side* of the Cash Book (representing the amount by which the debit side exceeds the credit side) and *brought down* on 1 February, as the *opening balances* for the new period. The balances, it will be noted, are in both cases *debit balances,* indicating the existence of an asset in the form of:

▶ cash in hand £26.00, and

▶ cash (or balance) at bank £370.00.

Before we move on from this example we will look at the Discount Allowed and Discount Received Accounts in the Nominal Ledger.

Considering Discount Allowed we notice that, while both the cheques received from *and* the discount allowed to Light Bros and Bilton Ltd appear on the *debit* side of the Cash Book, these customers will each receive *credit* for the total in their respective Ledger Accounts. But only the amount of the *actual money* they pay is debited in the cash and bank columns. Accordingly, to complete the double entry, we must have in the Nominal Ledger an account for *discounts allowed*, in which the further debit required will be shown, and correspondingly for *discounts received*.

Cash Book

V. TREAT

Dr						Cr				
Date	Fo	Discount	Cash	Bank	Date		Fo	Discount	Cash	Bank
		£	£	£				£	£	£
xxx1					xxx1					
Jan 1 Capital A/			60.00	325.00	Jan 4	Drawings				70.00
3 Cash Sales			336.00		4	Wages			260.00	
6 Capital A/c				1000.00	5	Rent				220.00
8 Light Bros		10.00	240.00		9	Brown and Sons		20.00		480.00
10 Bilton Ltd		5.00	140.00		11	Cash				120.00
11 Bank			120.00		12	Bank, cheques from Light Bros and Bilton Ltd			380.00	
12 Cash, cheques per contra				380.00						

Debit side

		Discount	Cash	Bank
16	Light Bros discount charged	(10.00)*		
		£5.00	£896.00	£1705.00
xxx1				
Feb 1	Balances b/d		26.00	370.00

Credit side

		Discount	Cash	Bank
13	Jennens Ltd	10.00		190.00
16	Light Bros cheque returned			240.00
18	Wages		230.00	
31	Interest and bank charges			15.00
31	Balances c/d		26.00	370.00
		£30.00	£896.00	£1705.00

*When Light Bros' cheque is returned the discount previously allowed to them must be *deducted* from discounts allowed and *debited* to their account.

Note that the original entry is not cancelled; the new transaction is recorded with an appropriate new entry.

The control account described and illustrated in Chapter 4 will also include the total payments made to creditors, month by month, and any discount received.

Cash Book postings to Ledger Accounts

It may be useful to now provide a summary of all we have covered in this chapter so far. **The Cash Book** is:

a   Book of Prime Entry, and

b   Ledger Account with the Cashier and Banker.

We post to the cash book as follows:

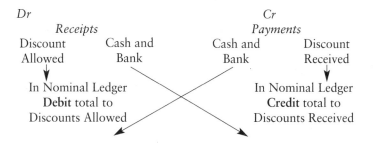

Dr
Receipts
Discount   Cash and
Allowed   Bank

In Nominal Ledger
Debit total to
Discounts Allowed

Cr
Payments
Cash and   Discount
Bank   Received

In Nominal Ledger
Credit total to
Discounts Received

a   In Purchase Ledger **debit** to individual suppliers total of cash and discount.

b   In Nominal Ledger **debit** to wages, cash purchases or other expense accounts.

c   In Private Ledger debit to Asset Accounts (if purchased) or Liability Accounts if loans or capital are repaid.

a   In Sales Ledger **credit** to individual customers total of cash and discount.

b   In Nominal Ledger **credit** to bank interest received, cash sales or other income accounts.

c   In Private Ledger **credit** to Asset Accounts (if sold) or Liability Accounts if, for example, money is borrowed or new capital introduced.

Other bank accounts

So far we have only considered the situation where a business has one bank account, a Current Account. A business may have several accounts, e.g. including at least a Deposit Account on which interest may be earned, or perhaps a Loan Account where the bank has lent money to the business on agreed terms of interest and repayment.

When the business has more money than it needs for day-to-day activities it could transfer the surplus from the Current Account to the Deposit Account. This is similar to a payment; the Current Account (which up to now we have called the bank account) will be credited and a new account, the Deposit Account, will be debited. This is just like the entries made when Cash is paid into the bank, Debit Bank and Credit Cash. We have already explained that the Cash and Bank Book is sometimes the Ledger Account as well, but the Deposit Account will usually have its own Ledger Account.

▶ **Example 5.2**

Joan Smith, a merchant, does not pay all cash received into her bank. She wants to record all cash received and paid and all her bank transactions in one Cash Book. Her transaction during the first few days of January xxx1 were as below:

xxx1			£
Jan	1	Cash in hand	150
		Bank overdraft	72
		Received cash from AB (after allowing him discount £10)	150
	2	Paid into bank	245
	3	Drew cheque for CD (after deducting discount £3)	27
	4	Received cheque from EF (after allowing his discount £30) and paid it into bank	270
	5	Drew from bank in cash	20

	Paid wages (on presentation of an open cheque at bank)	80
7	EF's cheque returned by bank, dishonoured	270
8	Received cash from GH (after allowing discount £2)	48
9	Paid into bank	25
10	Paid cash to JK (after deducting discount £4)	36

You are required (**a**) to record these transactions in a three-column Cash Book; (**b**) to rule off and balance the book; (**c**) to state clearly how the discounts are dealt with in the Ledger. (Prepare your own record and then compare it with the printed solution.)

A bank overdraft occurs when arrangements have been made for more to be withdrawn from the bank than has been paid into it. It is like a loan for a fixed amount and there is usually an upper limit placed on the 'loan' by the bank. Unlike a normal loan, interest is only paid to the bank if the account becomes overdrawn. If the business doesn't need an overdraft then no interest is paid. In effect it is a flexible loan.

An overdraft is **not** an asset, it is a liability and when there is an overdraft at the beginning or end of an accounting period it will appear as a **credit** balance in the Cash Book.

    a The three-column cash book is shown below.

    b To calculate the cash and bank balance it is useful to total the columns. For the cash Dr £368, Cr £306, so the net balance to be carried down (or forward) is £62. Similarly for the Bank Dr £540, Cr £469, £71 net. Record these balances so that the totals agree and complete the double entry by carrying them down to the opposite side. They will appear as debits, i.e. assets.

    c Discounts allowed. Individual items, e.g. £10.00 for AB, will be posted to Cr of AB in Sales Ledger and the total £12.00 to the Debit of Discount Allowed/Discounts Received. Individual items, e.g. £3.00 from CD, will be posted to Debit of CD in Purchase Ledger and the total of £7.00 to the Credit of Discounts Received.

Joan Smith

Cash Book

Dr

Date	Receipts	Discount	Cash	Bank
		£	£	£
xxx1				
Jan 1	Balance b/d		150.00	
1	AB	10.00	150.00	
2	Cash			245.00
4	EF	30.00		270.00
5	Bank		20.00	
7	EF discount not allowed	(30.00)*		
8	GH	2.00	48.00	
9	Cash			25.00
		£12.00	£368.00	£540.00
xxx1				
Jan 12	Balance b/d		62.00	71.00

→ Debited to 'Discount Allowed' Account

Cr

Jan xxx1

Date	Payments	Discount	Cash	Bank
		£	£	£
xxx1				
Jan 1	Balance b/d			72.00
2	Bank		245.00	
3	CD	3.00		27.00
5	Cash			20.00
6	Wages			80.00
7	EF cheque returned			270.00
9	Bank		25.00	
10	JK	4.00	36.00	71.00
11	Balances c/d		62.00	71.00
		£7.00	£368.00	£540.00

→ Credited to 'Discount Received' Account

* When EF's cheque is returned, the discount previously allowed to him, £30, must be recharged to him. It is therefore *deducted* in the discounts allowed column and *debited* to EF's account.

In practice *all* cash and cheques received would be paid into the bank. Any cash required for small purchases or other expenses would be recorded under the imprest (Petty cash) system (see Chapter 7).

Running balance account

So far ledger accounts have used the two-sided, Dr and Cr, format. An alternative way to display accounts is using a three-column running balance.

▶ **Example 5.3**

The nominal ledger account for VAT (Chapter 4, 'Nominal Ledger Account') could be recorded:

Date	Detail	Fo	Dr	Cr	Balance
xxx1			£	£	£
March 31	On purchases	PJ1	520.40		520.40 Dr
	On sales	SJ2		799.00	278.60 Cr
	On purchase returns	PRJ1		8.40	287.00 Cr
	On sales returns	SRJ2	40.40		246.60 Cr

The balance is calculated automatically after each posting and is indicated as Dr or Cr. Some systems use + and – instead of Dr and Cr as do other accounts. You may recognize this format from looking at your bank statements. This is the way these accounts are usually shown by a bank. See also 'Examination questions and sample solutions' at the back of the book where bank statements are presented in this format.

Testing Yourself

At this stage ignore VAT.

1 Define trade discount and cash discount. State clearly how these are treated in Books of Account.

2 A trader receives an account from XY, the landlord, for £250 in respect of one month's rent, which is paid on the date of receipt.

   Explain the different ways which might be adopted to record this item in books kept on the Double Entry System.

3 On 1 January xxx1, R Rich sold G Jones goods to the amount of £50.25; on 13 February Jones paid Rich £25 on account; on 27 February Rich sold Jones £48.50 of goods; on 3 March Jones returned to Rich £7.75 goods (not being up to sample); on 13 March Jones paid Rich £24 and was allowed £1.25 discount to clear the January account. On 31 March Rich sent a quarterly statement to Jones. Set out the statement in proper form.

4 From the following particulars write up A Bondman's Cash Book for the week commencing 5 July xxx1 and balance the Cash Book as at 10 July xxx1.

   July xxx1

   July 5 Cash in hand £15.50, and in bank £176.
          5 Paid by cheque to F Abbott his account of £47, less 5% cash discount.
          6 Paid in cash, postage stamps £2.75.
          7 Received cheque from R Beal in payment of his account of £40, less 2½% cash discount, and paid the cheque into bank.
          8 Purchased by cheque office desk £30.
         10 Paid wages in cash £120. Cash sales for week £150.75. Withdrew from bank for office purposes £20. Withdrew from bank for self £15.

   Post the items in your Cash Book to the Ledger.

5 Leslie Morris commences business on 1 January xxx1. Record in a suitable ruled Cash Book the following transactions for the first week of January xxx1 and bring down the balances on 7 January:

xxx1			£	
Jan	1	L Morris paid into bank on account of Capital.	700.00	
	2	Received and paid into bank direct the following:		
		Jones (after allowing discount £5)	45.00	
		Wilson (after allowing discount £0.50)	12.50	
		Graham (after allowing discount £0.75).	15.00	
	2	Drew cheque for office cash.	40.00	
	4	Wilson's cheque returned by bank unpaid.	12.50	
	5	Drew cheque for		330.00
		Paying wages	£200.00	
		salaries.	130.00	
	5	Bought goods for cash.		25.00
	6	Received the following (in cash):		
		Peters, payment for goods	£250.00	
		Rent receivable	10.00	
		Sanders (after allowing discount £1).	60.00	
				320.00
	6	Paid cash into bank.		300.00
	7	Paid by cheque:		
		Lister (after deducting discount £0.50)		19.50
		White (after deducting discount £1.50).		58.50

How would you deal with the totals of the columns Discounts Allowed and Discounts Received, when the Cash Book is ruled off on 7 January xxx1?

6 On 20 June xxx1, H Rivers received from S Wells an invoice for £514. Of this amount £510 represented the cost of goods purchased and £4 the carriage on them.

On 30 June xxx1, H Rivers returned to S Wells goods to the value of £60.

After the invoice had been entered in the books, it was discovered that a trade discount of 20% had not been deducted from the cost or from the item relating to goods returned and an adjusting entry was made to correct these mistakes.

The account was paid by cheque on 31 July xxx1, less 2½% discount.

Show the entries in the respective Books of Account of H Rivers to record the above transactions.

7 From the following particulars write up the Cash Book of Thomas Mixture for the month of January xxx2, and bring down the balances at the end of the month. It is not Mr Mixture's rule to bank all cash and make all payments by cheque.

xxx2			£
Jan 1	1	Cash in hand.	18.00
	1	Balance overdrawn at bank.	36.75
	2	Received cash sales.	242.50
	4	Banked cash.	115.00
	4	Paid Jackson & Co by cheque.	14.25
	5	Received Jones' cheque (direct to bank).	14.50
	6	Paid salaries in cash.	134.75
	7	Bought goods for cash (paid from office cash).	11.00
	8	Drew office cash from bank.	16.00
	9	Received cash sales.	225.00
	13	Paid salaries in cash.	133.50
	16	Received Smith's cheque (direct to bank).	56.75
	20	Paid Brown by cheque.	16.00
	20	Received from Jones in coins and notes.	55.50
	20	Paid salaries in cash.	134.75
	23	Drew office cash from bank.	135.00
	26	Received Jones' cheque (direct to bank).	17.50
	27	Paid salaries in cash.	134.75
	27	Paid office cash into bank.	20.00
	28	Jones' cheque returned by bank unpaid.	17.50

8 The Cash Book of Thomas Jones for the first week of January xxx1 is as follows:

xxx1		Discount £	Bank £	xxx1		Discount £	Bank £
Jan 1	Balance		752.00	Jan 3	Wages		159.00
2	Sundry customers:			5	Sundry suppliers:		
	L Smith	1.00	39.00		G Green	3.00	57.00
	V Latham	4.00	76.00		T Robson	2.00	78.00
4	Rents receivable		117.00	5	V Latham cheque returned		76.00
6	Plant A/c (machine tool sold)		26.00	6	Cash purchases		18.00
		£5.00	£1010.00			£5.00	£388.00

You should:

a indicate to which Ledger each entry in the Cash Book would be posted.
b make the cash postings in such Ledger Accounts, including the Discount Account.

9 From the following particulars you are required to write up the three-column Cash Book of K Walker. No posting to the Ledger is required:

xxx1

March	1	Cash in hand £246.50.
	1	Overdrawn at bank £93.60.
	2	Paid into bank £30.00.
	3	Paid wages by cash £141.50.
	4	Received cheque from R Francis value £35.75 in settlement of an amount owing £37.00.
	4	Cash sales £153.60.
	4	Received a cheque from M Scott £23.75, and allowed him discount £0.75.

5   Paid S Marsh cheque the balance of his account £34.00, less 5% discount.

5   Cash purchases £33.00.

6   Paid cheques from R Francis and M Scott into the bank.

8   K Walker paid into the bank addition capital £240.00.

9   Drew cheque £36.00 for office use.

10 Paid L Hopecraft cheque £18.80, being allowed discount £0.80.

10 Paid wages by cash £90.60.

10 M Scott's cheque was returned by the bank marked R/D.

11 Drew cheque £15.00 for private use.

11 Bought plant and machinery £370.00 and paid the amount by cheque.

12 Paid sundry small expenses by cash £16.40.

31 Bank charges £7.20.

Balance the Cash Book as on 31 March and bring down the balances.

10 Apart from in the Cash Book, in what Ledger or other accounts, and upon which side of these accounts, would you expect to find the following?

a £500 paid for new machinery.

b £170 received from J Robinson in full settlement of his account of £172.60.

c £600 received from an insurance company in settlement of a claim for damages to premises by fire.

d £750 received for the sale of old motor van.

e £250 paid to Jane Fitter in full settlement of an account due to her three months hence of £260.75.

The bank reconciliation

In this chapter you will learn:

► *About bank statements*
► *How to prepare a bank reconciliation statement*
► *About recording errors in the bank and cash books*

Objective

This chapter describes the importance of ensuring that the balance at the bank shown by the books of the business is the same as the balance shown by the records of the bank. The reconciliation should be carried out on a regular basis, and the chapter explains the procedure for achieving this.

Banks usually send to their customers at regular intervals a statement of their position in relation to the bank. This statement is a copy of the customer's (personal) account in the bank's Ledger, and usually will be shown from the bank's standpoint. That is to say, money paid in or *lodgements* by the customer will be shown as credits, and money withdrawn by cheque or direct bank transfer will be debited. At any time, there will be a balance either in favour of or against the customer.

Before the use of computers became common, *Bank Passbooks* were issued to all new customers, which were written up by the bank for the customer to compare with the bank columns in their own Cash Book. The customer could therefore be satisfied that the bank had given credit for all money which had been debited to it in the Cash Book. Similarly, when the bank *debited* the paid cheques, it could be seen that the name of the payee and the amount for which the cheque had been drawn were also in agreement with the *credit* side of the Cash Book.

At intervals it was, of course, necessary for the Passbook to be returned to the bank in order to be written up to date.

In most cases today, however, the bank's statement is given either in the form of *loose sheets*, so that there is a continuous record of the bank's version of the position between them and the customer, or is accessed online as and when the customer wishes.

We have seen elsewhere that it is the custom for suppliers of goods to the business to send statements of account which are valuable evidence of the accuracy of the Purchase Ledger Accounts.

The provision of a similar statement from the bank serves the same purpose particularly if the bank is the *creditor* of the business, as with a loan or overdraft account to which a limit has been set and the business needs to manage its account carefully if it is to avoid further charges and penalties.

It is rare for a bank to make a mistake in writing its version of the account, but we do find that at times mistakes are made by the cashier in the Cash Book at our end and also in *omitting to record* some particular receipt or payment.

As part of ordinary business practice, it is the custom to rule off and balance the Cash Book at monthly intervals, bringing down the balance to the beginning of the new period. For the bank columns in the Cash Book, as an asset account this balance represents either:

▶ cash at bank (Dr) or

▶ bank overdraft (Cr).

It will, also, be the cashier's duty to prepare at the end of each month what is termed a **bank reconciliation** or **bank agreement**, confirming the accuracy and completeness of their Cash Book records by comparing the bank's record with the business's account.

Remember this

Good practice suggests that, for internal control purposes, the person responsible for preparing or reviewing this reconciliation should not be the cashier, but someone independent, who is not involved with the actual handling of cash or cheques.

A bank reconciliation requires that every item entered in the Cash Book as being paid into the bank and each cheque or bank transfer recorded as paid be checked against the bank statement. This will identify cheques which have not been paid by the bank by those these were given to (called unpresented cheques) and receipts paid into the bank just before the balancing date but not yet appearing on the bank statement (uncleared or items not yet cleared). Note – direct bank transfers usually occur the same working day now, but may take longer than this so can also give rise to differences if paid at the end of the month.

In the affairs of a private individual, this reconciliation may be easily and quickly prepared; it may take a few minutes only, but with a business, where lodgements are being made daily throughout the month, and the number of cheques drawn and bank transfers made by the business is very large, the labour involved may be much greater.

We will now review the work to be done, bearing in mind that the bank statement shows the position of the business *in the light of the information in the bank's possession.*

Supposing the reconciliation is to be prepared on 31 January; we may commence with the statement balance at that date, using a sheet of cash-ruled paper which we can later file away for future reference (or similar on a spreadsheet or word-processed document of course). Our task is then to *reconcile* or *agree* the Cash Book balance with the balance appearing in the bank statement at that date.

If, as is usually the case, there is a difference between the two balances, it may be due to:

► Cheques drawn and issued by the business to its suppliers, or bank transfers authorized, and entered in the proper way on the credit side of the Cash Book, but not yet presented by the customer for payment or not cleared through the banking system. As the cheques so drawn have to be sent to suppliers, banked by them, and subsequently passed through the clearing system, several days may pass before they reach the paying bank. The same can apply with bank transfers where electronic transfer between banks isn't always instantaneous. We must therefore *add* the amount of the unpresented cheques to a debit balance, or deduct it from a credit balance.

Why? As we wrote the cheques, we credited the Cash Book to record the reduction in the assets of the business. As the bank has not recognized that reduction, we need to add back the amount we deducted as part of reconciling the two balances.

► *Cheques paid in by the business*, which on presentation to the paying bank are refused because of, for example:

▷ lack of funds to meet them

▷ countermand of instructions to pay by the Drawer

▷ death of the Drawer

▷ some irregularity on the face of the cheque, such as absence of Drawer's signature, difference between amount in words and figures, etc.

In these cases, the collecting banker will cancel the transfer of funds and return the unpaid cheque to the business. The business will take this up with its customer, and endeavour to resolve the difficulty.

In any event, as we saw earlier, the cashier should credit the bank with the amount involved, i.e. enter it as though it were a payment on the credit side of the Cash Book. Should they have omitted to do this, they must, for the purposes of reconciliation, deduct the amount from a debit balance (or add it to a credit balance).

► Bank interest paid (or charged if account is overdrawn), commission charged (such as regular charges to operate the the business account) and interest received from the bank (if the account is in credit and the bank pays interest – which is not always the case of course).

The bank will enter these items in its own account with the customer at regular intervals (usually monthly), but does not normally give the customer a separate advice that it has done so. The customer will be unaware of these items until they receive their statement. The correct action is then to debit the Bank Column in the Cash Book with the interest received by the business (as this increases the assets of the business), or credit it with the interest and commission charged (as this decreases the assets of the business).

If this has not already been done for this period in the Cash Book by the cashier, we therefore proceed as follows in preparing the Bank Reconciliation:

Interest received from the bank

> If a debit balance, add.

> If overdrawn, deduct.

Interest paid to the bank and bank charges

The reverse, of course, applies with interest and commission charged, i.e:

> If a debit balance, deduct.

> If overdrawn, add.

Let's review what we have learned so far with some examples:

▶ **Example 6.1**

The balance shown by the bank statement on 31 March xxx7 indicates an overdraft of £209.80, while, on the same date, the Bank Column in the Cash Book shows a credit balance of £419.00.

Comparing the two records, you find that two cheques drawn on 31 March, one for £204.00 and the other for £77.20, had not been presented for payment, while one of £72.00 paid into the bank on the same date had not yet been credited.

Prepare a Reconciliation Statement.

	£	£
Balance in hand as in Cash Book		(419.00)Cr
Add cheques drawn but unpresented:		
March 31	204.00	
March 31	77.20	
		281.20
Less cheque paid in but not yet credited by bank		(72.00)
Overdrawn as in bank statement		(209.80)

▶ **Example 6.2**

On 30 March xxx5, your Cash Book shows that you have in the bank the sum of £817.24. The bank statement shows a balance of £955.00.

On checking your Cash Book with the bank statement you find that a bank transfer authorized online amounting to £214.17 has not passed through the bank, that a cheque for £84.12 has not yet been credited to you, and that the bank has credited you with interest £22.07, and debited you with sundry charges £14.36. Draw up a reconciliation statement, showing adjustments between your Cash Book and Bank Statement.

	£	
Balance in hand as in Cash Book	817.24	Dr
Add uncleared bank transfer	214.17	
	1031.41	
Less cheque paid in but not credited	(84.12)	
	947.29	
Add interest credited by bank	22.07	
	969.36	
Less charges made by bank	(14.36)	
Balance as in bank statement	£955.00	

Note: After completing the reconciliation remember to enter the appropriate items in the cash book.

Example 6.3 introduces some of the errors which may be made in the Cash Book and entries which may have been omitted.

From the following particulars, prepare a reconciliation of the Cash Book balance with the bank statement balance.

	£
Balance as in bank statement (in customer's favour)	10.00
Credit balance as in Cash Book (overdrawn)	80.00
Unpresented cheques	144.00
(cheques paid by the business, sent to the suppliers but not yet paid by the bank)	
Uncleared cheques inwards	26.00
(cheques received from customers and paid into the bank, but not yet credited by the bank to the business account)	

Further,

▶ a cheque for £20 paid to J Jones has been entered in error in the Cash Column of the Cash Book

▶ the cashier has omitted to record bank commission charges of £8.

	£
Overdrawn as in Cash Book	(80.00) Cr
Add unpresented cheques	144.00
Favourable balance of	64.00
Less uncleared cheques inwards	(26.00)
	38.00
Less cheque to J Jones (paid by bank and therefore appearing in statement)	(20.00)
Less Commission charged by bank	(8.00)
Balance as in bank statement (in favour)	£10.00

Having identified these errors, we must remember to make the appropriate entries in the books of original entry. The reconciliation confirms that the data is correct but does not correct the original error. If these adjustments are not made, the balances in the statement and Cash Book will not agree next time a reconciliation is prepared.

We have produced a reconciliation between these two balances. If during this process we discover errors in or omissions from the Cash Book then the Cash Book must be corrected.

Using the data from Example 6.3:

a Dr Bank column, Cr Cash column £20

b Cr Bank column, Dr Bank Charges £8.

Starting with the original balances in the Cash Book:

Date	Receipts	Cash	Bank	Date	Payments	Cash	Bank
30.3. x 5	Balance b/d	200.00		30.3. x 5	Balance b/d		80.00
	Transfer (a)	20.00			Transfer (a)		20.00
					Bank charges (b)		8.00
		220.00	0.00			0.00	108.00
	Balance c/d		108.00		Balance c/d	220.00	
	Balance b/d	220.00			Balance b/d		108.00

Perhaps it will be worthwhile to check that these entries have been made correctly by preparing a new reconciliation:

Balance overdrawn as in Cash Book	(108.00) Cr
Add unpresented cheques	144.00
	36.00
Less uncleared cheques	(26.00)
Balance as in bank statement (in customer's favour)	10.00

The bank statement and Cash Book now agree. The unpresented and uncleared cheques should clear in due course and will appear therefore on the next bank statement.

The cash balance should also be checked with the cash actually held by the cashier from time to time. This should also identify any errors such as the recording of a payment in the wrong column of the cash book as appeared in this example. This is also important to help reduce the risk of theft of cash from the petty cash system. This process operates the same way as the bank statement reconciliation except that you are looking to reconcile the Cash Book record with actual cash left in the petty cash. We will review the petty cash process in more detail in the next chapter.

Customer/supplier statements

Where statements of account are received from customers or suppliers (debtors or creditors to the business) it is common practice to perform a similar reconciliation between the business's version of each account and the version illustrated by the statement received. Any differences not explainable by new sales/suppliers or payments made/received should be investigated.

Focus points

On completion of this chapter you should:

* know how to prepare a bank reconciliation statement
* recognize the need to record in the Cash and Bank Books any errors discovered by the reconciliation and any items correctly entered by the bank on their statement which have not been recorded by the business.

Testing yourself

1 A cashier receives the statement from the bank and finds that the amount of the overdraft differs from that shown by the Cash Book. Give the possible explanations for this difference.

2 From the following particulars prepare a statement showing how the differences between the bank statement balance and the Cash Book balance is reconciled:

	£
Statement balance – 30 June xxx1	1401.62
Cash Book balance – 30 June xxx1	577.52

Cheques drawn prior to 30 June xxx1, but not presented until after that date:

	£
P	29.20
Q	801.17
R	5.73
S	132.32

	£
Cheques paid into the bank on 30 June xxx1, not credited until 2 July xxx1	116.20
Bank charges and interest to 30 June xxx1, not entered in the Cash Book	8.12

3 On 30 November xxx1, the Cash Book of E Simpson disclosed a debit balance of £212, and his bank statement at the same date a balance in his favour of £361.

4 Prepare a bank reconciliation at 30 November, taking into account that a cheque payable to E Simpson in respect of a 3% dividend on this holding of 1000 ordinary shares of £1 each in Greystones Foundry Ltd was entered in the Cash Book on 30 November, but

not credited by the Bank until 1 December, and that cheques drawn by E Simpson on 28 November, as follows, were not presented at the bank by the payees until 3 December.

	£
H Simpson, salary	108.32
Corporation electric supply	35.68
Trade Supplies Ltd (a creditor)	35.00

5 On 31 December xxx9, Jane Smith found that her bank statement showed a balance in the bank of £88.62, whereas according to her Ledger the bank account was overdrawn by £57.69. On checking over the figures she discovered that the following cheques had not been presented:

	£
Wilkins & Co	96.17
Turnbull & Snow	63.00
Samuel & Son	85.50

while a payment in of £90 on 31 December had not yet been credited by the bank, and the bank's charges for the half-year amounting to £8.36 had not been entered in the Ledger.

Prepare a reconciliation between the two balances and state which other account would be affected.

6 A Shiner's Cash Book for July xxx6 is as follows:

Dr						Cr
xxx6			£	xxx6		£
June	30	Balance	817.22	July 3	Lomas & Co	151.23
July	4	J Bell	15.75	8	Smith Ltd	32.00
	9	Salt & Son	92.53	10	C Jervis	1.84
	18	Williams Ltd	31.22	20	Evans & Co	10.91

29	E Harris	81.17	27	PMG Telephones	35.32
31	James & Co	14.81	29	D Greene	1.80
			30	J Johnson	84.89
			31	Kenrick Ltd	25.72

His bank statement shows, for August xxx6, the following:

xxx6			£	xxx6			£
July	31	Balance	806.59	Aug	3	Kenrick Ltd	25.72
Aug	2	James & Co	14.81		6	F David	10.53
	3	Saul & Co	100.78		7	D Greene	1.80
					7	J Johnson	84.89

Prepare a Bank Reconciliation as at 31 July xxx6.

7 At 31 January xxx8, the Cash Book of Sue Gibson shows a balance overdrawn of £117, while according to her bank statement at that date there was a balance in her favour of £72. A comparison of the two records revealed the following:

a cheque for £25 sent to B Murray had been entered in the cash column of the Cash Book

b bank charges of £17 at 31 December xxx7 were not entered at all in the Cash Book

c the bank had debited Gibson's Account with a cheque for £11 received from D Carter, which had been returned dishonoured. The fact of dishonour was not shown in the Cash Book

d the Bank Column on the Receipts side of the Cash Book was found to be undercast £10

e unpresented cheques amount to £232.

You are required to prepare the Bank Reconciliation at 31 January xxx8, in proper form, setting out your adjustments clearly.

On 1 January xxx4, a trader obtained her statement and on comparing it with her Cash Book discovered that all items agreed except the following:

a cheques drawn and entered in the Cash Book, totalling £317.28, had not been presented at the bank

b a cheque for £17.50, lodged the previous day, did not appear in the statement

c the statement showed an item of interest on overdraft amounting to £14.09 not entered in the Cash Book.

The trader's Cash Book showed a balance, on 31 December xxx3, of £219.87 overdrawn.

State

a what balance the statement showed on the same day

b what would be the balance of the trader's Cash Book after making the necessary additional entries.

8 On 30 July xxx6, a trader's Cash Book showed his bank balance to be £71.18 overdrawn.

When he received his statement from the bank he found that a cheque for £19.50, lodged by him on 29 June, had not yet been credited by the bank, four cheques drawn on 30 June, amounting in total to £181.34, had not yet been presented for payment, and the bank on 30 June had entered a charge of £10.27 for commission and interest.

Draw up a statement showing the balance as shown by the Bank Statement.

Petty cash

In this chapter you will learn:

▶ *About the need for a petty cash book*
▶ *About the imprest system*
▶ *About posting totals to the ledger accounts*

Objective

This chapter describes the procedure for the recording of small items of cash purchases or reimbursements to employees. The use of the Imprest system to provide control is explained.

We have seen that the general rule in cash transactions is to pay all cash received into the bank on the day of receipt, and to make all payments by cheque or by bank transfer online. This helps to ensure our records are accurate and reduces the chances for fraud.

We have also seen that if wages and salaries are payable by the business to its employees in cash, some departure from this rule is inevitable, although in the first instance a cheque is issued to the Cashier so that they may obtain the necessary notes and coins from the bank for the payroll clerk to distribute.

However, it is necessary in all businesses, irrespective of their type or size, to make provision for the payment in notes or coins of a variety of *small amounts* which may be regarded as sundry or incidental expenses. They are usually termed **Petty Cash payments**, and must be considered because:

▶ they recur at regular intervals

▶ it is usually impracticable to issue a cheque or authorize a direct online bank transfer in payment of any one of them

▶ the person receiving payment may be an employee of the business

▶ in total they may amount, period by period, to a considerable amount and so need to be carefully tracked to reduce errors, keep our accounts in balance, and reduce the opportunities for fraud.

From the standpoint of the business it is most desirable to separate the records of Petty Cash payments from the main Cash Book records. It would clearly be inconvenient to include a large number of miscellaneous small payments in the Cash Book and for this reason, *as a separate Book of Prime Entry*, it is usual to keep a Petty Cash Book if cash transactions number more than a handful each month. The responsibility for the entries in this, and for the *Petty Cash balance* may be entrusted to the Cashier or to someone else whose job involves monitoring and managing the Petty Cash.

Weekly or monthly, the Petty Cashier will be handed cash sufficient to meet all demands for petty cash for the period. They will then submit a list of all their payments to the Cashier and receive a sum to replenish the reduced cash balance. This process is called the **Imprest System.**

It is usually a rule in most businesses that the Petty Cashier will take a receipt for each petty cash payment, and often specially printed forms bearing the name of the business are provided for this to be done – although these are not necessary, using specific notepaper like this (particularly if numbered pages are used) makes it harder for fraud to occur. These receipt forms, when completed with the name of the recipient, and details of the amount and nature of the expense, are kept by the Petty Cashier as independent evidence of payment.

To permit a suitable classification of expense items, the Petty Cash Book may be ruled with *analysis columns* into which the total paid can be detailed. This facilitates the subsequent posting of the analysis columns to the Nominal and other Ledger Accounts. The best way to illustrate the operation of a Petty Cash book is by an example:

▶ **Example 7.1**

Suppose A. Baldwin incurs the following petty cash transactions in March:

		£
March	1 Postage stamps	20.00
	3 Carriage	2.30
	4 Bus fare	1.80
	5 Shorthand note books	5.20
	6 Postage stamps	10.00
	8 Fare to London	12.55
	9 Sundry trade expenses	5.14

11 Pencils	1.40
14 Newspaper	1.50
16 Envelopes	2.41
18 Stationery	8.70
31 Carriage	7.20

Note: £100 is given to the Petty Cashier at the start of the month.

Rule a Petty Cash Book in analysis form, with five analysis columns headed Postages, Carriage, Travelling Expenses, Stationery and Sundry Trade Expenses respectively. (Other columns may apply in your case – the column headings can be chosen to suit your business.) Enter the above items and close the books as on 31 March, showing clearly the balance of Cash in Hand.

It should be noted that in certain cases, for example rail fares, the nature of the payment may not provide a receipt from an outside source. For this reason, the employee receiving the money should be required to fill in a pre-numbered Petty Cash Voucher Form giving the required details and approval by an appropriate authority when necessary. Wherever possible an independent receipt should always be filed with the firm's voucher. However, it is usually a good idea to insist employees provide a receipt in most cases – again as part of your fraud prevention process.

Further, *like the main Cash Book*, the Petty Cash Book is not only a Book of Prime Entry, it is also a Ledger Account with the Petty Cashier. In other words, they are debited with what is received (where the cash assets of the business are increased), and given credit for what is paid away on behalf of the business (where the cash assets are decreased). The balance of £21.80 is therefore the sum for which they are accountable at the end of the month. Since credit is given to them personally for payments, we have to consider *their effect upon the business*. Impersonally, the business must be debited with the **totals** of the expenses set out in the analysis columns. The debit reflects an increase in expenses where the business has consumed some benefit e.g.

Petty Cash Book

Dr Cash Received £	Date	Details	Receipt No	Total £	Postage £	Carriage £	Travelling Expenses £	Stationery £	Cr Sundry Trade Expenses £
100.00	xxx2 March 1	From Cashier							
	1	Brown, Stamps	1	20.00	20.00				
	3	Collins, Carriage	2	2.30		2.30			
	4	Hunt, Fares	3	1.80			1.80		
	5	White, Notebooks	4	5.20				5.20	
	6	Brown, Stamps	5	10.00	10.00				
	8	Lyle, Rail fare, London	6	12.55			12.55		
	9	Sundry expenses	7	5.14					5.14
	11	White, Pencils	8	1.40				1.40	
	14	Hunt, Newspaper	9	1.50					0.50
	16	White, Envelopes	10	2.41				2.41	
	18	White, Stationery	11	8.70				8.70	
	31	British Rail, Carriage	12	7.20		7.20			
				78.20	30.00	9.50	14.35	17.71	6.64
	31	Balance	c/d	21.80					
£100.00				£100.00					
21.80	April 1	Balance	b/d						

Note: If the business is registered for VAT then the analysis columns must include a VAT column.

postage. For each one an account will be opened in the Nominal Ledger. For example, in the case of Postage we should have:

POSTAGES

Dr							Cr
Date	Details	PCB Fo	Amount	Date	Details	Fo	Amount
			£				
xxx1 March 31	Petty Cash total	1	30.00				

Similar entries will need to be made in each account created in the Nominal Ledger for which a payment was made during the period. Ideally, the account created will match the column heading you have chosen.

Imprest system

When applied to Petty Cash, this means that a definite sum of money, say £100 (as in Example 7.1 above), is handed to the Petty Cashier when the Petty Cash system is established and at the end of each week or month the *amount expended* is reimbursed, e.g. £78.20 in the above example. The Petty Cash balance is thus restored to its original figure.

The merits of the system are that:

▶ at any time actual cash or vouchers and receipts should be available for the imprest of £100

▶ as the periodic reimbursements are the actual expenses paid, and not mere advances on account only, they are brought prominently to the notice of the Chief Cashier or other responsible official of the business.

Note: If the business is registered for VAT purposes, we should separate and record as VAT paid any VAT included in the payments made through the Petty Cash. An extra analysis column is required, headed VAT Paid, and any VAT identifiable from the invoices, receipts or vouchers supporting the payments should be included in this column. The total for the month will be posted to the debit of the VAT account (as for any other purchase) as shown in Chapter 4, 'Purchase returns and allowances'.

Focus points

On completion of this chapter you should:

❋ understand the need for a Petty Cash Book

❋ understand the principles and advantages of the Imprest System

❋ be able to enter receipts and payments into the Petty Cash Book

❋ be able to balance the book and calculate the amount required to reimburse the float

❋ be able to post the totals for the month to the appropriate ledger accounts.

1 What is the Imprest System of dealing with Petty Cash?

2 F Salmon keeps her Petty Cash Book on the Imprest System. The imprest figure was set at £350. On 1 November Year 8 the balance of petty cash brought forward was £155. The following transactions took place during November xxx8:

Year 8

1 Nov	Drew cash from the bank to restore the Imprest
4 Nov	Postage stamps £20
6 Nov	Train fare reimbursed £25
9 Nov	Petrol £15
10 Nov	Stationery £38
12 Nov	Bus fares £2
15 Nov	Paid £16 to P Gates – this was to refund an overpayment on his account in the Sales Ledger
16 Nov	Stamps £30
18 Nov	Motor van repairs £35
20 Nov	Stationery £47
23 Nov	Petrol £28
25 Nov	Miscellaneous expenses £17
28 Nov	Parcel post charges £19
30 Nov	Travelling expenses £38

Draw up F Salmon's Petty Cash Book, using the following analysis columns: Postage; Travelling expenses; Motor Van expenses; Stationery; Miscellaneous expenses; Ledger Accounts. Balance the account at 30 November, bring down the balance of cash in hand at that date, and show the amount of cash drawn from the bank to restore the Imprest on 1 December Year 8.

3 Alexander Field runs his own small business and he makes all payments of under £30 through his Petty Cash Book which is operated on an Imprest System. At the end of each week he restores the imprest to its nominated figure of £100. All other payments are made by cheque, and all receipts are paid into the bank.

The balance at the bank was £1605.27, and the petty cash balance was £48.83 at the beginning of the final week of April, and the following receipts and payments occurred:

April 24: The petty cash imprest was restored from the bank, not having been done at the end of the previous week.

: Paid amount owing to P Simpson of £200, less 7½% cash discount.

: Paid taxi fare – £6.80.

: Paid 15% salary advance on £500 to A Roe, a new employee.

Paid rail fare of £15.60 and parcel post of £5.20 (grouped on one voucher).

April 26: M Roe settled his credit account of £100 less 5% cash discount.

: Purchased large envelopes £2.45, pencils £3.69 and packing tape £1.93 (grouped on one voucher).

: J Lowbridge settled his account of £120, less 2½% discount.

Paid C Bell, a creditor, £10.95 (his account number is 251).

April 28: Paid cleaner £12.65 for work done in the office.

: E Gillard paid his credit account of £160, less 5% cash discount.

: Received 28% of annual rent income of £200.

: Purchased Postage Stamps – £7.45.

: Restored imprest account from Bank Cash Book.

Prepare a Petty Cash Book sheet and Bank Cash Book sheet as shown below and:

a Write up the Bank Cash Book for the week ending 30 April xxx9, and balance the book at that date. The name of the ledger account to be debited or credited in respect of each transaction should appear in the 'particulars' column.

b Write up the Petty Cash Book for the week ending 30 April xxx9, making use of the analysis columns and using petty cash voucher numbers with a separate voucher number for each transaction, except where otherwise indicated (the last voucher number issued in the previous week was 44).

Balance the Petty Cash Book at the end of the week and restore the imprest figure.

Petty Cash Book

Receipts	Date	Details	Voucher No.	Total Payments	Travelling	Cleaning	Postage & Stationery	Ledger

Bank Cash Book

Date	Particulars	Discount Allowed	Details	Bank	Date	Particulars	Discount Received	Details	Bank

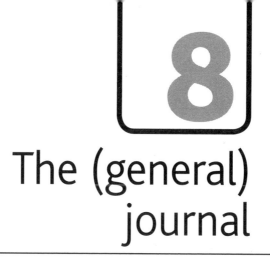

The (general) journal

In this chapter you will learn:

- ▶ *About narration*
- ▶ *About the general journal*
- ▶ *About making entries in the general journal*

Objectives

In this chapter you will be introduced to the General Journal as a Book of Prime Entry for items not appropriate for the Books met so far. A number of examples are used to illustrate the practice of completing this record.

Question You said in Chapter 3 that the Journal in its earliest form was still used for certain purposes, and that it would be referred to at a later stage?

Answer Yes. While the majority of the transactions carried out in a business relate to purchasing, selling and the receipt and payment of cash, there are nevertheless others which do not fall under these headings.

Question If there are transactions that do not relate to any of these items do we not use a Book of Prime Entry?

Answer As was stated earlier, *no entry should be made in a Ledger Account unless it has been recorded in a Book of Prime Entry*. Therefore in certain cases the use of the General Journal as it is sometimes termed, is essential. While the information that can be given in the ordinary Ledger Accounts is limited, as much information as is required, including reference to documents, correspondence, etc., may be shown in the General Journal. This we describe as the **Narration**.

Question Can you give me examples of such entries?

Answer It will help you to consider them as representing business transactions which are not capable of entry in the ordinary Purchase, Sales and Cash Books of Prime Entry. For example, if A Brown Ltd, a customer, owes the business £200 which he cannot pay after going bust, the business must recognize the non-payment as a *Bad Debt*. We must reduce the **accounts receivable assets** of the business as we will no longer receive a future benefit when the debt was paid. Therefore, we *credit* Brown with £200 in his Personal Account in the Sales Ledger. We *debit* a Bad Debts Account recognizing that the expenses have increased with that amount in the Nominal Ledger. This entry needs listing in the General Journal as the Book of Prime Entry.

Supposing also that Smith both buys goods from and sells goods to the business; in the Purchase Ledger there will be an account for him as a supplier, and in the Sales Ledger as a customer. If on balance he is indebted to the business he will only remit the difference in full settlement, therefore the balance on his Purchase Ledger Account must be transferred or posted to the credit on his Sales Ledger Account. This entry should be listed in the General Journal so you have a record of why the entries were made.

Question In effect for these and similar transactions the General Journal is the only book in which the prime or first entry can be made?

Answer Yes, but it is also appropriate, as we shall see shortly, for recording what are termed **opening** and **closing** entries. The former relate to the introduction into the business of Capital in one form or another; the latter refer either to the construction of the periodic **Profit and Loss Account** (or sometimes called the **Income Statement**).

Question And in all these cases it is important to give adequate *narration*?

Answer Yes, if this were not done, it might be difficult to explain the exact meaning of each entry at some later date (e.g. to an auditor or tax official). Also, the entry enables us conveniently to summarize the position for subsequent posting to the Ledger Accounts. A few examples will help to make the process clear.

▶ **Example 8.1**

Give the necessary General Journal entries to record the following:

▶ Having deducted 5% cash discount when paying the account of Lakeside Ltd, a letter is received from them notifying us that only 2½% can be allowed. The difference (£2.77) is being carried forward in their books.

▶ Goods to the value of £50 have been purchased from C Ridley and goods valuing £30 sold to him. Both accounts are subject to a cash discount of 5%, and a cheque for the net balance is forwarded to him.

Fo 1

			Dr	Cr
a				
	xxx8		£	£
	Feb 1	Discounts received	2.77	
		To Lakeside Ltd		2.77
		Being discount not allowed as per		
		their letter 29 January xxx8		
b				
	Feb 4			
		C Ridley (PL A/c)	30.00	
		To C Ridley (SL A/c)		30.00
		Being transfer of Sales Ledger		
		Balance to Bought Ledger on		
		settlement		

Should it happen that *either* the *debit* or *credit* aspect affects more than one Ledger Account, it is usual to prefix the word 'Sundries' to the entries.

C Ridley's account in the Purchase Ledger will then be as follows:

C RIDLEY

Dr								Cr
Date	Details	Fo	Amount	Date	Details	Fo	Amount
xxx8			£	xxx8			£
Feb 4	Sundries	J1	30.00	Feb 1	Balance b/d		50.00
4	Bank	CB2	19.00				
	Discount	2	1.00				
			£50.00				£50.00

The entries in the Sales Ledger would be:

C RIDLEY

Date	Details	Fo	Amount	Date	Details	Fo	Amount
xxx8			£	xxx8			£
Feb 1	Balance	b/d	30.00	Feb 4	Sundries	J1	30.00
			£30.00				£30.00

In posting from the General Journal to the Ledger Accounts, the word 'Sundries' appears in the 'Details' Column. It is unnecessary to repeat all of the information in the Ledger Account, when all that is required can be found on Fo 1 of the Journal.

The two entries for the cheque £19.00, and discount £1.00, will, of course, be posted from the Cash Book in the ordinary way.

The examples **a** and **b** illustrate that adequate narration is always an essential feature of Journal entries.

▶ **Example 8.2**

AB purchased from CD a delivery van for cash £8980 in April xxx5, and on 29 October he bought another for £11 210, giving the one bought in April in part payment, and paying the balance of £4360 in cash. Show these entries in AB's books of entry, and post to the relevant Ledger Accounts. Ignore VAT.

Fo 6

Purchase Journal

Date	Supplier	Description	Inv No	Ledger Fo	Total	Goods	Special Items	
xxx5					£		£	
Apr	CD	Delivery Van	1	2	8 980.00		8 980.00	Motors a/c PL8
Fo 34								
xxx5								Motors
Oct	CD	Delivery Van	40	2	11 210.00		11 210.00	a/c PL8

Fo 10

Cash Book

Date	Details	Fo	Amount	Date	Details	Fo	Amount
Dr							Cr
				xxx5			£
				April	CD	2	8980.00
	Fo 25			Oct	CD	2	4360.00
	(the October						
	entry)						

Fo 19

General Journal

xxx5		Fo	Dr	Cr
Oct	Sundries		£	£
	Motors A/C	PL8		8980.00
	CD	BL2	6850.00	
	Loss on Sale of Assets A/c	IL9	2130.00	
	Being Sale in part exchange			
	of Van per CD's invoice No 40,			
	29 October xxx5			

Fo 2

Purchase Ledger
CD

Date	Details	Fo	Amount	Date	Details	Fo	Amount
Dr							Cr
xxx5			£	xxx5			£
April	Bank	CB10	8 980.00	April	Goods	PJ6	8 980.00
Oct	Sundries	J19	6 850.00	Oct	Goods	34	11 210.00
	Bank	CB25	4 360.00				
			£11 210.00				£11 210.00

Private Ledger
MOTORS

Date	Details	Fo	Amount	Date	Details	Fo	Amount
Dr							Cr
xxx5			£	xxx5			£
April	Goods	PJ6	8 980.00	Oct			
Oct	Goods	34	11 210.00		Sundries	J19	8 980.00

In looking at this example, we see that the cost of the van purchased in April is extended in the Purchase Journal into the 'Special Items' column. It would be wrong to analyse it as *goods*, because it is apparently a *Fixed* Asset, i.e. an asset for use in the business not for resale. As such, it is debited to Motors Account in the Private Ledger of AB. When the second van is bought in October, exactly the same procedure is followed. At this point, however, a record has to be made of the disposal of the first van in part payment.

Having charged the business with two vans, we must, in effect, give it credit in *Motors Account* for:

▶ the part exchange value of £6850. As we paid £4360 for the new van which cost £11 210 the difference of £6850 is the value allowed on the old one

▶ Loss on Sale of £2130. The old van cost £8980 and its part exchange value was £6850, the difference of £2130 represents a loss. This amount will be recorded in the Profit and Loss Account at the end of the period. (**Note:** in practice we will also need to consider the impact of depreciation which we look at in Chapter 15.)

We may charge only the former to CD as we have done in his personal account. The latter is a special kind of expense remaining to be borne by the business and will be shown separately in the Nominal Ledger.

Nominal Ledger

LOSS ON SALE OF ASSETS

Dr							Cr
Date	Details	Fo	Amount	Date	Details	Fo	Amount
xxx5			£				
Oct	Sundries	J19	2130.00				

We will now consider the usefulness of the Folio Column in each Ledger Account. The insertion of the folio numbers prefixed by the initial letter of the Book of Prime Entry makes immediate reference a simple matter.

▶ **Example 8.3**

Give Journal entries for the following transaction in the books of L Denton.

Jan 1	L Denton commenced business with stock valued at £1493, cash at bank £2078 and fixtures value £655. £140 was owing to M Robinson.
March 10	Plant and machinery bought on credit from Langham Bros, value £523.
April 1	K Atkins, a debtor for £23, is known to be insolvent and the debt is written off as bad.
June 23	Goods valued £118.15 bought from Blake Bros entered in the Purchase Day Book and posted in error to the debit of Blake Bros' Account in the Bought Ledger.
June 28	Cheque £15.17 posted to the debit of Jones Bros instead of to the debit of Jones Ltd.

The entries on 1 January are an example of the use of the Journal for *opening* the books of a business. It is also apparent that the amount of Denton's Capital at this date is £4086, being Assets minus Liabilities.

The Cash Book balance will be debited in the bank column of the Cash Book, and the £140 owing to M Robinson credited to

his personal account in the *Purchase Ledger*. The other items
will be posted to accounts in the *Private Ledger*.

The purchase of machinery on 10 March could be shown in the
'Special Items' column of the Purchase Journal as seen in the
previous example. The following is an example of alternative
treatment where the Journal is used to record the private entry
of these transactions.

General Journal

		Fo	Dr	Cr
			£	£
Jan 1	Sundries			
	To Sundries			
	Cash at bank		2078.00	
	Stock		1493.00	
	Fixtures		655.00	
	M Robinson		140.00	
	Capital		4086.00	
	Being Assets and Liabilities introduced			
	this day.			
March 10	Plant and machinery		523.00	
	To Langham Bros			
	Being purchase on credit			523.00
	of drilling machinery			
	and lathe for tool shop.			
April 1	Bad debts		23.00	
	To K Atkins			23.00
	Being amount written off			
	per collector's report dated 1 April.			
June 23	To Blake Bros			236.30
	Being goods purchased £118.15			
	posted in error to the debit of A/c			
	and now adjusted.			
June 28	Jones Ltd		15.17	
	To Jones Bros			15.17
	Being cheque posted in error to			
	debit of Jones Bros			

The entry on 23 June is interesting as its shows the correction of an error in *one Ledger Account*, that of Blake Bros.

Purchases Account in the Impersonal Ledger will have been *debited* on 30 June with the total of the Purchase Day Book for the month, which includes the item of £118.15.

At the same time, because of the error, there is also a *debit* on a personal account in the Purchase Ledger of £118.15. Clearly Blake Bros should have been credited originally with £118.15, and to adjust the position it will now be necessary to enter in the Journal a credit to them of double the amount, i.e. £236.30. In so doing, we shall cancel the debit error and record their position as creditors for £118.15. Because the original error was two debits instead of a debit and a credit, the correcting entry must be a credit: either one credit of twice the amount of the error or two credits of the same amount, one cancelling the wrong entry and the other recording the correct entry.

The 28 June entry is simpler as a debit entry had been made, but to the wrong account. The credit to this account and debit to the correct one is straightforward.

The ability to make General Journal entries successfully presupposes a thorough understanding of double entry principles. Transactions of the kind dealt with in the above example, while not as common as purchasing, selling and cash transactions, will inevitably arise in all businesses at some time or another, and call for initial record in the General Journal, in the way illustrated.

Focus points

On completion of this chapter you should be:

✳ familiar with the purpose of the General Journal
✳ experienced in making entries in the General Journal for opening a business and for making day-to-day entries relating to the appropriate activities of the business.

Testing yourself

1 Explain the uses of the Journals in the system of Double Entry bookkeeping.

2 Explain the use of the General Journal. What entries, other than the opening entry, would you expect to find in this book?

3 The following errors are discovered in the books of a business concern:

   a £47.50 paid for new office furniture has been charged to office expenses.

   b £39.18, representing a monthly total of discounts allowed to debtors, has been posted from the debit side of the Cash Book to the *credit* of Discount Account

   c an entry of £10, representing the retail value of goods returned to X & Co, wholesalers, has been made in the Returns Outwards Book and posted. The amount should have been £7, the invoiced value of the goods in question.

   Show the entries necessary to correct these errors. The original wrong entries are not to be deleted. Subject to this restriction, make the corrections in whatever form you consider most appropriate.

4 You are required to give the Journal entries necessary to correct the undermentioned errors in the books of a business:

   a Cost of advertising the Prospectus, £2200, charged to Advertising Account. (A prospectus is the document produced in connection with the sale of shares in a company.)

   b Allowance of £50 made by a supplier of machinery entered in the Returns Outward Book and included in the total posted to Purchases Account.

   c £500 received from a customer for goods yet to be delivered posted to the credit of Sales Account.

   d Imprest of £100 handed to the Petty Cashier debited to General Expenses Account.

5 Give the Journal entries necessary to record the following facts in the books of I Markham, a manufacturer:

xxx4

Jan 1		I Markham commenced business with cash in hand, £136; cash at bank, £2141; plant and machinery, £2180; and stock value £1200.
	28	Bought plant and machinery on credit from Speed & Co Ltd, value £1130.
March 3		A debt for £25 owing by B Sykes proves worthless.
	10	The plant and machinery purchased on credit from Speed & Co was returned as not being according to specification.
	31	£25 interest on capital to be allowed.

6 Record by way of General Journal entry the following in the books of A, a merchant:

a X is both a supplier and a customer. The debit on his Sales Ledger Account is £40, and the credit on his account in the Bought Ledger is £60.

b On 28 February xxx6, a cheque in full settlement is sent to him, less 2½% cash discount.

c Purchase of office fixtures £400, and stationery, etc., £50, from Office Supplies Ltd.

d Sale of delivery van of book value of £4300 in part exchange at the price of £2250, against a new van costing £7500.

7 Give General Journal entries to record or correct the following:

Jan 6	£25 cheque received credited to John White, instead of James White, both being customers.
14	Cuthbert agreed to accept 0.75 in £ in full settlement of the balance of £180 appearing on his account in the Bought Ledger at 21 December xxx5.
17	Matthews, a customer, owed the business £200 on 31 December xxx5. It is agreed to allow him £50 for window display expenses, and 5% gross for special trade discount.

19   Arnold, a customer, to be charged by agreement £40 interest on his overdue account.

24   Wilkins, a supplier, takes over plant and tools valued at £200 as part payment of the balance due to him of £325.

8 (**Note**: Complete Chapters **9** and **10** before attempting this question.)

The bookkeeper employed by John Horton handed you a Trial Balance (see Example **9.1**) which included on the debit side an item: Suspense Account, £**90.90**. He stated that this was the difference between the two sides of the Trial Balance which he could not trace. On investigation you find that the difference is caused by the following errors:

a The Sales Day Book has been over-cast by £100.

b The Returns Outwards for November, amounting to £30.58, have been posted to personal accounts only.

c A cheque for £70.32 received from Barton Bros has been posted to their Sales Ledger account as £73.20.

d A first and final dividend amounting to £5.88, received from the trustee in bankruptcy of Huber Wilkins, has not been posted to the Sales Ledger account. The full amount of the debt (£19) has been written off as bad during the year.

e A cheque for £12.24, paid to J Smithson for goods supplied, has been posted to his credit in the Sales Ledger.

Show the entries (Journal or Ledger) which are necessary to correct the above errors.

Writing up
the books

In this chapter you will learn:

▶ *About bringing it all together*
▶ *About routine transactions in the double entry system*
▶ *About drawings accounts*

Objectives

The purpose of this chapter is to bring together all of the items illustrated in the chapters considered so far and prepare ourselves for producing summary financial statements.

We have now become acquainted with the various Books of Prime Entry and the Ledgers which they serve. You should have realized in particular that *double entry is completed within the Ledger* and that the Books of Prime Entry are not directly part of the double entry process itself.

The examples that have been used up to this point have largely dealt with the ordinary purchasing, selling and cash transactions of the business, and have been selected to illustrate the process of double entry.

We ought now, therefore, to be in a position to look at other examples which include these transactions and aim at the preparation of the **Final Statements**, the **Income Statement** (sometimes called the Profit and Loss Account) and the Statement of Financial Position (sometimes called the Balance Sheet).

It is important that in working through these accounts we try to put ourselves in the position of the bookkeeper, and consider *every transaction* from the standpoint of its effect on:

▶ the Revenues or Expenses of the business, and

▶ its Assets and Liabilities, or Capital position.

▶ Example 9.1

On 1 February xxx1, R Ready had the following Assets and Liabilities: Cash in hand £100; Cash at bank £1110; Accounts Payable: B Bright £75 and C Clowes £95; Accounts Receivable: R Wright £60 and S Tune £70; Furniture and fittings £180; Inventory £1340.

Open the books by Journal entry, find and credit the capital, and then enter the following transactions in the proper subsidiary books, post to the Ledger and extract a Trial Balance (a list of balances, see Sales Ledger below) at 28 February xxx1. The Cash Book and Personal Accounts should be balanced, and the balances brought down. Use a VAT rate of 20%.

xxx1			£
Feb 1	Received cash from R Wright		30.00
2	Sold on credit to M Moses goods		50.00 + VAT £10.00
4	Bought on credit from C Clowes goods		120.00 + VAT £24.00
5	Paid wages, cash		112.00
6	Drew cheque for personal use		125.00
	Cash sales for week		250.00 + VAT £50.00
9	Paid cash to bank		140.00
12	Received cash from S Tune	£67.00	
	Allowed him discount	3.00	
			70.00
	Paid wages, cash		115.00
13	Paid C Clowes by cheque	£90.00	
	Discount received	5.00	
			95.00
	Cash sales for week		387.00 + VAT £77.40
17	Sold on credit to R Wright, goods		252.00 + VAT £50.40
19	R Wright returned goods		10.00 + VAT £2.00
	Paid wages, cash		116.00
20	Cash sales for week		296.00 + VAT £59.20
22	Paid cash to bank		590.00
26	Paid wages, cash		119.00
27	Paid rent, cash		120.00
	Cash sales for week		182.00 + VAT £36.40

Before we begin the work of opening the books for the month, it will be helpful to first consider the transactions and the business practice relating to them.

▶ The amount of the proprietor's capital is not stated, but as we know it to be the excess of the Assets over the Liabilities we can easily discover it, *and record it together with the other opening balances.*

▶ It is apparent that in the Cash Book there must be columns for 'Cash' as well as for 'Bank' and Cash Discounts.

▶ Both Cash and Credit Sales are made. Only the Credit Sales will be recorded in the Sales Journal, in order to put on record the position of the customer as a debtor to the business, before payment is received.

▶ There is no need to open columnar or analysis Purchase and Sales Journals. The one word 'goods' is the only indication we have of the purchases and sales as a whole.

▶ This example includes VAT at the rate of 20%. If VAT is not applicable the only changes would be those connected with the VAT and the VAT account.

R. READY

General Journal

xxx1			Fo	Dr	Fo 1 Cr
Feb 1	Sundries	Dr		£	£
	To sundries				
	Cash in hand		CB2	100.00	
	Cash at bank		2	1110.00	
	R Wright		SL20	60.00	
	S Tune		25	70.00	
	Furniture and fittings		PL65	180.00	
	Stock to hand		70	1340.00	
	To: B Bright		BL15		75.00
	C Clowes		10		95.00
	Capital (balancing amount)		Pl75		2690.00
	Being Assets, Liabilities and Capital at this date				
				£2860.00	£2860.00

Purchase Journal

Date	Supplier	Fo	Total	Goods	VAT
xxx1			£	£	£
Feb 4	C Clowes	BL10	144.00	120.00	24.00
				NLFo 30	NLFo 52

Note:	Abbreviation
Cash Book	CB
Purchase Journal	PJ
Sales Journal	SJ
Sales Returns Journal	SRJ
General Journal	GJ
Bought Ledger (or Suppliers, or Creditors)	BL
Sales Ledger (or Customers, or Debtors)	SL
Nominal Impersonal Ledger	NL
Private Ledger	PL
Contra	C

The Journal entries as set out above enable us to post to the various Ledgers the balances outstanding on 1 February. If you are using a computer to do your bookkeeping, this will generally be automated.

In the manual accounts, the cash items will appear on the *debit* side of the Cash Book (as assets of the business); accounts will be opened in the Sales Ledger for Wright and Tune, again as *debits* (as they represent debtor assets of the business); and in the Purchase Ledger for Bright and Clowes, but on the *credit* side (as they represent creditor liabilities of the business).

Similarly, *debit* balances will appear in the Private Ledger for Furniture and Stock (as assets), while R Ready's Capital Account will be *credited* with £2690 (as the equity capital of the business).

Cash Book

Dr						Cr				
Date	Fo	Discount	Cash	Bank		Date	Fo	Discount	Cash	Bank
		£	£	£				£	£	£
xxx1						xxx1				
Feb 1 Balances	J1		100.00	1110.00		Feb 5 Wages	NL55		112.00	
1 R Wright	SL20		30.00			6 Drawings	PL80			125.00
6 Cash sales	NL40		250.00			9 Bank	C		140.00	
6 VAT	NL52		50.00			12 Wages	NL55		115.00	
9 Cash	C			140.00		13 C Clowes	BL10	5.00		90.00
12 S Tune	SL25	3.00	67.00			19 Wages	NL55		116.00	
13 Cash sales	NL40		387.00			22 Bank	C		590.00	
13 VAT	NL52		77.40			26 Wages	NL55		119.00	
20 Cash sales	NL40		296.00			27 Rent	NL60		120.00	
20 VAT	NL52		59.20			28 Balance	c/d		223.00	1625.00
22 Cash				590.00						
27 Cash sales	NL40		182.00							
27 VAT	NL52		36.40							
		3.00	1535.00	1840.00				5.00	1535.00	1840.00
		NL46						NL50		
March 1 Balances	b/d		223.00	1625.00						

If there are many cash sales, with associated VAT, it may be appropriate to have a VAT column.

Note: folio entry 'C' (9 and 22 Feb entries above) for contra refers to an entry in the books where a debit entry is matched by a credit entry in the same account. In this case illustrating taking money from the bank as petty cash.

172

Sales Journal

Date	Customer	Fo	Total	Goods	VAT
xxx1			£	£	£
Feb 2	M Moses	SL23	60.00	50.00	10.00
17	R Wright	SL20	302.40	252.00	50.40
			362.40	302.00	60.40
				NLFo 35	NLFo 52

Sales Return Journal
(Returns Inwards)

Date	Customer	Fo	Total	Goods	VAT
xxx1			£	£	£
Feb 19	R Wright	SL20	12.00	10.00	2.00
				NLFo 45	NLFo 52

Having first written up the Books of Prime *Entry for the transactions during the month*, and brought down the Cash and Bank Balances as instructed, we are able to post from the Journals to the appropriate Ledger Accounts.

Let us begin with the *Personal* Ledgers, dealing first with that section relating to the Accounts of Suppliers, or **Purchase Ledger.** You may find that it is useful to open up and post your own ledger accounts and then compare them with those that follow.

Purchase Ledger

C. CLOWES

Dr								Cr
Date	Details	Fo	Amount		Date	Details	Fo	Amount
xxx1			£		xxx1			£
Feb 13	Bank	CB2	90.00		Feb 1	Balance	GJ1	95.00
	Discount	CB2	5.00		4	Goods and VAT	PJ3	44.00
28	Balance	c/d	144.00					
			239.00					239.00
					March 1	Balance	b/d	144.00

B. BRIGHT

Dr								Cr
Date	Details	Fo	Amount		Date	Details	Fo	Amount
					xxx1			£
					Feb 1	Balance	GJ1	75.00

As no transactions have taken place on Bright's account, the opening balance on 1 February remains unchanged on 28 February.

Next we may turn to the **Sales Ledger**.

Sales Ledger

R. WRIGHT

Dr								Cr
Date	Details	Fo	Amount	Date	Details	Fo	Amount
xxx1			£	xxx1			£
Feb 1	Balance	GJ1	60.00	Feb 1	Cash	CB	30.00
17	Goods & VAT	SJ4	302.40	19	Returns & VAT	SRJ5	12.00
				28	Balance	c/d	320.00
			362.40				362.40
March 1	Balance	b/d	320.40				

M. MOSES

Dr							Cr
Date	Details	Fo	Amount	Date	Details	Fo	Amount
xxx1			£				
Feb 2	Goods & VAT	SJ4	60.00				

S. TUNE

Dr							Cr
Date	Details	Fo	Amount	Date	Details	Fo	Amount
xxx1			£	xxx1			£
Feb 1	Balance	GJ1	70.00	Feb 12	Cash	CB2	67.00
					Discount		3.00
			£70.00				£70.00

The **Nominal Ledger** can now be completed.

Within this, as we know, we shall expect to find the accounts dealing *with the effect upon the business* of the transactions entered into.

Nominal Ledger

Fo 30

PURCHASES

Dr							Cr
Date	Details	Fo	Amount	Date	Details	Fo	Amount
xxx1			£				
Feb 28	Total for month	PJ3	120.00				

Fo 35

CREDIT SALES

Dr							Cr
Date	Details	Fo	Amount	Date	Details	Fo	Amount
				xxx1			£
				Feb 28	Total for month	SJ4	302.00

Fo 40

CASH SALES

Dr							Cr
Date	Details	Fo	Amount	Date	Details	Fo	Amount
				xxx1			£
				Feb 6	Cash	CB2	250.00
				13	Cash	CB2	387.00
				20	Cash	CB2	296.00
				27	Cash	CB2	182.00
							£1115.00

SALES RETURNS

Dr				Cr			
Date	Details	Fo	Amount	Date	Details	Fo	Amount
xxx1			£				
Feb 28	Total for month	SRJ5	10.00				

DISCOUNTS ALLOWED

Dr				Cr			
Date	Details	Fo	Amount	Date	Details	Fo	Amount
xxx1			£				
Feb 28	Total for month	CB2	3.00				

DISCOUNTS RECEIVED

Dr				Cr			
Date	Details	Fo	Amount	Date	Details	Fo	Amount
				xxx1			£
				Feb 28	Total for month	CB2	5.00

Dr				VAT			Cr
Date	Details	Fo	Amount	Date	Details	Fo	Amount
xxx1			£	xxx1			£
Feb 28	Total for month	PJ3	24.00	Feb 28	Total for month	SJ4	60.40
				6	Cash sales	CB2	50.00
				13	Cash sales	CB2	77.40
28	Total for month	SRJ5	2.00	20	Cash sales	CB2	59.20
28	Balance	c/d	257.40	27	Cash sales	CB2	36.40
			£283.40				£283.40
				March 1	Balance	b/d	257.40

WAGES

Dr							Cr
Date	Details	Fo	Amount	Date	Details	Fo	Amount
xxx1			£				
Feb 5	Cash	CB2	112.00				
12	Cash	CB2	115.00				
19	Cash	CB2	116.00				
27	Cash	CB2	119.00				
			£462.00				

RENT

Dr							Cr
Date	Details	Fo	Amount	Date	Details	Fo	Amount
xxx1			£				
Feb 27	Cash	CB2	120.00				

Lastly, there is the **Private Ledger** to be considered.

Here we shall have first of all two Asset Accounts, for Furniture and Stock respectively, and one Capital Account, for the proprietor's equity capital.

Private Ledger

FURNITURE AND FITTINGS

Dr							Cr
Date	Details	Fo	Amount	Date	Details	Fo	Amount
xxx1			£				
Feb 1	Balance	GJ1	180.00				

STOCK

Dr							Cr
Date	Details	Fo	Amount	Date	Details	Fo	Amount
xxx1			£				
Feb 1	Balance	GJI	1340.00				

CAPITAL

Dr							Cr
Date	Details	Fo	Amount	Date	Details	Fo	Amount
				xxx1			£
				Feb 1	Balance	GJ1	2690.00

If, however, we look at the Cash Book, we see that on 6 February R Ready, the proprietor, drew a cheque £125 for personal use. This is withdrawing from the business a part of the proprietor's investment in the business and represents a decrease in Capital.

In either event, it must be debited in the Ledger in the Capital Account, or in a 'Drawings' Account opened for the purpose. Usually small withdrawals by the owner of a business will be accumulated in a Drawings Account until the year end before the total is debited to the Capital Account.

DRAWINGS

Dr				Cr			
Date	Details	Fo	Amount	Date	Details	Fo	Amount
xxx1			£				
Feb 6	Bank	CB2	125.00				

Having now posted all the transactions to the Ledgers, and recorded *their dual aspect*, it should be the case that arithmetical agreement has been obtained, i.e. the sum of the Debit Balances should equal the sum of the Credit Balances on 28 February xxx1.

Let us therefore extract the Balances on the Accounts, that is produce a copy of the balances as a list and categorize them as Debits or Credits, according to their nature:

Ledger	Account	Fo	Dr	Cr
			£	£
Cash Book	Cash	2	223.00	
	Bank	2	1625.00	
Bought	C Clowes	10		144.00
	B Bright	15		75.00
Sales	R Wright	20	320.40	
	M Moses	23	60.00	
Nominal	Purchases	30	120.00	
	Credit sales	35		302.00
	Cash sales	45		1115.00
	Sales returns	46	10.00	
	Discounts allowed	48	3.00	
	Discounts received	50		5.00
	VAT	52		257.40
	Wages	55	462.00	
	Rent	60	120.00	

Private	Furniture and fittings	65	180.00	
	Inventory, 1 February	70	1340.00	
	Capital	75		2690.00
	Drawings	80	125.00	
			£4588.40	£4588.40

In total therefore the Double Entry can be seen to be completed *within the Ledger Accounts,* using the Cash Book as a Ledger for this purpose.

This list, a summary of Ledger Balances, we call a **Trial Balance**. Its extraction at any time enables us:

▶ to satisfy ourselves of the **arithmetical accuracy** with which the routine work of writing up the Books of Prime Entry, and posting to the Ledgers, has been carried out; and

▶ to provide a basis for the preparation of the Final Statements the **Income Statement** and **Statement of Financial Position**.

Because of its importance, we will consider this statement at greater length in the next chapter.

Focus points

On completion of this chapter you should have a better understanding of the full process of recording routine transactions in the Double Entry System of a business. From this stage we will be able to consider how we present summaries of these records in the Final Accounts.

Testing yourself

1 N Bell was in business as a wholesale merchant and on 1 January xxx1 had the following assets and liabilities: Cash in hand, £450; Bank overdraft, £4680; Inventory, £7100; Motor vans, £2740; Fixtures and fittings, £920; Sundry Accounts Receivable: J Betts, £640; E Evans, £600; Sundry Accounts Payable; T Brown, £840; F Shaw, £580.

Enter the above and the following transactions into the proper subsidiary books, post to the Ledger and extract a Trial Balance. The Cash Book and, where necessary, the Ledger Accounts should be balanced and the balances brought down. Assume no VAT.

Jan 4 Received from J Betts cheque for £628 in full settlement of his account for £640. Paid cheque to bank.

6 Sold goods on credit to E Evans, £1200.

9 Paid wages in cash, £263.

11 Sold goods for cash, £443. E Evans returned goods. Sent him credit note for £48.

15 Sold a motor van for cash, £780.

18 Paid cash into the bank, £800.

23 Paid wages in cash, £263. Purchased on credit new motor van from the Albion Motor Co Ltd, for £8450.

25 Received cheque from E Evans for £1740 in full settlement of the amount due from him. Paid cheque to bank. Purchased goods on credit from F Shaw, £800.

27 Paid T Brown cheque for £820 in full settlement of the amount due to him on 1 January.

2 On 1 March xxx1, A Walker commences business with £10 000 in cash of which £9500 is paid into the bank. Enter the following transactions in the books of original entry, post to Ledger Accounts and extract a Trial Balance.

March 2 Bought premises and paid £1500 by cheque.

4 Purchased on credit from J Raleigh:15 gents' cycles at £125.00 + VAT £18.75 each. 20 ladies' cycles at £110.00 + VAT £16.50 each. 20 children's cycles at £77.00 + VAT £11.55 each.

5 Bought at an auction sale sundry goods for £268.00 and paid for them by cash. (No VAT.)

6 Sold to S Taylor:1 gents' cycle at £160.00 + VAT £24.00. 1 ladies' cycle at £140.00 + VAT £21.00. 1 child's cycle at £95.00 + VAT £14.25.

8 Returned to J Raleigh:10 children's cycles invoiced on the 4th and received a credit note.

10 Paid J Raleigh by cheque the amount due, less £167.00 cash discount.

12 Bought office furniture for cash £130.75. (No VAT.)

16 S Taylor paid by cheque the amount due.

18 Paid by cheque rent £250.00. (No VAT.) Paid by cash wages £150.60. Paid by cheque insurance £220.75. (No VAT.) Cash sales for the period £597 + VAT £89.55.

20 Paid all cash into the bank except £50.

3 R Simpson was in business as a wholesale cutler and jeweller. On 1 January xxx6, the financial position was as follows: Cash in hand, £440; Cash at bank, £2350; Inventory, £2000; Fixtures and fittings, £1160. Sundry Accounts Payable: M Marsh, £150; D Steele, £200. Sundry Accounts Receivable: H Robins, £275; J Long, £175.

Enter the above and the following transactions into the proper subsidiary books, post to the Ledger and extract a Trial Balance. The Cash Book and, where necessary, the Ledger Accounts should be balanced and the balances brought down. Assume VAT at 15%.

Jan 2   Received from H Robins on account, cheque for £200, which was paid to bank.

   3   Sold to D Dennis & Co Ltd: Goods £240 less 10% trade discount.

   4   Paid wages in cash £260.

   6   Cash sales paid to bank, £500.

   7   Bought from Silversmiths Ltd: Goods £340 subject to trade discount of 15%.

   8   Paid M Marsh by cheque £147.50 in settlement of the account of £150.

   11 Paid wages in cash £170.

   13 Cash sales paid to bank £250.

   15 Withdrew from bank for office cash £200.

   17 Sold to J Long: on credit £130.

   18 Paid wages in cash £160. R Simpson withdrew £80 for private purposes by cheque.

   18 Cash sales paid to bank £285.

   20 Received from J Long in full settlement of the amount due a cheque for £307. Paid cheque to bank.

4 On 1 January xxx1, the financial position of Rose Mason, owner of a children's clothes shop, is as follows: Cash in hand, £245.80; Inventory, £3750.00; H Atherton (Dr), £31.75; Fixtures and fittings, £750.00; A Baker (Cr), £390.00; Bank overdraft £176.75. Assume no VAT. Find and credit her capital. During the month her transactions were as follows:

Jan 2 Bought goods from G Henry & Co, to the value of £812.80 less 12½% trade discount.

6 Paid A Baker the amount owing, less 5% cash discount.

7 Returned to G Henry & Co, goods to the gross value of £103.25.

9 Sold goods to H Atherton, £68.60.

9 Received from G Henry & Co credit note for the net amount of goods returned.

10 H Atherton settled his account of 1 January, after deducting £1.75 cash discount.

14 Bought new showcase £75.75 from W Dixon.

19 Sold goods to N Dobbin £72.50.

20 R Mason paid £300 of her own money into the business bank account.

23 Sold shop fittings for cash £27.60.

26 Cash sales for the period £311.80.

28 Paid all cash into bank except £250.

Enter the transactions in the appropriate subsidiary books – post to the Ledger Accounts and extract a Trial Balance.

5 In the form of a three-column Cash Book, after properly heading each column, enter all the money transactions below and balance the Book. Assume no VAT.

1 Journalize the opening balances and remaining transactions. (**Note**: Purchases and Sales Books may be used, if preferred.)

Post the entries to the Ledger. Extract a Trial Balance. Close and balance the Ledger.

On 1 October xxx1, S Strong reopened the books with the following balances in addition to the Capital Account:

	£
Cash	47.80
K Knight & Co (Cr)	176.90
D Day (Dr)	225.75
Bank (overdraft)	217.90
Rent accrued, owing by S Strong (treat as a creditor)	120.00
Inventory	2741.25

The transactions during the month were:

		£
Oct 3	Received cheque from D Day to settle account	220.00
5	Paid same into bank	220.00
8	Sold to D Day: Goods	130.00
10	D Day returned goods	4.20
13	Sundry cash sales	183.70
14	Paid into bank	100.00
16	Bought of K Knight & Co: Goods	91.75
19	Paid landlord by cheque	120.00
21	Paid K Knight & Co on account	150.00
22	Sold to D Day sundry goods and received cheque (banked)	43.75
26	D Day's cheque returned dishonoured	43.75
27	Cash purchases	107.30
27	Sundry cash sales	249.40
28	Drew cheque for self	25.00
30	Wages and expenses for month paid by cheque and in cash	50.40
		111.50
31	Rent accrued (treat as an invoice)	120.00
	Bank charges	11.75
	Interest on capital at 6% per annum calculated on balance at 1 October xxx1 (treat as an invoice)	
	Inventory on hand valued at	2503.25

6 On 1 January xxx1, R Baxter commenced business as a fuel merchant with £10 650 in cash. On the same date he opened a current account at the bank and paid in £10 500. His transactions during the month were as follows:

Jan 3 Bought a second-hand lorry by cheque, £1256.00.
        Bought from the Victory Colliery Co Ltd:
        Coal £1970.00
  4 Cash sales £277.50.
  4 Sold to J Yates, Coal £184.00.
  6 Paid Victory Colliery Co £1000 on account by cheque.
  8 Bought from The Shell Oil Co Plc, Fuel oil £1685.00.
 10 J Yates settled his account by cheque and was allowed 5% cash discount. Cheque banked.
 12 Sold to W Jones, Fuel oil £473.00.
 12 Paid carriage by cheque £170.50.
 15 Settled the account of the Victory Colliery Co by cheque and was allowed 5% cash discount on the original account.
 16 Cash sales £106.
 16 Paid sundry expenses in cash £253.60.
 16 Paid all cash into the bank except £100 retained for business use.

You are required to enter the above transactions in the books of original entry, to post to Ledger Accounts and to extract a Trial Balance.

7 On 1 November xxx1, June Maynard commenced business as a sole trader, trading under the name The Bon Marché.

She paid £2000 into the bank account of the business on that date, and also borrowed £5000 from family sources to help finance the venture. She paid £4500 of this sum into the bank.

The following transactions were entered into during the month of November:

xxx1		£
Nov 1	Paid rent by cheque three months to 31 January xxx2	237.50
2	Bought material on credit:	
	Forrester & Co	126.50
	Arnold & Sons	439.75
	H Meyrick Ltd	112.95
3	Bought office fittings for cash	220.00
3	Drew cheque for cash for own use	45.00
4	Sold goods on credit:	
	E Walker	221.25
	J Roberts	51.00
	L Morley	147.45
	H Longden	4.85
10	Paid wages in cash	128.25
11	Sent cheque to Forrester & Co	125.00
	and obtained discount	1.50
16	Received cheque from Roberts, paid into bank	50.00
	and allowed discount	1.00
19	Received cheque from Morley, paid into bank	146.00
	and allowed discount	1.45
24	Paid wages in cash	128.25
27	Sent cheque to Arnold & Sons and obtained	435.00
	discount	4.75
30	Returned defective goods to H Meyrick Ltd	9.25

Enter the above transactions in the proper Books of Prime Entry, post to the Ledger, and extract a Trial Balance at 30 November.

The trial balance

In this chapter you will learn:

▶ *About the role of the trial balance*
▶ *How to prepare a trial balance*
▶ *About assurances it gives and errors that may exist*

Objectives

This chapter illustrates the role of the Trial Balance that was briefly introduced in Chapter 9. It also demonstrates its value to the accounting process and its limitations as a summary statement. It also discusses the idea of a four-column Trial Balance.

Question A key benefit of the Trial Balance is that it provides evidence of the *arithmetical accuracy* of the bookkeeping work. This is because of the dual aspect from which every transaction is regarded so debit entries should always equate to credit entries – or some problem exists with your accounts. Are we therefore justified in assuming that the routine work underlying the Trial Balance requires no further examination if this statement demonstrates arithmetical accuracy?

Answer No.

Apparent proof of accuracy is not the same as conclusive proof, and it may be the case that errors exist in the underlying work which the Trial Balance will not reveal.

If, for example, a *transaction has been omitted altogether* from the books, neither its *debit* nor its *credit* aspect can have been recorded.

Goods may have been purchased, say, from Brown, a supplier, and an invoice duly received. But if, in the course of checking prior to entry in the Purchase Journal, the invoice is lost or mislaid, nothing will ultimately appear to the *credit* of the Supplier's Account. Similarly as it has never been entered in the Purchase Journal, it cannot form part of the Total Purchases for the month which are posted to the *debit* of Purchases Account.

Such an **error of omission** would be discovered only when the supplier's Statement of Account is received.

Another example would be to neglect to record in the Cash Book any discount deducted by a customer.

The customer would be credited with too little in his Personal Account, causing an Asset in the form of a Book Debt to be *overstated*, and the Discounts Allowed Account would be underdebited, resulting in the *understatement* of an expense to the business.

There are also errors which we may describe as **compensating errors**. This is where an error in one direction is counterbalanced by an other error in the opposite direction of equal amount. Hence, again the lack of agreement is not disclosed by the Trial Balance.

The following are examples of *compensating errors*:

▶ The total of Sales Account on one page of the Nominal Ledger is inadvertently carried forward £10 less than it should be, i.e. there is *short credit* of £10. At the same time, the addition of Wages Account is made £10 too little, so that there is a *short debit* of £10.

▶ In extracting the balances on the Sales Ledger Accounts, an item of £110 is entered on the list of balances as £100, causing a *short debit* of £10, while a cheque for £10 from Jones, a customer, has been debited in the Cash Book but never posted to the credit of his account in the Sales Ledger. The *total book debts* are correctly shown in the List of Balances, *although the detail items are incorrect*.

We may also have to deal with **errors of principle**. Supposing £250 is paid as a deposit in connection with the supply of electricity to the business. This deposit is refundable if and when the business closes down, and therefore is an Asset. If the amount is debited to Heat, Light and Power Account in the Nominal Ledger it will in all probability be written off as an *expense* for the particular period, resulting in an *overstatement of working expenses*, and an *understatement of Assets*.

Secondly, should a part of the business's Fixtures and Fittings be disposed of to a dealer when the offices are being modernized, and entered as a sale in the Sales Journal, the Sales Account will be improperly inflated, *because the goods are not those in which the business is dealing*. Further, the Fixtures and Fittings Account will not record the reduction in value resulting from the disposal. Here also the Trial Balance is of no help in the detection of the errors.

We must not, however, assume that a Trial Balance's value as a basis for the preparation of the Final Accounts is seriously lessened. Accounts in the Nominal and Private Ledger are not usually numerous, nor are the number of entries appearing in them. Great care is taken in practice to record the true facts.

Similarly when the Sales and Purchase Ledger Balances are extracted and totalled, it is usual for the work to be checked before the figures are finally accepted.

As such, errors should be limited and careful accounting and checking should help to keep them to a minimum but a key reason for using an external auditor is to uncover these kinds of errors.

Errors which the Trial Balance will show

If there is a 'difference' on the Trial Balance, a search must be made for the probable cause as *any* difference will indicate that an error in recording *must* have occurred somewhere in the entry and recording process.

We can compare the names of the accounts appearing in it with those in some previous Trial Balance, and note any *omission*. We can also scrutinize each item in the light of its description and the definition that:

▶ a Debit Balance is either an Asset or an Expense, and

▶ a Credit Balance is either a Liability Capital or Revenue.

Therefore, we regard Sales as a Revenue (Credit Balance) whilst electricity, rent, discounts allowed, insurance and wages would be considered as Expenses, or Debit Balances.

It will not take long to go through the accounts in the Nominal and Private Ledgers to satisfy ourselves that they are apparently in order, and we should probably do this before re-examining the Sales and Purchase Ledger Accounts. Because they so rarely occur any Credit Balances on the Sales Ledger and Debit Balances on the Purchase Ledger should also be considered as a likely indication of error.

If the errors are not discovered by these checks, and assuming the (monthly) totals of the Books of Prime Entry have been checked to the Nominal Ledger, the following steps can be taken:

▶ Check the additions (or casts) of the Books of Prime Entry.

▶ Check the postings in detail from the Books of Prime Entry to the Sales and Purchase Ledgers.

The two latter checks involve a great deal of time and labour, but should result in locating the error, and obtaining agreement in the Trial Balance.

Remember this: Summary of errors

If the Trial Balance does not balance then check:

✳ arithmetical errors in primary records ledger accounts

✳ posting errors, e.g.
  ▷ wrong figures
  ▷ amounts omitted
  ▷ wrong side (debit instead of credit and vice versa)

✳ wrong balance extracted

If the Trial Balance balances there may still be:

✳ errors of omission

✳ compensating errors, e.g.
  ▷ unrelated, e.g. two or more offsetting errors of similar amounts
  ▷ related, e.g. cash from T Smith credited to LS Smith

✳ errors of principle.

Suspense Account

If the Trial Balance does not balance at the first attempt we may include another account, called a **Suspense Account** so that the Trial Balance balances and we can proceed. The suspense account should therefore be debited, or credited, with the total missing that makes the Trial Balance now balance.

This is only a temporary solution; sooner or later the errors and/or omissions which caused the difference must be identified and corrected. The net effect of correcting them will then offset the Suspense Account.

Example 10.1 summarizes work from this chapter so far.

▶ **Example 10.1**

The following Trial Balance was extracted from the books of F Briers on 31 December xxx1. Do you think that it is correct? If not, rewrite it in its correct form.

	Dr	Cr
	£	£
Capital Account		11 000.00
Inventory at 1 January xxx1	3 825.00	
Purchases and Sales	21 275.00	31 590.00
Returns Inwards		80.00
Returns Outwards	70.00	
Discounts Received	80.00	
Discounts Allowed		70.00
Motor Car		4 175.00
Wages and Salaries	10 250.00	
Carriage		70.00
Rent and Rates	3 185.00	
Accounts receivable	4 760.00	
Accounts payable		725.00
Cash in hand	20.00	
Bank Overdraft	4 245.00	
	£47 710.00	£47 710.00

Produce your own correct Trial Balance before looking at the answer below.

Although the total debits equal the total credits, the Trial Balance is very far from being correct. It should instead appear as below:

	Dr £	Cr £
Capital Account		11 000.00
Inventory at 1 January xxx1	3 825.00	
Purchases	21 275.00	
Sales		31 590.00
Returns Inwards	80.00	
Returns Outwards		70.00
Discounts Received		80.00
Discounts Allowed	70.00	
Motor Car	4 175.00	
Wages and Salaries	10 250.00	
Carriage	70.00	
Rent and Rates	3 185.00	
Accounts receivable	4 760.00	
Accounts payable		725.00
Cash in hand	20.00	
Bank Overdraft		4 245.00
	£47 710.00	£47 710.00

The adjustments made, and the reasons for them are:

▶ *Returns Inwards*. As an Expense or Asset (dependent upon whether the business can gain any future benefit from the returned stock) this is a Debit Balance.

▶ *Returns Outwards*, i.e. to *suppliers*. These are sometimes called Purchase Returns, and are a Credit Balance as they decrease our stock Assets.

▶ *Discount Received*. As Gain or Revenue of the business, the amount represents a Credit Balance.

▶ *Discounts Allowed*. An Expense, and so a Debit.

▶ *Motor cars* are an Asset of the business and will be a Debit Balance in the Private Ledger.

▶ *Carriage.* The cost of carriage is a business Expense, and a Debit in the Nominal Ledger.

▶ *Bank Overdraft.* As a Liability due to the bank this must be a Credit Balance in the Cash Book.

Remember this

If you find a Trial Balance doesn't balance, calculate the difference between the left and right columns. Does the figure look familiar? (e.g. an invoice that has been credited but not debited). Also, halve that figure (where a transaction has been debited or credited twice).

Four-column Trial Balance

The purpose of this form of Trial Balance is to assist us further in the preparation of the Income Statement and Statement of Financial Position. It demonstrates in a manner which is not apparent in the ordinary form of Trial Balance, the fact that:

▶ a *Debit* Balance is either an *Asset* or an *Expense*, and

▶ a *Credit* Balance is either a *Liability*, *Capital* or *Revenue*.

The Expense and Revenue accounts are generally listed in the Income Statement and used to determine the profit of the business over a particular period of time. The Asset, Liability and Equity Capital accounts are generally listed in the Statement of Financial Position and show how the Capital of the business is represented.

Let us redraft the Trial Balance of R Ready, shown in Chapter 9, in *four-column* form:

Trial Balance

R. READY   28 February xxx1

Account	Ledger	Fo	Profits (IS) Dr	Cr	Capital (SFP) Dr	Cr
			£	£	£	£
Cash	Cash Book	2			223.00	
Bank		2			1625.00	
C Clowes	Bought	10				144.00
B Bright						75.00
R Wright	Sales	20			320.40	
M Moses		23			60.00	
Purchases	Nominal	30	120.00			
Credit sales		35		302.00		
Cash sales		40		1115.00		
Sales returns		45	10.00			
Discounts allowed		46	3.00			
Discounts received		50		5.00		
VAT		52				257.40
Wages		55	462.00			
Rent		60	120.00			
Furniture and fittings	Private	65			180.00	
Inventory, 1 Feb		70	1340.00			
Capital		75				2690.00
Drawings		80			125.00	
			£2055.00	£1422.00	£2533.40	£3166.40

Opening Inventory, although an Asset, is entered in the *Profits* column because it represents goods in which the business is dealing.

The Inventory on hand at 28 February xxx1 will be recorded and will be used (see Chapter 11) in:

▶ the Profits (IS) column (Credit), and

▶ the Capital (Statement of Financial Position) column (Debit), thus enabling us to record:

► the true Profit, and

► the existence of the Asset of Inventory at this date.

► Summary

	Dr	Cr
	£	£
Revenue	2055.00	1422.00
Capital	2533.40	3166.00
	£4588.40	£4588.40

What we have now done is to show in the *first two columns* of the four-column Trial Balance all those items which are detailed in the Income Statement and help to determine the profit of the business for that period.

In the *third and fourth columns* are found the accounts which relate to Assets (except Closing Stock), Liabilities and Equity Capital, and as such comprise the Statement of Financial Position of the business.

Focus points

On completion of this chapter you should be:
* aware of the role of the Trial Balance in the records of a business
* able to prepare a Trial Balance
* aware of what assurances of correctness it gives
* aware of errors that may still exist
* able to prepare a four-column Trial Balance.

Testing yourself

1 An arithmetical agreement of the Debit and Credit Columns in a Trial Balance cannot be considered conclusive proof of the accuracy of the bookkeeping work.

   Give at least three examples of errors that might have occurred.

2 Write short notes on:

   a errors of omission
   b errors of commission
   c compensating errors

   giving two examples of each.

3 On taking out a Trial Balance from a set of books, a bookkeeper found that the Dr side exceeded the Cr by £9.

   Assuming that this 'difference' was due to a single mistake, mention as many types of error as you can think of, each different in principle, any one of which could have caused it.

4 On preparing a Trial Balance from a set of books the sides are found not to agree, the Dr total being £2530.20, and the Cr £2580.60. You are convinced that nothing has been omitted and that all the figures are arithmetically correct, all postings, additions, etc., having been independently checked.

   What is the probable nature of the error made and what will be the correct totals of the Trial Balance?

5 The following errors were discovered in a set of books kept by Double Entry:

   a An item of £52 in the Sales Day Book posted to the customer's account as £50.20.
   b Bank interest amounting to £60 charged by the bank on an overdraft, entered on the debit side of the Cash Book in the bank column.

   c An item of £15 for goods returned by a customer entered in the Returns Outwards Book and omitted to be posted.

   d A payment by cheque of £10 to XY, entered in the Cash Book on the credit side in the cash column.

State by what amount the totals of the Trial Balance disagreed.

6 A Trial Balance is extracted to check the arithmetical accuracy of a set of books. If the Trial Balance fails to agree, errors must have been made. However, if the Trial Balance does agree, it does not prove the accuracy of the accounts. There are errors which a Trial Balance does not reveal.

Name and briefly describe four types of error which would not stop a Trial Balance from balancing. Give one example for each type of error.

7 State what 'difference' would be caused in the books of a business by each of the following errors:

   a The omission from the list of debtors' balances, compiled for the purpose of the Trial Balance, of a debt of £12.25, due from P & Co.

   b Omitting to post from the Cash Book to the Discount Account the sum of £5.35, representing discounts allowed to debtors during July.

   c Omitting to make any entry in respect of an allowance of £8.50 due to Q & Co. in respect of damaged goods.

   d Posting an item of wages paid, correctly entered as £231.75 in the Cash Book as £231.25 in the Ledger Account.

   e Posting £20 being cash received from the sale of an old office typewriter, to the debit side of 'Office Equipment' Account.

Note: These errors are to be taken as affecting different sets of books having no relation to one another.

8 The following Trial Balance contains certain errors. You are required to discover them and draw up a correct Trial Balance.

	Dr £	Cr £
H Jones, Capital Account		6 000.00
Current Account (Cr)		1 091.00
S Brown, Capital Account		4 000.00
Current Account (Dr)		57.00
Salaries and wages	11 140.00	
Rents and rates	2 520.00	
Sales, less returns		32 556.00
Purchases, less returns	17 245.00	
Inventory, opening	5 472.00	
Trade accounts receivable	10 314.00	
Trade accounts payable		3 591.00
Fixtures and fittings	550.00	
Manufacturing expenses	926.00	
Manufacturing expenses (unpaid)	102.00	
Office expenses	341.00	
Carriage inwards	559.00	
Carriage outwards		253.00
Bank overdraft		1 956.00
Interest on overdraft		42.00
Bad Debts written off	112.00	
Bad Debts reserve	250.00	
Cash in hand	15.00	
	£49 546.00	£49 546.00

9 The following is the 'Trial Balance' of Diminishing Returns owned by XY at 31 December xxx1:

	Dr £	Cr £
Capital		2 650.00
Bank	126.00	
Machinery	1 452.00	
Fixtures	78.00	
Inventory, 1 January xxx1		340.00
Purchases	12 242.00	
Wages	7 135.00	
Salaries	3 312.00	
Rent	1 100.00	
Sales		24 612.00
Repairs	357.00	
Bad debts	24.00	
Heat and light	748.00	
Accounts Receivable	970.00	
Accounts Payable		475.00
	£27 544.00	£28 077.00

Amend the Trial Balance, taking the following into account:

a The Sales Day book had been undercast £89.

b The bank confirmed the overdraft at the sum shown on 31 December xxx1.

c XY's private drawings of £184 had not been posted to the Ledger.

10 A sale of £10 had not been posted to the account of I Jones, a customer. At 31 December xxx1, the accountant of ABC Ltd has failed to balance her Books of Account. The difference has been carried to the debit of a Suspense Account.

Subsequently, the following errors are discovered:

a The total of the Sales Day Book for June has been posted to Sales Account in the Impersonal Ledger as £2784.25. The Day Book total is £2748.25.

b For the month of November, cash discounts allowed, £37.10, and Discounts received, £19.85, have been posted to the wrong sides of the Ledger Account.

c An allowance to a customer of £1.95 has been posted in the debit of his account in the Sales Ledger.

d A book debt of £14.55, due by L, a customer, has been omitted from the list of Sales Ledger balances.

e Cash drawings of the proprietor, amounting to £20, have not been posted to the Ledger.

f Goods purchased costing £21.10 were posted to the credit of the Supplier's Ledger Account, and also to the credit of 'Sundry Purchases' Account in the Bought Ledger.

After the discovery and correction of the errors mentioned, the books balanced. You are required:

a to show the Suspense Account as it originally appeared

b to make the requisite corrective entries.

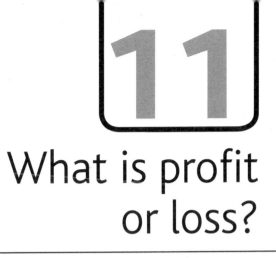

What is profit or loss?

In this chapter you will learn:

▶ *About revenue or capital profit or loss*

▶ *How profit and loss relate to assets and capital*

▶ *About closing stock*

Objectives

This chapter explains the accounting aspects of profit and loss, in particular its relationship to changes in Assets and Capital of a business. It also discusses the inclusion of closing stock in the Trial Balance.

Question The profit made seems to be represented by an increase in the Assets of the business during the period. Is this always the case?

Answer Yes. The word 'Profit' has no meaning in accounting terms except in the sense of an increase of Net Assets. As the business Assets are directly related to the Capital, you could just as truly say that Profit represents an increase in Capital. Put in another way, if the Capital invested at the commencement is a liability of the business, the liability is greater at the end of the period by the amount of the Profit earned.

Question What, then, is a Loss?

Answer A shrinkage in the Net Assets, i.e. the extent to which they fall short of the Initial Capital for the period. If the initial capital had at one time comprised £100 worth of stock which owing to a general drop in prices had to be sold for £90 cash, an Asset of £90 would replace one of £100 and a Loss of £10 would have been incurred.

Such a loss would be described as a Revenue Loss, because stock is a part of the Current Assets of the business, or its Trading property. But if Fixed Assets, like Plant and Machinery, are sold at a figure below their book value, this is called a Capital Loss.

Question Referring again to example 10.1 (Chapter 10) in Chapter 10, the proprietor had withdrawn £125 from the business for personal use, and yet you put the item in the third, or *Asset* column of the Trial Balance. Should it not have been entered in the first or *Expense* column?

Answer No. In the majority of businesses the owners will periodically withdraw either cash or goods (sometimes both) for their private use. If these withdrawals are made to cover personal expenses, and have no relation whatever to the *expenses of the business*, we regard them as withdrawals *on account of accruing profits*. Therefore, they properly appear elsewhere than in the Revenue columns of the Trial Balance. To enter them in the third or *Asset* column is the only alternative and is justified if we think of the initial Capital as a *Liability* to the business. In withdrawing money or goods from the business, the proprietor has really reduced the Capital invested.

Question Should drawings then be set against *Profits* rather than against Capital?

Answer Often it is convenient to do this, yes. The Capital Account, as we have seen, is credited with whatever the proprietor first introduces. Any drawings are then debited to a separate, or *Drawings*, Account. This is sometimes called a *Current Account* (particularly if your business is a partnership). Subsequently, when the profit is determined for each period, it is credited to the Capital Account. At the end of the year the total drawings are also transferred from the Drawings Account to the debit of the Capital Account. This is the treatment that several examining institutions expect. An alternative approach would credit the profit for the year to the Drawings or Current Account. The balance would then represent the difference between the amounts withdrawn by the proprietor during the year and the net profit for the year. If the proprietor decided to retain that surplus within the business it will be transferred to the Capital Account (Dr Drawings, Cr Capital). If they wish to use it for private purposes it will be paid out to them (Dr Drawings, Cr Bank). Withdrawals may be made on account of Capital, and would be debited to Capital Account, but these would not occur regularly in most businesses.

Question Am I right in thinking that the Trial Balance, whether in the ordinary or in the four-column form, does not give all the information needed for preparing the Final Accounts?

Answer Yes. Even in the simple case of R Ready, in Chapters 9 and 10, certain *adjustments* may have to be made. It is true, however, to say, as we did, that it provides a *basis* for their preparation.

Question What are these adjustments?

Answer It will be better for us to fully consider them after we have become familiar with the ordinary form of Revenue Account and Statement of Financial Position, because they affect both (so we look at adjustments in Chapter 14). However, one of the adjustments we have to take into account is that of Inventory. In determining our profit figure, it is not enough to compare the cost of goods purchased with the proceeds of goods sold. Since a minimum amount of Inventory has to be held by the business and will usually have been included as part of the cost of purchases, an adjustment is necessary to calculate the cost of goods sold. Thus, at any particular date, for example the date to which the business makes up its accounts, allowance must be made for the existence of the Inventory *then in hand*, and its proper value.

In the case of a new business, if we thought in terms of *quantities* only, we might say *purchases* equal *sales* plus *Inventory in hand at the end* of the period. Therefore, closing Inventory must be included in the second column of the four-column Trial Balance, and as it is a part of the property of the business at the same date, it *also appears* in the third or *Asset* column, i.e. in the former as a credit, and in the latter as a debit, which maintains the 'double entry'.

We determine our closing stock by doing a stock take (i.e. counting the inventory we have on hand at the year end). If you ever wonder why businesses does a stock take at the year end, you now know the answer. It is part of the year end adjustment in producing our accounts and we can't complete these without the stock take.

The need for the explicit inclusion of closing stock into our accounts as an adjustment at the end of the period arises as a conventional Double Entry bookkeeping system does not support the management of goods/stock values during the year. Inventory purchased during the year is recorded at cost (minus trade discount) in the *Purchases* account and inventory sold is recorded at Sales price in the Sales account. These two accounts are brought together in the Profit and Loss account as we will see in the next chapter. Remember we talked about how we use both a Purchases account and a Sales account to track inventory but only a single cash account to record cash in and out of the business. The Purchases and Sales accounts do need to be brought together as part of the year-end procedure to create the Revenue account, as we will see in Chapter 12.

The following example illustrates how we create the inventory adjustments.

▶ **Example 11.1**

At the beginning of the year the business held inventory to the value of £2300. During the year purchases of goods for resale amounted to £35 764, and sales to £57 891. At the end of the year the inventory in hand was estimated to have cost £4229.

	£
Opening inventory	2 300
add Purchases during the year	35 764
Cost of goods available for sale	38 064
(the whole of this amount will either have been sold during the year or not sold; if not sold it will still be in inventory)	
Deduct cost of closing inventory	4 229
Cost of goods sold	33 835

It is the amount of	£33 835
which will be deducted from the sales figure of	£57 891
to give the gross profit for the year of	£24 056

Clearly any error in estimating the cost (or in practice we need to use the inventory value if that is lower than cost for any inventory items) will have a corresponding effect on the profit for the year. Auditors therefore take particular notice of how you do your stock-take to make sure this produces an accurate figure for closing inventory for the accounts. The amount of £4229 is an asset of the business at the year end.

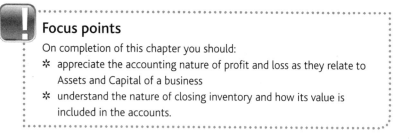

Focus points

On completion of this chapter you should:

* appreciate the accounting nature of profit and loss as they relate to Assets and Capital of a business

* understand the nature of closing inventory and how its value is included in the accounts.

The revenue account: the trading, profit and loss and appropriation accounts

In this chapter you will learn:

▶ *About trading, profit and loss accounts*
▶ *About differences between merchanting and manufacturing businesses*
▶ *How to produce the different forms of account*

Objectives

The purpose of this chapter is to introduce you to the Profit or Loss calculation for a business. It describes the calculation for retail businesses and for manufacturing businesses – these being slightly different from each other. It demonstrates that the profit and loss calculation is part of the process of Double Entry recording.

Having prepared a Trial Balance, corrected any errors and made some of the year end adjustments (for inventory), we are now able to proceed to the first section of the Final Accounts.

Our task for the Final Accounts production is two-fold; first is to determine the Profit or Loss which has resulted from the carrying on of the ordinary transactions of the business. Secondly it is to produce a balanced list of all the assets of the business and the liabilities it owes to its suppliers, funders or owners. Our final accounts are primarily made up of these two reports.

One of the major objectives of our Final Accounts is to produce the information for these two tasks in such a way that it is clear and informative, and free from unnecessary detail.

The period for which these Final Accounts are drawn up will vary according to the requirements of the owner of the business. It is customary to prepare them at least at yearly intervals, or at the date of the business's financial year end. This may be 31 December, 31 March or some other date when perhaps there is least pressure of work on the office staff. The reporting of profit to the Government is normally required once a year for all businesses in the UK (e.g. for tax purposes).

In this chapter we will consider the first of these tasks – namely determining the Profit or Loss we have produced by carrying out the normal activities of our business. The account that provides this for us is part of the double entry system as part of the Nominal Ledger. It is called the **Revenue Account** (although it is also called the **Income Statement** once presented in its final form).

The **Revenue Account** is usually divided into three sections:

- the Trading Account
- the Profit and Loss Account
- the Appropriation Account.

We will look at the first two sections of the Revenue Account first in this chapter.

The Trading Account

The purpose of this account is to determine what is called the **gross profit** (or sometimes called gross income) or **loss**.

In this account, after making allowance for stocks carried at the beginning and the end of the period, we compare the proceeds of sales with the cost of goods sold. We will use an example to show how this account is created.

▶ **Example 12.1**

On 1 January xx1x, A Graham had a stock of goods valued at £1216 (based on his stock-take exercise at the end of last year). Purchases for the year amounted to £10 340, and sales to £15 000 (both determined by balances at year end from the respective accounts). Transport charges on incoming goods amount to £208. Stock on 31 December xx1x was valued at £1764 (based on his year end stock-take exercise). Show the Trading Account.

Trading Account

Year ended 31 December xx1x

Dr				Cr
		£		£
Inventory, 1 January xx1x		1216.00	Sales	15 000.00
Purchases	£10 340.00		Inventory, 31 December xx1x	1 764.00
Carriage inward	208.00			
		10 548.00		
Gross Profit		5 000.00		
		£16 764.00		£16 764.00

It is important we should notice the following points:

- The account is headed 'Year ended 31 December xx1x', implying that it is a summary of the transactions throughout the year.

- The cost of purchases is increased by the transport charges paid, and represents delivered cost to the business. Apart from this no other kind of expense is included if this is a merchanting or retail business.

- Gross Profit is seen to be the excess of sales over the purchased cost of the goods sold, i.e. the balancing item in ruling off the account (if it was a credit entry it would have been a gross loss as it meant that purchases exceeded sales in the year)

- It is the first stage in the determination of the final or net profit.

INVENTORY

Sometimes a difficulty may arise as to the measurement of the quantity and value of the Inventory at 31 December xx1x, which is shown above at £1764.

We saw in Chapter 11 how necessary it is to take it into account and an essential step in this process is to determine the quantities, usually by means of an actual stocktaking.

In this process the goods on hand will be counted, weighed, measured, etc., listed on Inventory sheets and priced at purchased cost. They cannot be valued at their selling price because they are not yet sold, and may never be sold. It is reasonable to value them at cost price, because in doing so we are merely carrying forward *from one period into another* a part of the Cost of Purchases.

It may be that at the date of stocktaking the market price (or present buying price) is less than the cost price. Provided, however, that there is no selling deficiency, i.e. the cost price, together with any selling expenses yet to be incurred, does not exceed the selling price, no adjustment is required. The general rule for inventory valuation is 'cost or market value', whichever is lower.

A point to note is that in the Trading Account the ratio of **gross profit** to **sales** or **turnover** is an important one in all businesses. Expressed as a percentage it amounts in this case to 33% of the Sales (15 000 ÷ 5000) = $^1/_3$, or $33^1/_3$%.

Let us now consider the closing entries in the Ledger Accounts concerned.

Private Ledger

INVENTORY

Dr								Cr
Date	Details		Fo	Amount	Date	Details	Fo	Amount
xx1x				£	xx1x			£
Jan 1	Balance		b/d	1216.00	Dec 31	Transfer to Trading A/c		1216.00
Dec 31	Transfer to Trading A/c			1764.00	Dec 31	Balance	c/d	1764.00
Jan 1	Balance		b/d	1764.00				

▶ On 1 January xx1x, *inventory then in hand* of course appears as a Debit Balance and is transferred on 31 December to the *debit* of the Trading Account.

▶ At the same time the closing inventory figure of £1764 is debited above and posted to the *credit* of Trading Account.

▶ The debit of £1764 is then brought down on 1 January of the next year.

In making these entries in the inventory Account we are transgressing the rule that no first entry should be made in any Ledger Account. It may be preferred to use the General Journal as the proper Book of Prime Entry. Its use for this purpose was referred to in Chapter 8. The record in this Journal would then be:

		Dr	Cr
xx1x		£	£
Dec 31	Trading A/c, xx1x Dr	1216.00	
	Inventory		1216.00
	Being Transfer of Inventory		
	at January 1, xx1x		
xx1x			
Dec 31	Inventory Dr	1764.00	
	Trading A/c, xx1x		1764.00
	Being Inventory at this date		
	transferred		

It should be noted that the Trading Account is produced by transferring each item from its ledger account to the Trading Account. It is also necessary to journalize the transfers from the other Accounts which will be found in the Nominal Ledger and the closing entries in the accounts will appear as follows:

PURCHASES

Dr							Cr
Date	Details	Fo	Amount	Date	Details	Fo	Amount
xx1x			£	xx1x			£
Dec 31	Total						
	purchases			Dec 31	Transfer to		
	for year*	10 340.00			Trading A/c		10 340.00

*the total of the totals for each month.

CARRIAGE INWARDS

Dr							Cr
Date	Details		Fo	Amount	Date	Details	Fo Amount
xx1x				£	xx1x		£
Dec 31	Total expenses			208.00	Dec 31	Transfer to	
	for year					Trading A/c	208.00

As regards *Sales* the transfer will be made from the *debit* of Sales Account to the credit of Trading Account.

SALES

Dr							Cr
Date	Details	Fo	Amount	Date	Details	Fo	Amount
xx1x			£	xx1x			£
Dec 31	Transfer to Trading A/c		15 000.00	Dec 31	Total sales for year		15 000.00

These entries will, in effect, move the balances for the individual accounts to the Trading Account ready to calculate the profit or loss they represent in total thereby enabling the gross profit to be calculated.

In a *manufacturing* business, on the other hand, the Trading Account will be in a different form. In addition to purchases, remuneration paid to staff employed in the actual production of the goods will be debited.

Purchases here will include in the main raw materials and component parts.

As *gross profit* in a *merchanting* business is determined after comparing the proceeds of sales with the cost of goods sold, similarly in a *manufacturing* business the proceeds of sales are compared with the *Direct Cost*, or Prime Cost, of production, which covers *both purchases and manufacturing wages and salaries* and any other identifiable direct expenses (i.e. ones directly linked to production).

Our justification for dealing with it in this way is as follows:

a Merchanting business. Every sales order booked involves a direct and proportionate increase in Purchases.

b Manufacturing business. Every sales order requires not only a direct increase in purchases, but also a direct increase in at least some of the manufacturing expenses.

In the case of **b**, apart from these direct expenses of production, there are also the general factory expenses to be considered.

These could include rates on the factory premises, repairs to plant and machinery, power costs for operating the plant and so on. It would be incorrect for us to include these in the Trading Account unless we are instructed to do so, because their inclusion would convert the Account into a Manufacturing, or Production Account, not simply a Trading Account.

In practice this will usually mean that a merchanting business will produce a trading account, and a manufacturing business will produce a manufacturing account and a trading account. The manufacturing account will provide a cost of goods manufactured which will be transferred to the trading account where it will take the place of 'goods purchased'.

The Profit and Loss Account

The Profit and Loss Account follows immediately after the Trading Account, of which it is really a continuation.

If the total Revenue is greater than the total cost charged in the Trading Account the balancing figure will be a Gross Profit. This will be debited in the Trading Account and carried down as a credit in the Profit and Loss Account, and vice versa.

Its purpose is to ascertain the final or *net profit* of the business for the period by including:

▶ the remaining *expenses*, other than those already dealt with in the Trading Account

▶ the *incidental sources of income*, such as Cash Discounts received, Bank Interest received, etc. that are not associated with trading directly.

In form it is similar to the Trading Account, the expenses or debits appearing on the left-hand side, and the incidental sources of income or credits on the right-hand side. That is, it too is produced as part of the Double Entry process, including the need to transfer the items included in it from their Nominal Ledger accounts.

As regards debits and credits in the Profit and Loss Account, care must be taken that:

- ▶ the expenses included are those of the *business only (excluding* such items as Proprietor's drawings, or private payments made by the business on their behalf)

- ▶ the *whole of the expenses* relating to the period under review are brought in.

We shall see at a later stage the importance of the latter point, but meanwhile let us look at the form and construction of the Trading Profit and Loss Account using an example to illustrate how this is created.

▶ **Example 12.2**

From the items set out below select those which should appear in the Trading, Profit and Loss Account, prepare those accounts (only) showing the Gross Profit and the Net Profit or Loss.

	£
Capital	22 400.00
Freehold Premises	21 350.00
Inventory at 1 January xx1x	650.00
Accounts Receivable	360.00
Accounts Payable	1 512.00
Purchases	13 500.00
Sales	25 000.00
Returns Inwards	20.00
Discounts Allowed	52.00
Salaries	7 220.00
Sundry Expenses	2 753.00
Rates	490.00
Fixtures and Fittings	1 062.00
Cash at Bank	450.00

The inventory in hand at 31 December xx1x was £215.

Trading, Profit and Loss Account

Year ended 31 December xx1x

Dr	£		Cr	£
Inventory, 1 January xx1x	650.00	Sales	£25 000.00	
Purchases	13 500.00	*Less* Returns	20.00	
Gross profit c/d	11 045.00			24 980.00
		Inventory, 31 Dec xx1x		215.00
	£25 195.00			£25 195.00
Salaries	7 220.00	Gross profit b/d		11 045.00
Sundry expenses	2 753.00			
Rates	490.00			
Discounts allowed	52.00			
Net profit	530.00			
	£11 045.00			£11 045.00

The remaining items in the list are of a Capital nature, and will appear in the Statement of Assets and Liabilities (the Statement of Financial Position) of the business.

The information below the 'Gross Profit' b/d line comprises the *Profit and Loss Account*. If required the Trading Account could be presented separately from the Profit and Loss Account. The matching credit entry for the Net profit figure will appear in the Capital Account recording the net effect on the capital of the business transactions of the period.

An alternative form of presentation of this summary account which is increasingly being adopted is a vertical one. The same example is shown below in this format. The information presented is identical and is still produced as part of the Double Entry System. The only thing that has changed is the layout of the Account. The vertical form of layout is usually preferred as it improves the understandability of the information – one of the major aims of the Final Accounts.

Trading, Profit and Loss Account
Year ended 31 December xx1x

	£	£
Sales	£25 000.00	
less Returns	20.00	
		24 980.00
deduct		
Cost of goods sold:		
Inventory, 1 January	650.00	
Purchases during year	13 500.00	
Available for sale	14 150.00	
Inventory, 31 December	215.00	13 935.00
Gross profit		11 045.00
deduct expenses:		
Salaries	7 220.00	
Sundry expenses	2 753.00	
Rates	490.00	
Discounts allowed	52.00	
		10 515.00
Net profit		£ 530.00

In this form – as is typically used by businesses to present this information – it usually now referred as an **Income Statement** (although this usually also includes the **Appropriation Account** also to be completed – as we will see later). The transfer from the Accounts in the Nominal Ledger will be made as follows:

SALARIES

Dr							Cr
Date	Details	Fo	Amount	Date	Details	Fo	Amount
xx1x			£	xx1x			£
Dec 31	Total salaries for year		7220.00	Dec 31	Transfer to Profit and Loss A/c		7220.00

TRADE EXPENSES

Dr				Cr			
Date	Details	Fo	Amount	Date	Details	Fo	Amount
xx1x			£	xx1x			£
Dec 31	Total for year		2753.00	Dec 31	Transfer to Profit and Loss A/c		2753.00

RATES AND TAXES

Dr				Cr			
Date	Details	Fo	Amount	Date	Details	Fo	Amount
xx1x			£	xx1x			£
Dec 31	Total for year		490.00	Dec 31	Transfer to Profit and Loss A/c		490.00

DISCOUNTS ALLOWED

Dr				Cr			
Date	Details	Fo	Amount	Date	Details	Fo	Amount
xx1x			£	xx1x			£
Dec 31	Total for year		52.00	Dec 31	Transfer to Profit and Loss A/c		52.00

Alternatively, instead of making the transfers directly to the Profit and Loss Account, we could use the *General Journal*, with the result that the following Journal entries will appear as *closing entries*:

			Dr	Cr
xx1x			£	£
Dec 31	Sundries			
	Profit and Loss A/c	Dr	10 515.00	
	Sundries			
	Salaries			7220.00
	Sundry expenses			2753.00
	Rates			490.00
	Discounts allowed			52.00
	Being transfer of Expense			
	Account balances to Profit			
	and Loss Account as above.			

If the latter method is adopted the word 'Sundries' with the appropriate Journal reference will describe the credit entries in each of the Ledger Accounts, in place of 'Transfer to Profit and Loss Account'.

We can now review a full example of a Manufacturing, Trading, Profit and Loss Account to bring together all we have discussed in this chapter.

▶ **Example 12.3**

The financial year of Excelsior Pressings, a manufacturer of small household equipment, ends on 31 December. The following balances are in the books of the firm as at 31 December xx1x:

	£
Inventory as at 1 January xx1x:	
Raw materials	28 315
Work in progress (at factory cost)	6 200
Finished goods	33 700
Heating and lighting	3 450
Wages of indirect manufacturing personnel	45 820
Rent and rates	16 400
Purchase of raw materials	172 300
Manufacturing wages	194 500

Factory power	4 760
Factory expenses and maintenance	3 700
Salaries	32 400
Sales of finished goods	652 500
Advertising	60 800
Administration expenses	27 500

The following information is also available:

▶ Inventory has been valued as at 31 December xx1x as follows:

	£
Raw materials	*30 200*
Work in progress (at factory cost)	*7 100*
Finished goods	*37 500*

▶ In respect of xx1x, the following apportionments are to be made:

	Factory	*General Office*
Heating and lighting	*4/5*	*1/5*
Rent and rates	*3/4*	*1/4*
Salaries	*1/3*	*2/3*

▶ Depreciation is to be allowed as follows:

Plant and machinery	*£20 000*
Office equipment	*£4 000*

You are required to prepare the Manufacturing, Trading, Profit and Loss Accounts of Excelsior Pressings for the year ended 31 December xx1x.

Note: Try to prepare your own accounts and then compare them with the solution that follows. The slightly new requirement means that you have to consider, using the description of the balance and the additional data, the amounts which will be included in each particular account.

Excelsior Pressings

Manufacturing account for the year ended 31 December xx1x

	£	£
Raw materials used		
Opening inventory	28 315	
Purchases	172 300	
Available	200 615	
Closing inventory	30 200	
Used during the year		170 415
Manufacturing wages		194 500
Other expenses		
Heating and lighting	2 760	
Indirect personnel	45 820	
Rent and rates	12 300	
Factory power	4 760	
Sundry and maintenance	3 700	
Salaries	10 800	
Depreciation plant and machinery	20 000	
		100 140
Cost of manufacturing during the year		465 055
add opening work in progress		6 200
deduct closing work in progress		7 100
Cost of goods completed during the year		464 155

Trading account for the year ended 31 December xx1x

	£	£
Sales		652 500
Cost of goods sold		
Opening inventory	33 700	
Completed during the year	464 155	
Available for sale	497 855	
Closing inventory	37 500	
Used during the year		460 355
Gross profit		192 145

Profit and loss account for the year ended 31 December xx1x

	£	£
Gross profit		192 145
Expenses		
Heating and lighting	690	
Rent and rates	3 100	
Salaries	21 600	
Advertising	60 800	
Administration expenses	27 500	
Depreciation of office equipment	4 000	
		117 690
Net profit, before taxation		74 455

Appropriation (or Net Profit and Loss) Account

As its name implies, this third section deals with the Net Profit or Loss that has been computed by the Trading, Profit and Loss Account, and its distribution among the proprietors of the business.

In a partnership firm the Net Profit figure will here be divided in the ratio in which the partners share profits and losses (see Chapter 18).

In the case of a Limited Company, the appropriation account shows how the Net Profits are divided in dividend to the shareholders according to their respective rights and interests and this appropriation sometimes appears in the Profit and Loss Account (see Chapter 19).

The necessity for such an account rarely, if ever, arises where the position of a sole trader is being computed, the Net Profit being carried direct to the Capital or Current Account of the proprietor, as already explained.

Focus points

On completion of this chapter you should:

✳ understand the purpose of the Trading, Profit and Loss Account
✳ appreciate the difference between the Trading and Profit and Loss Account and the Manufacturing, Trading, Profit and Loss Account
✳ be able to produce either form of account by transferring appropriate items from the Nominal Ledger Accounts.

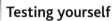

Testing yourself

1 What do you understand by

   a Capital Expenditure
   b Revenue Expenditure?

   State some items coming under each of these headings in the case of a company carrying on business as manufacturers of aeroplanes.

2 What is the object in preparing a Trading Account as distinct from a Profit and Loss Account? Explain what information may be obtained from the former and its importance to a trader.

3 PQ carries on business as a merchant, but, although stock is taken regularly at the end of December in each year, proper Books of Account are not kept. A Cash Book, Petty Cash Book and Personal Ledger are the only books.

   Explain briefly how you would proceed if requested to ascertain the result of the trading for the past year.

4 What is the object of calculating gross profit and net profit? Does gross profit measure the prosperity of a business? Explain.

5 On 5 January xx1x, Ambrose sold goods to Applejohn.

   The goods had cost Ambrose £100, and the selling price was 50% on cost, payment being due on monthly account less 2% for cash.

   On 28 January xx1x, Applejohn returned some of the goods, and Ambrose sent him a credit note for £30.

   The amount due was paid by cheque on 28 February xx1x, but three days later the cheque was returned by the bank unpaid. Ultimately full settlement was received from Applejohn.

Show:

a Applejohn's account in the books of Ambrose.

b What profit or loss Ambrose made on the whole transaction.

6 A business has three departments, A, B and C. You are asked to calculate the working profit in each department, by reference to the following:

	£
Opening Inventory, B	1280.00
Opening Inventory, C	640.00
Closing Inventory, B	1320.00
Closing Inventory, C	650.00
Purchases	6000.00
Wages	1800.00
General Expenses	1250.00
Sales, B	6800.00
Sales, C	3200.00

All purchases are made for A department in the first instance. A department (which has no sales) processes the goods and then re-issues them to B and C departments at fixed prices.

The issues to B were valued at £5000 and to C at £2400.

25% of the wages are charged to B, 20% to C, 10% to general expenses and the balance to A.

The general expenses are recharged as follows:

Department A, 7% on output value,

Department B, 10% on sales value,

Department C, 7% on sales value,

any difference being carried to the Profit and Loss Account.

This may seem to be a question that you have not been taught how to answer; but think about it. There are three departments and general expenses. You are told how wages and general expenses are charged to the three departments. The output of A is not sales to customers but transfers to B and C at a given value which become the 'purchases' of B and C departments.

The Statement of Financial Position

In this chapter you will learn:

- ▶ *About the purpose of the balance sheet*
- ▶ *How it relates to the profit and loss account*
- ▶ *How to produce a Statement of Financial Position in various formats*

Objectives

In this chapter you will be introduced to the second of the Final Accounts of a business – the Statement of Financial Position. This chapter describes the purpose of this statement and explains how it is prepared (drawn up) from the Trial Balance. Its relationship with the Income Statement is also described.

Together with the **Income Statement** (Profit and Loss Account), we have described the **Statement of Financial Position** (or sometimes called the **Balance Sheet**) as a part of the Final Accounts of the business. It can be thought of as 'a photograph of the position of affairs of the business at a particular date' as it summarizes the financial position of a business at a specific point in time.

More precisely, it is a Statement of Assets and Liabilities, including the balance of the Profit and Loss Account made up to the date at which the Statement of Financial Position is prepared.

The fact that it includes the balance on the Profit and Loss Account implies that this balance, if a Credit, will be shown as a Liability and if a Debit, as an Asset.

In other words, the business having an *initial liability* to its proprietor for the amount of Capital invested, now has a *further liability* in respect of the profit earned.

It is important for us to remember that the Statement of Financial Position is the complement to the Income Statement and is an essential part of the Final Accounts for this reason. When the business was started, Capital was invested in it, probably in the first place in the form of cash. Almost at once this cash would be spent in the acquisition of various forms of property the business needed to operate of the kind we have defined as Fixed Assets or Current Assets.

The former represented property which the business must possess as part of its equipment; the latter consisted of property in which the business was dealing.

Once the Current Assets are used by the proprietor or the manager to produce a Profit it would clearly be necessary to draw up a further Statement of Financial Position at *the end of each trading period*, showing just what Assets then existed in the business at that date. Provided no additions to or withdrawals from Capital had taken place, and each Asset held was reasonably and properly valued in each succeeding Statement of Financial Position, any increase in the Total Assets would represent a *profit*, and conversely any decrease a *loss*.

In the latter case, as the loss appeared in the Statement of Financial Position as an 'Asset', it could quite well be deducted from the liability of the business to its proprietor on Capital Account, disclosing at that point a *loss of Capital*, which, of course, is in line with the facts.

Assets = Liabilities

and the assets and liabilities will consist of:

Fixed Assets

+ Current Assets

= Owner's Capital

+ Liability to Other Creditors

or rearranged

Owner's Capital = Fixed Assets + Current Assets – Creditors

Earning a profit means therefore increasing our total assets over time. For example, for a retail business, we have bought something for, say, £100 and sold it for £150. If these were cash transactions they could be represented as changes in current assets. Buying for £100 merely means

–£100 cash asset
+£100 stock asset

i.e. a change within the current assets.

Selling for £150 means   +£150 cash asset
                                 –£100 stock asset
and   –£50 profit

The form of the Statement of Financial Position

We have seen that the Profit and Loss Account is prepared just like any ordinary Ledger Account, although before presentation to others it may be redrafted into a vertical format (to become the Income Statement).

In form, it is a summarized Ledger Account to which all the Revenue balances appearing in the Trial Balance are transferred at the end of the financial year of the business. By so doing, an ultimate balance (either of Profit or Loss) is determined.

But we still have to deal with the 'Capital' columns remaining in the Trial Balance. It is these remaining balances, **and the balance of the Profit and Loss Account**, which are entered in a 'sheet of balances' or **Statement of Financial Position.**

We could, if we wished, show this Statement of Financial Position in the form of an ordinary Ledger Account, debiting to it the Assets, and putting the Liabilities on the credit side.

As a result, in reading the Statement of Financial Position in the ordinary way, from left to right, we begin with the Assets, and then see the Liabilities out of which they have been financed.

We can also however, regard the Statement of Financial Position as a *classified summary* of the Ledger Balances remaining on the books after the preparation of the Revenue Account and including the balance of the Revenue Account. This is probably more commonly how a Balance Sheet is created so is then outside the normal Double Entry process.

THE STATEMENT OF FINANCIAL POSITION AND THE TRIAL BALANCE CONTRASTED

While both are drawn up at a particular date, the former includes only those balances which are, or have become, *Assets and Liabilities*; the latter also includes the various Nominal Ledger balances relating to *expenses* and *gains*.

The Statement of Financial Position is a properly structured statement of the Assets and Liabilities. The Trial Balance merely lists all the balances as they appear in the Ledgers.

The purpose of the Statement of Financial Position is to give information to the proprietor of the business as to its financial position, whereas the Trial Balance is extracted primarily to prove the arithmetical accuracy of the bookkeeping work i.e. that the principles of Double Entry have been adhered to.

Finally, the Statement of Financial Position always includes the value of the inventory at the end of the period; the Trial Balance does not necessarily show this Asset for reasons we saw in earlier chapters on the unique features of stock accounting.

Let us now take two examples illustrating the points we have been discussing.

▶ **Example 13.1**

From the following items construct the Statement of Financial Position of L Redfern as on 31 December xxx1 or 'as at' or 'at' to show this is valid only at a point in time.

	£
Capital as at 1 January xxx1	2000
Motor vans as at 31 December xxx1	2200
Cash at bank as at 31 December xxx1	700
Profit for the year	3000
Land and buildings as at 31 December xxx1	4100
Drawings for the year	1500
Inventory of goods, 31 December xxx1	2300
Loan from A Herbert repayable 30 Nov xxx2	4000
Accounts Receivable as at 31 December xxx1	2000
Accounts Payable as at 31 December xxx1	3800

In this first case, it may be helpful if we list the items as *Assets* (Debits) or *Liabilities* (Credits):

	Dr	Cr
	£	£
Capital, 1 January xxx1		2 000.00
Motor vans, 31 December xxx1	2 200.00	
Cash at bank, 31 December xxx1	700.00	
Profit for the year		3 000.00
Land and buildings, 31 December xxx1	4 100.00	
Drawings	1 500.00	
Inventory of goods, 31 December xxx1	2 300.00	
Loan from A Herbert, repayable xxx2		4 000.00
Accounts receivable as at 31 December xxx1	2 000.00	
Accounts payable as at 31 December xxx1		3 800.00
	£12 800.00	£12 800.00

We may then proceed as follows, remembering:

▶ that a Statement of Financial Position is always prepared at some definite date

▶ that the balances on the various Accounts of which it is made up are not transferred to it as is the case with the Revenue Account.

L. REDFERN
Statement of Financial Position
as at 31 December xxx1

Assets	£	£	Liabilities	£	£
Fixed Assets			Capital Account	2 000	
Land and Buildings	4 100		Profit for year	3 000	
Motor Vans	2 200			5 000	
Total fixed assets		6 300	Less drawings	1 500	
Current Assets					
Inventory	2 300		Capital at 31.12.x1		3 500
Accounts receivable	2 000		Current Liabilities		
Cash at bank	700		A Herbert	4 000	
			Accounts payable	3 800	
Total current assets		5 000			7 800
TOTAL ASSETS		£11 300	TOTAL LIABILITIES		£11 300

It should be noted that:

- the Assets are stated in their order of permanence beginning with the least liquid asset of 'Land and Buildings'

- Cash, Accounts receivable and Inventory represent Current Assets, while Motor Vans and Land and Buildings are Fixed Assets

- although Profit and Drawings have been shown in a Capital Account they might equally well have been recorded in Current Account

- the loan from A Herbert is shown as a Current liability as it is due to be repaid within twelve months of the Statement of Financial Position date.

As with the Trading, Profit and Loss Account, the Statement of Financial Position may be presented in a vertical format to help understanding. This is the format you will most often see a Statement of Financial Position presented as. For example:

L. REDFERN
Statement of Financial Position
as at 31 December xxx1

	£	£
Fixed Assets		
Land and buildings	4 100.00	
Motor vans	2 200.00	
Total Fixed Assets		6 300.00
Current Assets		
Inventory	2 300.00	
Accounts receivable	2 000.00	
Cash at bank	700.00	
Total Current Assets		5 000.00
Total Assets		£11 300.00

(Continued)

Capital account		
As at 1 January xxx1	2 000.00	
Add profit for year	3 000.00	
Deduct drawings	(1 500.00)	
As at 31 December xxx1		3 500.00
Current Liabilities		
Loan from A Herbert	4 000.00	
Accounts payable	3 800.00	
Total Current Liabilities		7 800.00
Total Liabilities		**£11 300.00**

You should notice that in this vertical presentation the assets and liabilities are still listed in the order of permanence. Whilst this is not critical, it is normal practice.

▶ **Example 13.2**

From the following particulars construct the Statement of Financial Position of T Tomlinson as on 31 March xxx2.

Capital 1 April xxx1 was £5000. The loss for the year to 31 March xxx2 was £1200 and drawings were £220. On 31 March xxx2 the Inventory was £2480, and the Bank Overdraft £1320, Accounts receivable £3260, the Loan from F Weston £2200 repayable on 31 March xxx8, the Fixtures and Fittings £1480, Accounts payable £2900, Cash in Hand £50, Machinery £2730.

If you have studied Example 13.1 carefully, it should not be necessary to list the balances again before constructing the Balance Sheet. Try to produce your own Statement of Financial Position (and make it balance!).

Looking at the information given, we see, however, that a *trading loss* of £1200 has been sustained, and in addition there are drawings of £220. The initial Capital has thus *decreased* by £1420.

As regards the Liabilities, we may note here that the Loan is not repayable until xxx8; an Overdraft is usually considered a Current Liability; the item 'Accounts payable' referring to the Purchase Ledger Accounts of suppliers for *goods* or *services*.

T. TOMLINSON

Statement of Financial Position

as at 31 March xxx2

Assets	£	£	£	Liabilities	£	£	£
Fixed Assets				Capital Account:			
Machinery	2 730.00			1 April xxx1		5 000.00	
Fixtures and Fittings	1 480.00			Less Loss year to			
Total Fixed Assets		4 210.00		31 March xxx1	200.00		
					220.00		
Current Assets				Drawings		1 420.00	
Inventory	2 480.00						3 580.00
Accounts receivable	3 260.00			At 31 March xxx1			
Cash in hand	50.00			Longer-term Liability Loan			2 200.00
Total Current Assets		5 790.00		Current Liabilities			
				Bank overdraft		1 320.00	
				Accounts payable		2 900.00	
				Total Current Liabilities			4 220.00
Total Assets		£10 000.00		Total Liabilities			£10 000.00

Having considered separately the Trading, Profit and Loss Accounts, and the Statement of Financial Position, we may now prepare each of them from an ordinary two-column Trial Balance.

▶ **Example 13.3**

From the following balances prepare the Trading Account, Profit and Loss Account, and Statement of Financial Position of J Farmer, a retailer, for half year ended 30 June xxx1:

	£	£
Petty cash	50.00	
Accounts payable		493.00
Cash at bank	986.00	
Furniture, fixtures and equipment	400.00	
Purchases	8 417.00	
Sales		11 618.00
Inventory, 1 January xxx1	1 117.00	
Office expenses	45.00	
Rent and rates	997.00	
Lighting and heating	186.00	
Advertising	75.00	
Delivery expenses	66.00	
Capital		2 000.00
Drawings	1 560.00	
Carriage on purchases	212.00	
	£14 111.00	£14 111.00

Inventory on 30 June xxx1, £1084. Not registered for VAT.

J. FARMER

Trading, Profit and Loss Account

Six Months ended 30 June xxx1

Dr	£	£		£	Cr £
Inventory, 1 January xxx1		1 117.00	Sales		11 618.00
Purchases	8 417.00		Inventory, 30 June xxx1		1 084.00
Carriage on purchases	212.00				
		8 629.00			
		2 956.00			
		£12 702.00			£12 702.00
Gross profit c/d			Gross profit, b/d		2 956.00
Rent and rates		997.00			
Lighting and heating		186.00			
Advertising		75.00			
Delivery expenses		66.00			
Office expenses		45.00			
Net profit, carried to Capital A/c		1 587.00			
		£2 956.00			£2 956.00

J. FARMER
Statement of Financial Position
as at 30 June xxx1

Dr				Cr
Assets	£	£	£	£
Fixed Assets				
Furniture, fixtures and		400.00	*Liabilities*	
equipment			Capital Account	2000.00
Current Assets			*Add* Net profit for	
Inventory	1084.00		half year to date	1587.00
Cash at bank	986.00			3587.00
Petty Cash	50.00		*Less Drawings*	1560.00
Total current				
assets		2120.00	At 30 June xxx1	2027.00
			Current liabilities	
			Accounts payable	493.00
Total Assets		£2520.00	Total Liabilities	£2520.00

Note that as the Trading Account and the Profit and Loss Account are only divisions of the Revenue Account, they may conveniently be shown together in one statement.

Focus points

On completion of this chapter you should:

✳ be clear on the purpose of the Statement of Financial Position

✳ understand how it relates to the Profit and Loss Account

✳ be able to draw up a Statement of Financial Position from a Trial Balance

✳ be aware of the use of various formats for presenting the information contained in a Statement of Financial Position.

1 What effect would the following errors made by a bookkeeper have upon (a) the Trial Balance, (b) the annual accounts for a business:

   a An item of £50 for goods sold to CD posted from the Sales Journal to the credit of CD's Ledger Account.
   b An item of £212, representing the purchase of a desk, placed in the general expenses column of the Purchase Journal.
   c A sum of £15, representing interest allowed by the banker, entered in the bank column on the credit side of the Cash Book.

2 List the assets you would expect to find on the Statement of Financial Position of AB, a motor-car manufacturer, grouping them into the different classes.

   Why is the distinction between different types of asset important?

3 From the following particulars draw up the Balance Sheet of B Wilton as on 31 December xxx1. Land and buildings, £51 000; Machinery, £7325; Motor vans, £12 120; Fixtures and fittings, £3070; Inventory at 31 December xx1x, £5950; Accounts receivable, £3856; Cash in hand, £29; Accounts payable, £7820; Bank overdraft, £1200; Loan from A Mather, £40 000; Capital as at 1 January xx1x, £30 230; Loss for the year, £4100. State briefly your opinion of the financial position of B Wilton.

4 AB, an engineer, decides to erect a new machine in his works. He dismantles an old machine and uses material from it to the value of £250 in the erection of the new machine. Additional materials are purchased from outside sources at a cost of £840, and the wages amount to £560.

   Explain how the items would be dealt with in his books.

5 The following balances were extracted from the books of D Wright on 31 December xx1x. You are required to prepare a Trading Account, Profit and Loss Account and Statement of Financial Position as on that date.

	Dr	Cr
	£	£
Cash in hand	17.00	
Bank overdraft		175.00
Inventory, 1 January xx1x	6 794.00	
Purchases and sales	14 976.00	26 497.00
Wages	3 719.00	
Insurance	155.00	
Bank charges	110.00	
Furniture and fittings	1 115.00	
Returns inwards and outwards	309.00	237.00
Accounts receivable/payable	1 753.00	615.00
Land and buildings	20 000.00	
Discount		154.00
Capital		21 270.00
	£48 948.00	£48 948.00

Stock at end £1169.00

6 From the following Trial Balance of J Lowe, prepare Trading, Profit and Loss Accounts for the year ended 31 March xxx2, and a Statement of Financial Position as on that date.

	£	£
Purchases	21 300.00	
Carriage inwards	350.00	
Sales		36 600.00
Inventory, 1 April xxx1	4 000.00	
Trade expenses	850.00	
Fixtures and fittings	2 000.00	

(Contd)

Discounts allowed	900.00	
J Lowe: Capital		6 000.00
Returns inwards	750.00	
Cash in hand	150.00	
Accounts receivable	2 400.00	
Salaries	7 200.00	
J Lowe: Drawings	2 500.00	
Discounts received		400.00
Sundry accounts payable		4 000.00
Cash at bank	2 700.00	
Rent	500.00	
Rates	1 400.00	
	£47 000.00	£47 000.00

Stock at 31 March xxx2 was £5500

7 The following Trial Balance was extracted from the books of R Parr on 31 December xx1x:

	Dr £	Cr £
Capital		35 000.00
Drawings	1 450.00	
Inventory at 1 January xxx1	26 000.00	
Purchases and sales	45 000.00	65 000.00
Returns outwards		600.00
Returns inwards	1 000.00	
Salaries	4 750.00	
Trade expenses	2 050.00	
Bad debts	230.00	
Discount account (balance)		350.00
Accounts receivable	35 750.00	
Accounts payable including VAT		19 600.00
Insurance	220.00	
Fixtures and fittings	1 850.00	

	Dr	Cr
	£	£
Motor vans	2 650.00	
Rent and rates	3 550.00	
Bank overdraft		3 950.00
	£124 500.00	£124 500.00

The value of the stock on hand was £17 950.

You are required to prepare Trading, Profit and Loss Accounts for the year ended 31 December xx1x, and a Statement of Financial Position as on that date.

8 The following balances were extracted at 30 April xxx2, from the books of CD:

   a Prepare a Trading, Profit and Loss Account for the year ended on that date, and also a Statement of Financial Position.
   b Do the results of the business for the year justify the drawings of £350 by CD? Explain.

	£
Office salaries	7 628.00
Insurance of plant	61.00
Discounts received	33.00
Sales	27 350.00
Bad debts	69.00
Plant and machinery	7 430.00
Commission	127.00
Investment interest received	30.00
Inventory, 1 May xxx1	1 110.00
Repairs	98.00
Sundries	46.00
Goods returned by customers	100.00

Discounts allowed	115.00
Rent and rates	1 322.00
Purchases	4 290.00
Accounts receivable	3 143.00
Travelling expenses	263.00
Wages and National Insurance	13 004.00
General insurance	34.00
Carriage inwards	87.00
Accounts payable	1 426.00
CD: Capital, 1 May xxx1	13 250.00
Cash at bank	109.00
Coal, gas and water	2 177.00
Goods returned to suppliers	74.00
Investment in Utopia Ltd	600.00

The stock at 30 April xxx2 was valued at £1275.00.

9 The following is the Trial Balance extracted at 31 December xx1x from the books of S Printer, who carries on business as a manufacturer of sports equipment:

	Dr	Cr
	£	£
Petty Cash Book	28.00	
Nominal Ledger:		
Carriage outwards	504.00	
Carriage inwards	266.00	
Travelling expenses	2 169.00	
Discount allowed	933.00	
Discount received		218.00
Repairs and incidentals	820.00	
Rent and rates	872.00	
Factory wages	10 655.00	
Heating and lighting	137.00	
Sales, less returns		30 750.00

	Dr	Cr
	£	£
Factory National Insurance	318.00	
Packing and dispatch expenses	1 252.00	
Purchases, less returns	10 546.00	
Salaries and National Insurance	2 735.00	
Private Cash Book		853.00
Private Ledger:		
Inventory, 1 January xx1x	3 915.00	
S Printer: Capital at 1 January xx1x		10 000.00
S Printer: Drawings	1 200.00	
Office fixtures and general equipment		
1 January xx1x	1 567.00	
Equipment sold		136.00
Equipment purchase	608.00	
Bank interest account	46.00	
Sales Ledgers:		
Accounts receivable		6 002.00
Purchase Ledger:		
Accounts payable		2 616.00
	£44 573.00	£44 573.00

The stock at 31 December xx1x was valued at £5200.

You are required to:

a Prepare a Trading, Profit and Loss Account for the year ended 31 December xx1x, and a Statement of Financial Position at that date.

b State the percentages of Gross Profit and of Net Profit to Turnover.

c Show the Office Fixtures and General Equipment Account as it would appear in the Private Ledger.

10 In the form of a three-column Cash Book, after properly heading each column, enter all the money transactions below and balance the book.

Journalize the opening balances and remaining transactions. (**Note**: Purchases and Sales Books may be used, if preferred.) Post the entries to the Ledger. Extract a Trial Balance. Draw up a Profit and Loss Account and Statement of Financial Position.

On 1 May xx1x, D Robinson, nurseryman, reopened his books with the following balances in addition to his Capital Account: Cash, £40; Rent outstanding, £80; Bank overdraft, £470; M Merritt (Cr), £232; S Service (Dr), £327; Stock, £1565.

During the month his transactions were:

			£
May	3	Received cheque from S Service and paid into bank	300.00
	5	Sold to S Service:	
		Rose bushes	146.00
		Rose standards	139.00
		Misc plants	127.00
	7	S Service's cheque returned dishonoured	300.00
	10	S Service paid in cash (banked)	275.00
	14	Bought from M Merritt:	
		Fruit trees	356.00
		Shrubs	42.00
	18	Paid M Merritt by cheque to settle account to 1 May	230.00
	21	Returned to M Merritt damaged shrubs	4.00
	25	Cash sales	48.00
	26	Bought for cash sundry plants at auction	17.00
	27	Paid rent outstanding by cheque	80.00

29	Drew cheque for self	80.00
31	Wages and expenses for month:	
	Paid by cheque	120.00
	And in cash	52.00
	Bank charges	6.00
	Rent accrued	40.00
	Interest on capital at 6% pa	
	Stock on hand valued at	1701.00

11 The following is the Trial Balance extracted from the books of JB as at 31 December xx1x.

	Dr	Cr
	£	£
Private Ledger:		
Capital, 1 January xx1x		4 137.00
Drawings	1 000.00	
Inventory, 1 January xx1x	2 035.00	
Fixtures and fittings, 1 January xx1x	2 119.00	
Accounts payable		268.00
Accounts receivable	238.00	
Nominal Ledger:		
Purchases	5 911.00	
Sales		30 782.00
Discounts allowed	223.00	
Discounts received		104.00
Packing expenses	192.00	
Office expenses	74.00	
Salaries	7 826.00	
Repairs	58.00	
Lighting and heating	1 087.00	
Rates	1 146.00	
Rent	1 200.00	
Wages (employees)	11 644.00	

Sundry expenses	61.00	
Cash book		781.00
Petty cash book	27.00	
Accounts payable (Personal Ledger)		1 433.00
Accounts receivable (Personal Ledger)	2 664.00	
	£37 505.00	£37 505.00

The inventory at 31 December xx1x, was valued by JB in the sum of £3157.

Prepare a Trading, Profit and Loss Account, and Statement of Financial Position.

Adjustments in the final accounts

In this chapter you will learn:

- ▶ *About year end adjustments*
- ▶ *How adjustments are made to various accounts*
- ▶ *How adjustments are reflected in the Income Statement and Statement of Financial Position*

Objectives

Having been introduced to the Income Statement and the Statement of Financial Position as two Final Accounts produced by a business, you now need to ensure that these accounts contain all the correct information. This chapter introduces you to a number of so called 'adjustments' which need to be made to ensure that the Final Accounts accurately reflect the reality of the financial activities and position of the business.

Question You said in Chapter 11 that certain adjustments may be necessary in preparing the Final Accounts, and that the Trial Balance does not show what they are. Can we consider them now?

Answer As we have dealt with the simple form of Profit and Loss Account and Statement of Financial Position, in which no adjustments were called for, we may now look a little more closely at the problem of ascertaining *true Profit and Loss* as it arises in practice.

In the first place, our task is not merely to prepare the Final Accounts from the information given in the books of the business as they may stand. We must examine the Ledger Accounts, particularly the accounts in the Nominal Ledger, to see that they are *complete for the period under review*.

Question Is there any likelihood of their being incomplete?

Answer When we talk about the function of the Profit and Loss Account, for example, as the statement of the Profit or Loss over a definite period, it is essential that we include in it *all the expenses incurred as well as the whole of the gross income* of the business.

If any expenses *attributable to the period* were inadvertently omitted, the final figure of Profit would be untrue, and would be *overstating the position*. Similarly, Profit is *understated* if we neglect to bring in every kind of income that belongs to the business, however incidental to the main purpose of the business, which has been *earned* during the period and for which it may properly take credit.

Question Can you give me examples of such items, and explain why they are termed 'adjustments'?

Answer Examples of the most commonly occurring adjustments are those for wages, inventory, debts, rent, rates and insurance. We also need to consider depreciation adjustments on our fixed assets (we'll do this in the next chapter).

Wages

It is quite typical for businesses to pay wages on Fridays for the week ended on the preceding Wednesday. The wage sheets or cards for the week have to be checked and certified, the pay roll prepared, deductions made for National Insurance, and so on. Consequently, if the financial year ended on a Thursday, wages for a whole week and one day would be outstanding, no payment would have been made, and there would be no Credit entry in the Cash Book and no Debit entry in the Wages Account for the amounts involved when the books were closed.

In effect, the *expense* figure for wages would be less than the true amount, and the fact that the employees were *creditors* of the business would be ignored. The expense should be included in the Profit and Loss Account and the creditors in the Balance Sheet. Therefore we must make an adjustment raising the wage figure to its true level (an additional Debit), and at the same time record the liability for wages in the Balance Sheet (an additional Credit).

Inventory

The adjustment to purchases of goods for resale to reflect the opening and closing inventory has been explained earlier but these are, in effect, adjustments.

Debts: good, bad or doubtful

Another instance arises in connection with the Book Debts, or 'Accounts Receivable', as we have described them.

At the end of the financial year, a certain amount will be due from customers for goods sold to them. The value of these goods appears as 'Sales' in the Trading Account, as a result of our Double Entry process, and is the main source of our Profit. However, unless we are quite convinced that all our customers are willing and able to pay what they owe in full, a part of the Book Debts may eventually not be paid and will become **Bad Debts**. Any loss that is likely to arise in this way must be charged against the Profit earned in the same period it was recorded, if possible, otherwise the loss will become a burden on the Profits of a *subsequent* trading year. As such, when debts go bad we have to write them off against the personal debtor's account (Cr) (and the bad debt account as the other entry (Dr)).

However some debts from this period may go bad in a future period. To prevent this needing to reduce that period's Profit (and so this period's Profit is not overstated) we will usually reserve a certain amount of this period's Profit for when this occurs. Neglecting to reserve an estimated sum for Bad or Doubtful Debts has the effect of *overstating Profits* in this period, and *also overstating Assets* (as the accounts receivable appear in the Statement of Financial Position of the business at more than they will ultimately realize).

The adjustment required in this case is to *debit* a sum to the Profit and Loss Account as a **'Provision for doubtful debts'**, along with the debts actually written off as Bad during the period.

The amount of this provision should be calculated by analysing each debt by the date of sale. For a year ending 31 December any sales made in September but not yet paid would be considered unusual as credit terms won't usually be as low as three months for payment. Careful assessment should be undertaken therefore of all the September and earlier months' sales, looking at the terms of trade and any particular circumstances, would lead to an estimate of those considered doubtful. Many businesses would also make a general provision in respect of October, November and December sales – a general percentage provision reflecting the expectation that some of the outstanding debt will not be paid but we don't know which ones. (If we did we probably wouldn't have allowed them credit in the first place!)

The corresponding Credit balance can be shown on the Liabilities side of the Statement of Financial Position, or perhaps better shown as a deduction from the total Accounts receivable on the Assets side, thereby reducing them to their estimated collectible value.

Why do bad debts arise? Because the business has agreed to sell to a customer on a credit basis instead of requiring cash. Nobody *has* to grant credit, but it is often essential if you wish to sell your products and services. The decision should only be made after a review of the information provided by the customer when credit was requested. Usually this will include a bank reference and details of other suppliers who already give credit or you can use one of the trade or commercial organizations who provide detailed credit reports. The credit controller can then decide whether to grant credit, and if so, what the limit will be. (Similar to the procedure for a credit card from a bank for individuals.) After some experience using this basic (often low initial) limit the account will be reviewed and if there is a satisfactory record of payments the credit limit will be increased, and if poor the facility will be withdrawn.

We will use an example to illustrate how this works.

▶ Example 14.1

During xx11, the first year of business, a merchant wrote off Bad Debts amounting to £100, and at 31 December made a Provision for Doubtful Debts, amounting to £50.

During xx12, a payment of £30, was received in respect of one of the debts (£40) written off in xx11, further debts amounting to £60 were written off, and at 31 December xx12, the merchant considered it prudent to make a provision against existing debts of 60% for one owed of £40, and 30% for one owed of £30.

In addition, it was estimated that a final payment of £0.75 in the £ would be received in xx13 in respect of a debt on the books at £28.

You are required to produce, for the two years, the Bad Debts Account, Provision for Doubtful Debts Account and (as far as possible for these elements) the Profit and Loss Account.

In this example, we are instructed to open an account for the Provision for Doubtful Debts.

The recovery of £30 during xx12 serves to reduce the expense of £60 for debts written off during that year, and the balance is transferred at the year end to the Provision Account. The Provision required at 31 December xx12 is brought down as a Credit Balance on 1 January xx13, and may as such be termed a Liability Provision.

Alternatively, the Profit and Loss Account for xx12 could show a debit (charge) for Bad Debts of £30 and a credit of £10, being the difference between the opening provision of £50 and the required closing provision of £40. This would be a more accurate use of the two accounts.

Nominal Ledger
BAD DEBTS

Dr						Cr
xx11		£	xx11			£
Dec 31	Sundry customers' debts written off	100.00	Dec 31	Transfer to Profit and Loss A/c		100.00
xx12			xx12			
Dec 31	Sundry customers' debts written off	60.00	Jan 1	Cash, final payment of £0.75 in £ on debt of £40.00 written off in xx11		30.00
			Dec 31	Transfer to Provision For Doubtful Debts A/c		30.00
		£60.00				£60.00

Nominal Ledger
PROVISION FOR DOUBTFUL DEBTS

Dr					Cr		
xx11			£	xx11			£
Dec 31	Provision c/d, being provision at this date		50.00	Dec 31	Transfer to Profit and Loss A/c		50.00
xx12				xx12			
Dec 31	Transfer from Bad Debts A/c		30.00	Jan 1	Provision b/d		50.00
				Dec 31	Transfer to Profit and Loss A/c		20.00
31	Provision c/d, being provisions at this date:						
	X 60% of £40.00	£24.00					
	Y 30% of £30.00	9.00					
	Z 25% of £28.00	7.00					
			40.00				
			£70.00				£70.00
				xx13			
				Jan 1	Provision b/d		40.00

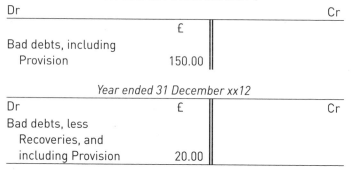

Profit and Loss Accounts (extract)

Year ended 31 December xx11

Dr	£	Cr
Bad debts, including Provision	150.00	

Year ended 31 December xx12

Dr	£	Cr
Bad debts, less Recoveries, and including Provision	20.00	

Rent and Rates

Sometimes expenses are incurred during the year which don't fully relate to that year – either as it is settling expenses partly related to a previous period, or because some of the payment relates to the next period. Where this occurs we need to make adjustments in what we transfer to the Profit and Loss Account to ensure only expenses related to this period are listed there.

We can best illustrate this adjustment with an example.

▶ **Example 14.2**

Merryweather & Co. pay a rent of £2400 per annum for their business premises. The estimated business rates are £3000 payable half yearly in advance on 31 March and 30 September.

The rent is payable in advance on the usual quarter days, and on 30 September xx12, the firm sublet a part of the premises to Tenant & Co at £800 per annum, the first half-yearly payment being due on 31 March xx13.

The Rates and Rent Accounts in Merryweather's books was as follows on 1 January xx12:

Rates

Dr				Cr
xx12		£		
Jan 31	Balance b/d, Rates prepaid	750.00		

Rent

		xx12		£
		Jan 31	Balance b/d, Rent due 25 December	600.00

You are required:

▶ to write up the account for the year, bringing down any necessary balances at 31 December xx12

▶ to state in which section of the Final Accounts for the year xx12 these balances would appear, giving reasons in brief.

Before we begin, let us take the information given, and consider it. The following points must be borne in mind:

▶ The financial year end of the business is 31 December xx12.

▶ In the year ended on that date we shall expect to find in the Profit and Loss Account:

▷ an expense for rent payable of £2400

▷ an expense for rates of £3000

▷ a provision for rent receivable from Tenant & Co. of £200 (3 months at £800 per annum).

▶ And in the Statement of Financial Position:

▷ an Asset or Debit Balance of £750 representing rates *paid in advance for the 3 months to 31 March xx*13.

▷ a similar Asset of £200, being rent accrued due at 31 December xx12.

> The opening balances represent half the rates paid on 30 September xx12 (one half of £1500) and the rent due (one quarter £2400).

The Rent and Rates Accounts in the Nominal Ledger will then appear as shown below assuming all payments are made on the due dates, and apportionments are made on a monthly basis.

Rates

Dr					Cr
Date		Rates	Date		Rates
xx12		£	xx12		£
Jan	1 Balance b/d, Rates prepaid	750.00	Dec 31	Provision for 3 months, Rates paid in advance c/d	750.00
Mar	31 Cash, Rates 6 months to 30 September xx12	1500.00	31	Transfer to Profit and Loss A/c: Rates	3000.00
Sept	30 Cash, Rates 6 months to 31 March xx13	1500.00			
		£3750.00			£3750.00
xx13					
Jan	1 Balance b/d, Rates prepaid	750.00			

Rent

Dr   Cr

Date			Rates	Date			Rates
xx12			£	xx12			£
Jan	2	Cash, Rent	600.00	Jan	1	Balance b/d, Rent due December 25	600.00
Mar	25	Cash, Rent	600.00	Dec	31	Provision for	
June	24	Cash, Rent	600.00			3 months' Rent	
Sept	29	Cash, Rent	600.00			accrued from	
Dec	25	Cash, Rent	600.00			Tenant & Co at this	
						date at £800.00 per	
						annum c/d	200.00
	31	Transfer to			31	Transfer to Profit	
		Profit and				and Loss A/c:	
		Loss A/c: Rent				Rent Payable	2400.00
		Receivable	200.00				
			£3200.00				£3200.00
xx13		Balance b/d					
Jan	1	Rent accrued					
		due	200.00				

Note: If there were many properties it would be useful to open separate Rent receivable and Rent payable accounts.

We notice that the *two provisions* carried down appear as the opening figures for the year xx13. Since they are Debit Balances they may rightly be described as Asset Provisions.

Let's use another illustration of another provision, this time in the reverse direction.

► **Example 14.3**

This illustrates the preparation of financial statements after the Trial Balance has been adjusted.

The Trial Balance of Bilton Potteries prepared after calculation of the gross profit is shown below.

Bilton Potteries

Trial Balance as at 31 January xx11

Details	Debit £	Credit £
Capital		7 000
Premises	5 000	
Bank	3 218	
Accounts receivable	434	
Inventory (31 January xx11)	1 000	
Accounts payable		870
Drawings	3 800	
Insurance	450	
Rent Receivable		225
Rates	500	
Wages	5 200	
Gross Profit for year ended 31 January xx11		11 507
	£19 602	£19 602

A detailed review by the accountant revealed that the following adjustments were outstanding:

► Rates amounting to £100 had been paid in advance.

► Rent receivable of £75 was still outstanding at 31 January xx11.

► The insurance total included the payment of £50 for private house contents insurance.

► Wages owing amounted to £300. An example of an accrual.

You are required to:

▶ Open up the appropriate ledger accounts and post the above adjustments. Balance off these ledger accounts.

▶ Prepare a Profit and Loss account for the year ended 31 January xx11 and a Statement of Financial Position as at that date, after the above adjustments have been posted.

Note: As the gross profit has already been calculated the Trial Balance includes this item and the Inventory at 31 January xx11.

There are four accounts to be amended. All follow the same principle but think about them carefully and attempt to produce them before comparing with the solution.

Rates

Dr			£				Cr	£
xx11				xx11				
Jan	31	Balance	500	Jan	31	In advance c/f		100
					31	P & L a/c		400
			_500_					_500_
Feb	1	In adv b/f	100					

Rent

Dr			£				Cr	£
xx11				xx11				
Jan	31	P & L a/c	300	Jan	31	Balance		225
					31	Due c/f		75
			_300_					_300_
Feb	1	Due b/f	75					

Note that these are both debit balances, i.e. assets, but one is a payment in advance made by Bilton and the other is rent due to Bilton.

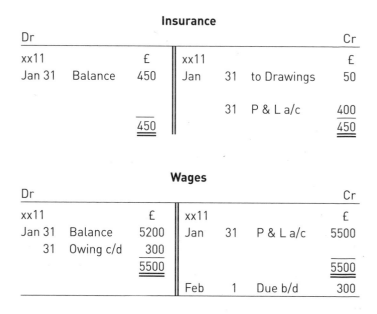

Insurance

Dr		£	Cr				£
xx11			xx11				
Jan 31	Balance	450	Jan	31	to Drawings		50
				31	P & L a/c		400
		450					450

Wages

Dr		£	Cr			£
xx11			xx11			
Jan 31	Balance	5200	Jan	31	P & L a/c	5500
31	Owing c/d	300				
		5500				5500
			Feb	1	Due b/d	300

You should be able to see that now different amounts will appear in the Profit and Loss account for each of these adjusted expenses. They will now just reflect the relevant amounts for this year and balances created will move some of the expenses and reserves in to the next period where they correctly relate to or will be collected in.

Bilton Potteries

Profit and Loss Account for the year ended 31 January xx11

		£	£
Gross profit brought forward			11 507
Rent receivable	(225 + 75)		300
			11 807
deduct Expenses			
Wages	(5 200 + 300)	5 500	
Rates	(500 ± 100)	400	
Insurance	(450 ± 50)	400	
			6 300
Net profit			£5 507

Balance sheet as 31 January xx11

		£	£	£
Fixed assets	Premises		1 000	5 000
Current assets	Inventory		100	
	Payment in advance			
	Accounts receivable	(434 + 75)	509	
	Bank		3 218	
			4 827	
deduct Current liabilities				
	Accounts payable	870		
	Wages due	300	1 170	
	Net current assets			3 657
	Total net assets			8 657
Representing			7 000	
Capital			5 507	
Profit for the year			12 507	
deduct drawings		(3 800 + 50)	3 850	
				£8 657

Consignment and Branch accounts

A Consignment account is used when a supplier has agreed to provide a customer with goods stored under the control of the customer but which remain the property of the supplier until the customer uses them. Under this circumstance the revenue and profit will not be recorded until the sale takes place, so the Sales Account should not be used. Until then it is usual to record the transfer of the inventory from the supplier to the customer in a separate account, 'Inventory on consignment'.

When the customer notifies the supplier that he has used items that were transferred to the Inventory or Consignment account at a cost of £1060 these will be converted to selling price. A sales invoice will be prepared for the customer's records in the usual way and a transfer (supported by a Journal entry) from 'Inventory on consignment' to Sales account will be made.

Similar accounting procedures may arise when there is a Branch for which some separate records are kept. The amount of authority given to the Branch manager will affect the precise form of these records and accounts. Usually these will include separate Branch accounts for inventory, expenses and perhaps debtors subject to local control.

We will illustrate how this works in practice with an example.

▶ **Example 14.4**

Smart Goods Ltd has a branch at Southness and for control purposes keeps the Books of Account at head office.

All goods are purchased by head office and invoiced to the branch at cost price plus 50%.

The branch transactions during the year ended 31 December xx11 were:

	£
Opening inventory at invoice price	12 000
Branch accounts receivable at 1 January xx11	16 600
Goods sent by head office at invoice price	147 000
Credit Sales during the year	85 600
Cash Sales during the year	56 600
Goods returned to head office at invoice price	6 300
Petty cash balance at 31 December xx11	30
Cash received from debtors and paid direct into head office Bank Account	83 900
Branch expenses paid direct by head office	14 500
Petty cash balance at 1 January xx11	20

On the first day of each week the head office sent £40 to the branch for petty cash payments.

The result of the physical stocktaking on 31 December xx11 agreed with the inventory account.

You are required to write up the following accounts for the year ended 31 December xx11 for the Southness branch:

▶ Inventory account

▶ Branch adjustment account

▶ Accounts receivable account

▶ Petty cash account

▶ Profit and Loss account

The books are kept by head office – the Branch may also keep its own memorandum (i.e. subsidiary – not part of the double entry system) records but we are not considering those.

In this example it is the 'Branch adjustment account' which reflects the unrealized profit movements following the transfer of inventory and its subsequent sale.

The given data includes the assets of the branch at the beginning of the year, inventory, accounts receivable, petty cash balance and the unrealized profit on the inventory. These four accounts can be opened remembering that the first three are debit balances and the last one, unrealized profit, a credit balance. Inventory (Dr) at selling price minus unrealized profit (Cr) equals Inventory (Dr) at cost price. The transactions for the year can be recorded in the accounts and the end of the year transfers to the Branch Profit and Loss Account provide a summary of the activities.

Prepare your own accounts before checking with the solution.

INVENTORY ACCOUNTS

Dr		Fo	£			Fo	£
xx11				xx11			
Jan 1	Opening inventory b/d		12 000	Dec 31	Goods returned		6 300
Dec 31	Goods from HO		147 000	31	Credit sales		85 600
				31	Cash sales		56 600
				31	Closing inventory c/d		10 500
			£159 000				£159 000
	Opening stock b/d		10 500				

Dr	SOUTHNESS BRANCH ADJUSTMENT ACCOUNT		Cr
xx11		£	
Dec 31	Unrealized profit on goods returned	2 100	
31	Gross profit realized during year	47 400	
31	Unrealized profit in closing inventory c/d	3 500	
		£53 000	

xx11		£
Jan 1	Unrealized profit on opening inventory b/d	4 000
Dec 31	Unrealized profit on goods transferred	49 000
		£53 000
	Unrealized profit b/d	3 500

Dr			SOUTHNESS BRANCH			Cr
			ACCOUNTS RECEIVABLE ACCOUNT			
xx11		Fo	£	xx11	Fo	£
Jan 1	Balances b/d		16 600	Dec 31 Cash		83 900
				received		
Dec 31	Credit sales		85 600	31 Balances		18 300
				c/d		
			£102 200			£102 200
	Balances b/d		18 300			

SOUTHNESS PETTY CASH ACCOUNT

xx11		£	xx11		£
Jan 1	Balances b/d	20	Dec 31 Sundry expenses		2 070
Dec 31	Cash from HO	2 080	31 Balances c/d		30
		£2 100			£2 100
	Balances b/d	30			

SOUTHNESS BRANCH ACCOUNTS RECEIVABLE ACCOUNT

Profit and Loss Account

year to 31 December xx11

	£		£
Expenses by HO	14 500	Gross profit	47 400
Sundry petty cash expenses	2 070		
Profit	30 830		
	£47 400		£47 400

Focus points

On completion of this chapter you should:

* be aware of the reason for year end adjustments to the double entry accounts
* be clear as to how adjustments to expenses (e.g. wages), inventory and income (e.g. accounts receivable) are made
* be aware of how the adjustments are reflected in the Profit and Loss Account and Statement of Financial Position
* be able to write up the appropriate records for consignment transactions and branch accounts.

Testing yourself

1 Explain briefly the object of a bad debts reserve. Upon what basis is it usually formed? How does it affect the Profit and Loss Account and the Statement of Financial Position? Illustrate your answer with a specimen account.

2 During the year ended 31 December xx1x, CP Kilham made the following bad debts: AB, £13.13; XY, £5.49; and RZ, £12.91.

Submit the entries Kilham should make when closing books as on 31 December xx1x.

3 X sets up in practice as a doctor on 1 January xx11. During xx11 the fees received were £33 545, and at the end of the year £237 was owing. During xx12 the fees received were £33 831, and at the end of the year £364 was owing. The expenses amounted to £11 265 in xx11 and £11 320 in xx12, there being no liabilities outstanding at the end of either year.

Ascertain the profit for each of these years.

4 On 1 October xx11, the Bad Debts Reserve Account of a business stood at £3768. During the ensuing twelve months bad debts amounting to £3389 were written off. On 30 June xx12, a payment of £80 was received on account of a debt which had been treated as irrecoverable two years previously. The debts outstanding at 30 September xx12 were examined, and the bookkeeper was instructed to make a reserve of £3400 to cover the anticipated loss.

Show the Ledger Account or Accounts as they appear after the closing of the books had been completed.

5 On 1 January xx11, H Jacks owed J Dixon £220. On 31 March Jacks purchased goods from Dixon valued at £246, of which he returned goods to the value of £16 on 3 April. On 6 April Jacks paid Dixon £120 on account. On 1 July Dixon received notice of the bankruptcy of Jacks, and on 5 October he received the first and final dividend of £0.35 in the £ from the Trustee in Bankruptcy. Show the account of H Jacks in the Ledger of J Dixon as it should appear after Dixon had balanced his books at 31 December xx11.

6 The Rates Account of G Baker is shown in the Ledger as follows:

RATES ACCOUNT

xx12

31 Dec   To Balance, in advance, b/f £360.

xx13

31 May   To Cash, half-year to 30 September
xx13, £734.50.

18 Nov   To Cash, half-year to 31 March xx14,
£734.50.

Balance the account by transfer to Profit and Loss Account at
31 December xx13, bringing forward the appropriate amount
in advance. (Remember that rates are due on 31 March and 30
September.)

7 At 31 December xx11, the Ledger of T Atkins contained the
following balances for accounts receivable:

	£
Arthur	436.08
Carol	215.50
Henry	314.09
Peggy	120.50

The estate of Arthur is being administered in Bankruptcy, and it
is feared, pending realization, that not more than £0.50 in the £
will be recoverable. Henry has died and his estate has no assets
whatever. For the sake of prudence 5% is to be reserved on the
debts of Carol and Peggy.

Show the four accounts, together with Bad Debts Account and
Reserve for Doubtful Debts Account. Journal need not be given.

8 In xx12 a trader, X, wrote off as a bad debt £319.77, the balance of an account due to him by Y.

In xx13 Y paid the debt in full. Show by means of Journal entries how the recovery of this debt would be dealt with in closing X's book for xx13, on the assumption that:

a the cash received was posted to the credit of Y's account.
b the cash was posted to a nominal account.

9 The payments made by X Ltd to its travellers on account of commission and salaries during xx11 amounted to £121 547.18 and during xx12 to £141 752.67. The amounts accrued and unpaid under this heading were as follows:

	£
31 December xx10	2036.96
31 December xx11	3441.18
31 December xx12	3122.89

Draw up a statement showing the amount to be charged against profits in xx11 and xx12 respectively, and show what would have been the effect of accidentally omitting to make the proper reserve at the end of xx11.

10 The Rent and Rates Account in the Ledger of Riley Bros showed that on 31 December xx11, the rent for the quarter to Christmas was outstanding, and that the rates for the half-year ending 31 March xx12, amounting to £876.38, had been paid. During the ensuing year the following payments relating to the rent and rates were made:

			£
Jan	4	Rent for Christmas quarter	590.00
Mar	29	Rent for Ladyday quarter	590.00
June	26	Rates for half-year ending 30 September xx12	974.73
July	7	Rent for Midsummer quarter	590.00
Sept	30	Rent for Michaelmas quarter	590.00
Dec	28	Rent for Christmas quarter	590.00

The rates for the half-year ending 31 March xx13, which amounted to £980.88, were paid on 6 January xx13.

You are required to show the Rent and Rates Account as it would appear after the books for the year ended 31 December xx12 had been closed. Make any calculations in months.

11 The financial year of Sanctions Ltd ended on 31 December xx11.

At that date, the following balances appeared, among others, in their Nominal Ledger:

Rates, £3225 (15 months to 31 March xx12).

Wages, £47 098 (to 27 December xx11).

Stationery, Advertising, etc., £864.

Bad and Doubtful Debts, written off, £126.

The wages for the week ending 3 January xx12 were £2562 (7-day week).

Stationery inventory for which an adjustment is required amounted to £117.

The Accounts receivable totalled £5660, and a reserve is to be made of 5% for doubtful debts and 2% for discounts.

Show the Ledger Accounts involved after giving effect to the above.

12 XY, who owed £200 to AB for goods supplied on 1 June xx11, became unable to pay his debts in full and offered a composition of £0.25 in the £ to his accounts payable and this was accepted. A cheque for the dividend was received by AB on 1 December xx11.

When XY called his creditors together, AB had on his premises a machine belonging to XY and claimed a right of lien in respect of it. This was admitted and the machine was valued at £80. AB's claim was consequently reduced by this amount.

AB decided that instead of selling the machine he would retain it as part of his plant. When making up his annual accounts on 31 December xx11, the balance of XY's account was written off as a bad debt.

You are required to show, by means of Journal entries and Ledger Accounts, how the transactions would be recorded in AB's books.

13 In the books of Hazel Holborn at 31 December xx12, the financial year end, the Ledger Account for 'Heat, Light, Power and Water' shows a Debit Balance of £1253. Investigation discloses the following points:

A deposit of £100 (returnable on cessation of supply) was paid on 1 April xx12, in respect of electric power.
The charge for electric power is made quarterly, and the last debit in the account is for the three months to 30 November xx12. The demand note for the three months to 28 February xx12, amounted to £135.
A half-year's water rate, amounting to £94, was debited to the account in October xx12, in respect of the period to 31 March xx13.

Make such adjustments in the Ledger Account as appear to you to be necessary and state how, if at all, they would be shown in Holborn's Statement of Financial Position at 31 December xx12.

14 The firm of J Clark & Son trades from both Head Office and a Branch depot. All purchases are made by Head Office and goods sent to the Branch are invoiced at cost. The Branch sells goods on credit and for cash.

The following information relates to the Branch for the financial year ended 31 December xx13:

	£
Accounts receivable at 1 January xx13	5 720
Inventory at 1 January xx13	9 000
Inventory at 31 December xx13	8 340
Goods sent from Head Office	40 480
Goods returned to Head Office at cost	420
Cash sales	20 100
Credit sales	36 000
Allowances to credit customers	210
Returns from credit customers	330
Discount allowed to credit customers	1 440
Bad debts	360
Cash received from credit customers	29 520
Rates	1 080
Wages and salaries	3 600
Selling expenses	780

In the Head Office ledger of J Clark & Son, you are required to prepare the following accounts for the year ended 31 December xx13:

- Goods sent to Branch.
- Branch Inventory.
- Branch Accounts receivable.
- Branch Profit and Loss.

Depreciation

In this chapter you will learn:

- ▶ *About depreciation of fixed assets*
- ▶ *About two methods of calculation*
- ▶ *How depreciation affects profit or loss and financial position*

Objective

In this chapter you will be introduced to the concept and practice of depreciation as a 'cost-spreading' activity performed by businesses who purchase and use Fixed Assets. This chapter introduces the two primary depreciation methods commonly used – the straight-line method and the diminishing (or reducing) balance method.

We have seen in the preceding chapter how important it is that everything affecting the determination of true profit is properly taken into account whenever an attempt is made to produce a Trading, Profit and Loss Account and a Statement of Financial Position. Any outstanding income, even though not actually received yet in cash, and any expense incurred but not yet paid must, if relating to the period under review, be provided for either as an *Asset or a Liability Provision.*

In doing so, we are taking steps to ensure *the genuineness of the profit figure* which the Profit and Loss Account discloses, but we should not forget that the Statement of Financial Position drawn up at the end of the period is also important. As the Statement of Financial Position is concerned with the proprietor's Capital, and the property or Assets by which it is represented, it is just as necessary to consider the correctness of the values put upon these Assets. Generally speaking, it is sufficient for the Assets as a whole to be shown at their 'going concern' values, i.e. at a figure which reflects their worth to the business as an established concern, producing a normal and reasonable profit on the total Capital invested. By way of contrast we can speak of break-up values of the property, representing its realizable value if sold in the market. Between these two valid, but very different values for our assets, there may be a wide gap. Therefore we need rules for what values we should use in our accounts.

Examples of Current Assets are:

▶ Inventory, and

▶ Accounts receivable

and we have seen that they are typical of the property *in which the business is dealing from day to day*. The Inventory held by the business should be capable of sale at the prevailing market price; Book Accounts receivable must also (usually) be capable of collection from customers at their full value.

We can, therefore, appreciate that for Current Assets, the test of their *realizable value* (i.e. what we can sell them for) is all-important, and their *book value* shown in the Books of Account should not be in excess of this value, or we will be reflecting values that are more than we could sell them for. As selling them is our primary objective for these assets, this is the basis we need to be guided by.

In the case of Non-Current Assets, however, being property *purchased for retention and not primarily for resale*, altogether different considerations apply. Examples of this class of assets are:

▶ plant and machinery

▶ motor vehicles for delivering goods to customers.

Although these assets may last for a number of years, we have to recognize that they will not last forever. Therefore, although they may be retained within the business, a limit must be set to their *effective working life*, or the period of time during which they can be economically operated. Beyond this period, no matter how carefully they have been repaired and overhauled, it will usually be found that charges for renewals and replacements of parts are increasing to the point that *these Assets must be replaced*.

The effective working life will naturally vary between one class of Fixed Asset and another; sometimes it may be more than 20 years, while with motor vehicles three to five years is often the maximum period during which useful service can be given to the business. For a computer, its life is unlikely to be more than three years.

As a result, we can think of this as a progressive shrinkage in value of these classes of property year on year. This we term **depreciation**. It is important that we take a note of it in our accounts as a *shrinkage of value caused by the use of the property for the purpose of profit-earning.*

The logical extension of this idea is that against the profits earned in each trading year we should be put as an expense for the depreciation estimated to have taken place during that trading year.

In other words, we could say that the loss in value of our non-current assets year by year is just as much a business expense as wages paid, or the charge for rent and rates or any other business expense we incur to generate our profits.

The real working expenses will therefore be understated in our accounts if the factor of depreciation is ignored year by year, and ultimately, when the machinery is worn out, or obsolete, the proprietor of the business may have to introduce fresh Capital to replace it.

This point of view brings us to the second reason for charging depreciation. Net Profit, as determined by the preparation of the Trading, Profit and Loss Account, is the yield upon the Capital invested, and may be wholly withdrawn by the proprietor in the form of cash. If depreciation is charged as a business expense, this Profit figure will be accordingly reduced, and also therefore so will the amount of *cash withdrawable from the business.* Put in yet another way, cash or its equivalent, representing the charge for depreciation, will be retained within the business, and may, over a period of time, accumulate to provide the amount required for eventual replacement. Although making a charge for depreciation reduces profit, the charge by itself does not provide extra cash for the business. The cash that is not distributed becomes part of the total resources of the business and may be used for any purpose. As such, if it is used for some other purpose it will not necessarily be available to buy a replacement.

For these reasons, it is the general practice to depreciate or *write down* the Non-Current Assets, as this is called, usually on a percentage per year basis. This calculation is usually performed annually when the Final Accounts are to be prepared and is therefore one of our year end adjustments in reality (as per discussion in Chapter 14).

The result is that we have to create a double entry record for these costs. This we will do by:

▶ a Debit to Profit and Loss Account, and

▶ a Credit to the particular Asset Depreciation Account.

The two methods most generally employed to compute how much we should depreciate assets by each year are:

▶ the Straight Line, or Fixed Instalment method

▶ the Diminishing Balance, or Reducing Instalment method.

The next sections review each of these methods in turn in more detail.

Straight-line (or fixed instalment) method

The straight-line method of depreciation computation relies on writing off yearly a part of the original or purchase cost. When the Asset is bought its effective working life is estimated as being a certain number of years, and the difference between cost and any estimated value expected to be left at the end of this life (called **residual value**) is recovered at the same rate per month or year over this period.

We can use an example to illustrate how this works in practice.

▶ **Example 15.1**

Sanders and Son have a delivery van which cost £ 13 185 on 1 January xx11. Depreciation is to be provided using the straight-line method over a period of three years, at the end of which it is expected that it will be bought back by the supplier for £2400. Show the Ledger Account of the Asset and the Asset Depreciation Account in the firm's books for the years xx11, xx12 and xx13.

Calculation of depreciation

		£	
Original cost		13 185	
Resale value		2 400	
Loss in value	=	10 785	
Over 3 years, i.e.		£3 595	*per annum*

At 31 December xx11 the van would appear in the Statement of Financial position as below, being the balances on the two accounts:

	Assets	
	£	£
Delivery van at cost	13 185.00	
Less depreciation	3 595.00	
		£9 590.00

i.e. its net book value would then be £9590 only, the cost minus the depreciation.

At 31 December xx11 the depreciation balance relates to the charge for the year. At 31 December xx12 it will be £7190 and is the total (or **aggregate**) for the two years. At 31 December xx13, the van will be sold so will not appear in the Statement of Financial position for that date. There will be a charge for Depreciation in the Profit and Loss Account for the year ended on that date, 31 December xx13.

Depreciation is usually charged on assets in use at the beginning of a year if they are sold during the year. Sometimes, particularly for high cost items, straight-line depreciation may be charged in relation to months instead of on a yearly basis.

Private Ledger
DELIVERY VAN

| Dr | | | | | | | Cr |
Date	Details	Fo	Amount	Date	Details	Fo	Amount
xx11			£	xx11			£
Jan 1	Cash, Purchase cost		13 185.00	Dec 31	Balance	c/d	13 185.00
			£13 185.00				£13 185.00
xx12				xx12			
Jan 1	Balance	b/d	£13 185.00	Dec 31	Balance	c/d	£13 185.00
xx13				xx13			
Jan 1	Balance	b/d	£13 185.00	Dec 31	Transfer to disposal of delivery van A/c		13 185.00
			£13 185.00				£13 185.00

PROVISION FOR DEPRECIATION OF DELIVERY VAN

Dr				Cr			
Date	Details	Fo	Amount	Date	Details	Fo	Amount
xx11			£	xx11			£
Dec 31	Balance	c/d	3 595.00	Dec 31	Transfer to Profit & Loss A/c		3 595.00
xx12				xx12			
Dec 31	Balance	c/d	7 190.00	Jan 1	Balance	b/d	3 595.00
				Dec 31	Transfer to Profit & Loss A/c		3 595.00
			£7 190.00				£7 190.00
xx13				xx13			
Dec 31	Transfer to disposal of delivery van A/c		10 785.00	Jan 1	Balance	b/d	7 190.00
				Dec 31	Transfer to Profit & Loss A/c		3 595.00
			£10 785.00				£10 785.00

DELIVERY VAN DISPOSAL ACCOUNT

Dr				Cr			
Date	Details	Fo	Amount	Date	Details	Fo	Amount
xx13			£	xx13			£
Dec 31	Transfer cost	JI	13 185.00	Dec31	Transfer Accumulated depreciation	JI	10 785.00
				31	Sale	CBI	2 400.00
			£13 185.00				£13 185.00

When the van has been sold at 31 December xx13 journal entries will transfer the cost of the van and the balance on the van depreciation accounts to a 'Van Disposal Account'. The Debits and Credits are equal and this means that all the loss in value over the three years has been charged to the Profit and Loss Account already (as charges for depreciation over the van's life).

If the then accumulated depreciation plus sales proceeds did not equal cost then the difference would be transferred to the Profit and Loss Account. In practice it is not uncommon to have a difference. As for predicting residual value in advance: this is of course difficult to do. A large difference might suggest that the depreciation rate had not been estimated correctly but may occur in practice, if for example the machine becomes irreparable sooner than expected.

If the accumulated depreciation plus sales proceeds are less than the cost then we have to add the extra depreciation too to the Profit and Loss Account so we maintain balance in our accounts., i.e. Dr Profit and Loss Account, Cr Disposal Account. This would imply not enough depreciation had previously been charged than, with hindsight, should have been.

The same can occur of course if we overcharge depreciation (i.e. keep the machine longer than we expected). If this occurs we simply do the reverse entries to add back 'profit' to the Profit and Loss Account, i.e. Cr Profit and Loss Account and Dr Disposal Account.

Diminishing (or reducing) balance method

With this method for computing depreciation, *a fixed percentage is written off the book value* of the Asset as it appears in the books *at the commencement of each year*. This method is sometimes used by smaller firms, usually for assets with a small value, but is in practice harder to use as firms must keep a detailed register for each asset and for each significant item of plant and machinery to calculate the correct total depreciation each year. This is unnecessary if using the straight-line method, as the total value of all assets can just be used each year given a fixed percentage is applied to all assets with this method.

We will illustrate how this works in practice with an example.

▶ **Example 15.2**

At 1 January xx12, the balance on the Plant and Tools Account was £4730. During the year a lathe was purchased costing £575, and on 31 March xx13, three drilling machines, which cost £900 when purchased at the start year three years ago, were sold for £520.

Show the Asset Account, calculating depreciation at 10% per annum on the diminishing balance method.

Private Ledger

PLANT AND TOOLS

Dr							Cr
Date	Details	Fo	Amount	Date	Details	Fo	Amount
xx12			£	xx12			£
Jan 1	Balance	b/d	4730.00	Dec 31	Profit & Loss A/c		
June 30	Cash Lathe		575.00		Depreciation 10% of £4730.00		473.00
				31	Balance	c/d	4832.00
			£5305.00				£5305.00
xx13				xx13			
Jan 1	Balance	b/d	4832.00	Dec 31	Cash		
					3 Drilling Machines sold		520.00
				31	Profit & Loss A/c Loss on sale		136.10
				31	Profit & Loss Depreciation 10% on £4832.00		483.20
				31	Balance	c/d	3692.70
			£4832.00				£4832.00
xx14							
Jan 1	Balance	b/d	£3692.70				

N.B.	Cost three years ago	900.00
	1 year 10%	90.00
		810.00
	2nd year 10%	81.00
		729.00
	3rd year 10%	72.90
		656.10
	Selling price	520.00
	Loss:	£136.10

At 31 December xx12, the following would appear in the Balance Sheet:

	Assets	
Plant	£	£
At 1.1.xx12	4730.00	
Add Additions at Cost	575.00	
	5305.00	
Less Depreciation at		
10% per annum	473.00	
		£4832.00

Although the method used in this example correctly produces the net book value (NBV) it does not show the aggregate cost and depreciation provided which 'best practice' would consider desirable. This is why separate asset and depreciation accounts, as in example 15.1, are preferable. Review both examples to ensure you can see how the different methods operate.

The reducing balance method is open to the criticism that Non-current Assets depreciated this way tend to be dealt with in groups, and that with ordinary rates of depreciation its slowness in writing down the values is not sufficiently recognized. If the life of the asset is short the percentage required may be prohibitively high; e.g. to depreciate a tool having a life of three years only would require a 90% rate.

The General Journal should be used to avoid making a Prime Entry in the particular Ledger Account as usual. For example:

▶ **Example 15.3**

xx12			Dr	Cr
Dec 31			£	£
	Profit and Loss A/c	Dr	473.00	
	Plant and Tools Depreciation A/c			473.00
	Being depreciation at 10% p.a. now written off.			

As the example shows, an account for Depreciation as a business expense may be opened in the Nominal or Private Ledger, *but the Debit Balance on it must ultimately be transferred to Profit and Loss Account.*

Comparison of the two methods

A comparison of the two methods using the data in 15.1 is shown below.

The reducing (or diminishing) balance would require 43½% (approximately) to be written off each year.

		Reducing-balance depreciation	Straight-line depreciation
		£	£
Cost		13 185	13 185
Yr11	Depreciation	5 735	3 595
	Net book value	7 450	9 590
Yr12	Depreciation	3 241	3 595
	Net book value	4 209	5 995
Yr13	Depreciation	1 831	3 595
	Net book value	2 378	2 400

This is less than the amount received for the van at 31 December xx13 so there would be a small surplus on the sale of the motor van.

The depreciation charged using the straight-line method is shown above for comparison. You can see that the straight-line method charges much less in xx11 but much more in xx13.

Focus points

On completion of this chapter you should:

* be aware of the need for depreciation of fixed assets
* be capable of calculating depreciation charges for the final accounts using the two methods shown – straight-line line method and reducing balance method
* be able to draw up the double entry records for depreciation
* be clear as to how these accounts affect the calculation of Profit or Loss of a business and its Statement of Financial Position.

Testing Yourself

1 How is the shrinkage in the value of fixed assets provided for in accounts kept on the double entry principle?

2 Explain why it is generally necessary when preparing the accounts of a business to make provision for depreciation of the fixed assets.

   If you know of any exceptions to this general rule, mention them and give your reasons.

3 On 1 January xx11, a business purchased a delivery van for £8800. Show how the account would appear in the books of the business for the four following years assuming that depreciation is written off (a) by the fixed instalment method, and (b) by the diminishing balance method, the rate of depreciation being 20% in each case.

   State, giving your reasons briefly, which method of depreciation you consider is more appropriate for an asset of this sort.

4 On 1 January xx12, Dix Ltd purchased machinery costing £1240. For the years xx12, xx13 and xx14 depreciation was written off at the rate of 5% on the diminishing balance. During xx15, it became apparent that the machinery would not be of service after 31 December xx16, and for these latter two years the fixed instalment method was substituted to write off the remaining balance. In December xx16, the machinery realized £15 on sale. You are required to write up the Machinery Account (including depreciation) from the commencement, determining depreciation to the nearest £.

5 X Ltd purchased a seven-year lease of certain shop premises for £8000. A further sum of £2000 was expended in various alterations, and it was estimated that at the end of the lease the cost of restoring the premises to their original condition (for which the company was liable) would be about £500.

   Show the Ledger Account for the first two years, providing for depreciation.

6 From the following particulars, write up the Machinery Account for the year ended 30 November xx12.

   The balance from the previous year was £26 882.

On 31 May xx12, new machinery was purchased for £1164, and wages amounting to £124 were paid for its instalment. The old machinery replaced by the above was sold for £144, which was its written-down value on 30 November xx11.

Depreciation at the rate of 12½% per annum is to be written off (for this question half a year is significant – only half a year of depreciation should be included for the items purchased and sold).

7 The Statement of Financial Position of PQ & Co Ltd, drawn up as on 31 March xx13, showed plant and machinery valued, after writing off depreciation, at £25 500.

Depreciation had been written off regularly, from the dates of purchase of the various items, at the rate of 10% per annum on the diminishing value.

On 1 June xx13, a vehicle, which had been bought on 1 November xxx8, for £5750, was sold for £1250 and replaced by a new one costing £7700.

Show the Plant and Machinery Account as it would appear in the Company's books for the year ended 31 March xx14, after writing off the appropriate depreciation for the year. (For this question work in months.)

8 CD purchased factory premises (subject to a lease of 10 years from 30 June xx10) from the Liquidator of H Ltd on 30 June xx14, the purchase price being £30 000.

To enable him to complete the purchase, he borrowed £16 500 from Happy Bank Ltd, the loan being repayable in three years by equal annual instalments of principal, reckoning interest at 10% per annum. Provide depreciation on the fixed instalment basis, and show the Property Account and the Loan Account in CD's books for the three years to 30 June xx17.

9 On 1 January xx11, a manufacturer acquired a machine at a cost of £1200.

During xx11 repairs to the machine cost £50 and a new attachment, which cost £250, was added to it.

The repairs during the year xx12 amounted to £180.

It was decided to depreciate the machine at the rate of 10% per annum on the reducing balance method.

From the foregoing particulars you are required to write up the Machinery Account for the two years ended 31 December xx12.

10 The following is the Trial Balance extracted from the books of J Falconer at 31 December xx13.

	Dr	Cr
	£	£
Salaries	12 414.00	
Discounts received		132.00
Repairs and renewals	318.00	
Sales		68 505.00
Carriage outwards	163.00	
Accounts payable, including VAT		674.00
Wages	26 116.00	
Sundry expenses	86.00	
Accounts receivable	3 445.00	
Commission	196.00	
Capital, 1 January xx13		7 200.00
Inventory, 1 January xx13	1 572.00	
Discounts allowed	578.00	
Returns outwards		295.00
Plant and machinery, 1 January xx13	7 460.00	
Cash in hand	2.00	
Purchases	7 336.00	
Rates	3 575.00	
Warehouse expenses	4 537.00	
Office fixtures, etc., 1 January xx13	4 200.00	
Cash at bank	1 200.00	
Rent of premises	2 788.00	
Drawings	1 000.00	
Bad debts reserve, 1 January xx13		200.00
	£77 006.00	£77 006.00

You are required to prepare:

a Trading, Profit and Loss Account for the year to 31 December xx13.

b Statement of Financial Position at 31 December xx13 showing per cent net Profit to Capital at 1 January xx13.

Note: The following adjustments are necessary:

a the stock on hand at 31 December xx13 was valued at £1769

b three months' rates are prepaid in the sum of £715

c the rent of premises is £3717 per annum, payable quarterly, and has been paid to 29 September xx13

d depreciation is to be charged at 5% on plant and machinery, and 10% on office fixtures, etc.

11 Give the Journal entries necessary to record the following transactions:

Dec 2   Bought fixtures and fittings value £345 on credit from S Maxton and Sons.

     15   A cheque value £76.25 received from Perkins Ltd was wrongly posted to Brampton Bros' Account.

     19   Exchanged one motor car value £1220 for three typewriters value £200 each and the balance in cash.

     31   Plant and machinery is to be depreciated by £2173.

     31   O Carfax, a debtor for £55, having become insolvent, pays £0.20 in the £ settlement of the amount owing.

12 A firm acquired a 25 years' lease of its business premises for £18 000 at the beginning of the year. The firm's bankers advanced £12 000 towards the purchase price on the security of the lease.

Repayment of the bank loan is made by monthly instalments, in advance, of £250 which the bank debit to the firm's current account together with interest at the rate of 10% per annum on the balance at the beginning of the year.

You are required to make the entries in the firm's books at the end of the first year to record the above arrangements, including depreciation of the lease according to the method you consider most suitable in the circumstances.

13 The following 'statement of affairs' has been drawn up to give the financial position, as on 31 March xx11, and 31 March xx12, respectively, of A Brown who keeps her books on a single entry basis:

Statement of Financial Position, 31 March xx11

	£		£
Capital	6192.00	Fixtures	250.00
Accounts payable	742.00	Inventory	2305.00
		Accounts receivable	4176.00
		Cash	203.00
	£6934.00		£6934.00

Statement of Affairs, 31 March xx12

	£		£
Capital	5933.00	Fixtures	230.00
Accounts payable	817.00	Inventory	2562.00
		Accounts receivable	3777.00
		Cash	181.00
	£6750.00		£6750.00

Brown has transferred £100 a month regularly from her business banking account to her private banking account by way of drawings, and she has taken £25 worth of stock for her private use. The alteration in the value of the fixtures represents an amount written off by way of depreciation.

Calculate Brown's trading profit for the year.

14 The only books kept by Green are Personal Ledgers. At 1 January his position is as follows:

	£		£
Capital	17.00	Accounts payable	635.00
Accounts receivable	3109.00	Capital	3023.00
Inventory	102.00		
Equipment at cost	430.00		
	£3658.00		£3658.00

At 31 December following, he informs you that the following are the figures concerning his Assets and Liabilities:

	£
Cash	15.00
Bank (overdraft)	230.00
Inventory	98.00
Accounts receivable	3036.00
Accounts payable	502.00

He has had his equipment valued, and thinks that it is now only worth £350. He has taken notes as to his drawings, and informs you that he has spent £1332 for household purposes, etc., £140 for a life assurance premium and £110 for fire insurance for business assets. In addition, he has taken home goods, of which the cost price was £90 and the sale price £120.

Prepare a Statement showing Green's profit for the year, and his general position at 31 December.

15   Statement of Financial Position

	£		£
Accounts payable	721.00	Freehold premises	21 560.00
Capital	33 150.00	Machinery and plant	7 420.00
		Inventory	2 876.00
		Accounts receivable	1 982.00
		Cash	33.00
	£33 871.00		£33 871.00

The above is a copy of Samuel Wood's Statement of Financial Position as on 31 December xx11. The only books kept are a Cash Book and a Ledger. The following is a summary of his receipts and payments for the year ended 31 December xx12.

	Receipts		Payments
	£		£
Cash on account		Accounts payable for	
of credit sales	4 276.00	goods purchased	3 954.00
Cash sales	12 863.00	Wages	10 743.00
Capital paid in	4 200.00	General expenses	627.00
		Additions to machinery	4 160.00
		Drawings	536.00
	£21 339.00		£20 020.00

On 31 December xx12, the amount due to Creditors was £816, and the Accounts receivable and Inventory amounted to £2918 and £1854 respectively. You are required to prepare Trading, Profit and Loss Accounts for the year ended 31 December xx12, and a Statement of Financial Position as on that date, after making adjustments in respect of the following:

a Depreciation of 10% is to be written off the Machinery and Plant, including additions during the year.

b £150 is to be provided as a Reserve for Doubtful Debts.

c The sum of £38 for goods supplied to the proprietor was included in the Accounts receivable balance at 31 December xx12.

Clubs, societies and charities bookkeeping

In this chapter you will learn:

▶ *About simpler forms for 'not for profit' organizations*

▶ *About receipts and payments accounts*

▶ *About income and expenditure accounts and Statements of Financial Position*

Basic recording

In small 'not-for-profit' organizations like charities or sports clubs the usual basic objective for accounting records will be to record the receipt and payment of cash and cheques – i.e. the role of the Cash and Bank Books. Without the use of a Purchases or Sales journal the Cash and Bank Books provide most of the required information by the use of analysis columns – just like those we have already used for the analysis of purchases and sales journals, and illustrated for the Petty Cash Book (Chapters 3 and 7).

A similar analysis, totalled for the year, provides the total receipts and payments. These can then be used to produce a **Receipts and Payments Account** or an Income and **Expenditure Account**.

Receipts and Payments Account

If the organization is so small that it does not bother with the adjustments for accounts receivable, accounts payable, accrued expenses or prepayments then the revenue statement is called a Receipts and Payments Account. Without these adjustments, this is simply a summary of the cash and bank book. In the horizontal layout it will show, as the cash book does, the income on the debit (left-hand) side. A Statement of Financial Position will not be likely to be required.

Like the cash book, the first entry will be the balance of cash in hand and at the bank, followed by all the receipts suitably classified and the total will represent the whole of the resources available to the organization. Similarly with the payments. All the payments will be shown as expenditure, whether they are revenue items or capital items. The balance – the difference between the opening balance plus receipts minus the payments – equals the closing balance of cash in hand and at the bank.

There is strictly no need for a Statement of Financial Position with this form of basic accounting but it may be appropriate to show in a brief note the value of assets used and any liabilities.

We can illustrate this with the following example.

▶ **Example 16.1**

The Hixley Arts Club started meeting on 1 April xx12. The analysis and summary of the Cash and Bank receipts and Expenditure Book for the year to 31 March xx13 produced the following amounts:

	£
Members' subscriptions	475
Sales of refreshments	275
Annual outing ticket sales	200
Sundry expenses	160
Rent	230
Purchase of refreshments	235
Annual outing expenses	50
Purchase of equipment	75

Prepare a Receipts and Payments Account for the financial year ended 31 March xx13.

Using the vertical layout:

THE HIXLEY ARTS CLUB
Receipts and Payments Account
year ended 31 March xx13

	£	£
Balance at beginning of the year		0
Receipts: Members' subscriptions	475	
Sales of refreshments	275	
Ticket sales for annual outing	200	
Total receipts	950	
Payments: Rent	230	
Sundry expenses	160	
Purchase of refreshments	235	
Annual outing expenses	50	
Purchase of equipment	75	
Total payments	750	
Surplus of receipts over payments		200
Balance at end of year (represented by cash in hand and at bank)		£200

Although this layout provides totals for receipts and expenditure, which may be useful, most readers would prefer to see related items brought together, to show the net result of that activity:

		£	£
Members' subscriptions			475
Refreshments:	Sales	275	
	Purchases	235	
	Surplus		40
Annual outing:	Receipts	200	
	Expenses	50	
	Surplus		150
			665
Rent		230	
Sundry expenses		160	
Purchases of equipment		75	
			465
Surplus for the year			200
Add: Balance at beginning of year			0
Balance at end of year			£200

There is no particular need for the distinction between revenue and capital items as all expenditure has been included in this statement so there is nothing to record in a balance sheet. The only asset is the amount of cash in hand and at the bank which is shown at the end of the statement. Equipment costing £75 has been purchased and in practice a note would be made so that it was not forgotten or lost.

Remember that both these formats reflect only the Receipts and Payments. No adjustments have been made to reflect Accounts receivable, Accounts payable, unpaid bills, etc. If these items are significant to the entity you are doing accounting for then to show a fairer picture they should be reflected in a slightly more complicated statement – the Income and Expenditure Account.

Income and Expenditure Account

Like the Receipts and Payments Account this is based on an analysis and summary of the cash receipts and payments. Adjustments are made for accounts receivable, accounts payable and other items, in particular subscriptions and capital items, to ensure that everything relating to the accounting period is included. A Statement of Financial Position will also be prepared.

We can illustrate this using an example.

▶ **Example 16.2**

The Statement of Financial Position of the Spartan Fitness Society at 31 December xx14 showed:

		£
Equipment at valuation		23 100
Subscriptions due for xx14		265
Prepaid rent		126
Bank		2 976
	£	26 467
Less: Subscriptions in advance for xx15	195	
Accrued expenses	55	
		250
Total net assets		26 217
Club Fund		£26 217

During xx15:

	£
► Subscriptions received were:	
▷ for xx14	265
▷ for xx15	20 975
▷ for xx16	94
► Rent paid	4 840
► Staff salaries paid	13 280
► Equipment purchased	2 940
► Other expenses paid	1 086
At the end of xx15:	
► Club equipment is valued at	24 190
► Subscriptions are owing for xx15	180
► Other expenses due	40
► Rent prepaid	135

You are required to:

► Prepare an Income and Expenditure Account for the Spartan Fitness Society for the year ended 31 December xx15.

Note: In a horizontal Income and Expenditure Account, income appears on the Credit (right-hand) side and expenditure on the Debit (left-hand) side.

► Present the Statement of Financial Position of the Society as at 31 December xx15.

There are several new items in this example.

Firstly the subscriptions. Many societies treat this on a cash basis, but not Spartan. No new principles are used but you should think carefully about the entries which should appear in the account.

Subscriptions

			£				£
xx15				**xx15**			
Jan 1	Due for xx14	b/f	265	Jan 1	In advance for xx15	b/f	195
Dec 31	In advance for xx16	c/f	94	Dec 31	Subs received during year	c/f	21 334
31	I & E a/c		21 350	31	Due for xx15	c/f	180
			21 709				21 709
xx16				**xx16**			
Jan 1	Due for xx15	b/f	180	Jan 1	In advance for xx16	b/f	94

Secondly there is the equipment at valuation. At the beginning of the year this was £23 100 and equipment purchased during the year amounted to £2940. Adding these together gives a total of £26 040 but the year end valuation was £24 190, a difference of £1850. At this stage it can be recognized as a loss of value, i.e. an expense for the year, usually called depreciation, as was discussed in Chapter 15.

Finally, before the financial statements are produced, the bank balance should be calculated.

	£	£
Opening balance, from the old balance sheet		2 976
add receipts during the year: subscriptions		21 334
		24 310
deduct payments, Rent	4 840	
Staff salaries	13 280	
Equipment	2 940	
Other expenses	1 086	
		22 146
Balance at 31 December xx15		£2 164

Note: this reconciliation should be made at regular intervals, say monthly.

Spartan Fitness Society
Income and expenditure account for the year ended
31 December xx15

Expenditure		Income	
	£		£
Staff salaries	13 280	Subscriptions for xx15	21 350
Loss in value of equipment	1 850		
Rent paid (126 + 4840 − 135)	4 831		
Other expenses (1086 − 55 + 40)	1 071		
Surplus for the year	318		
	21 350		21 350

Statement of Financial Position at 31 December xx15

		£	£	£	£ (xx14)
Non-current assets	Equipment at valuation			24 190	23 100
Current assets	Subscriptions owing		180		
	Rent in advance		135		
	Bank balance		2 164		
Total current assets			2 479		
deduct current liabilities	Subscriptions in advance	94			
	Other expenses due	40			
Total current liabilities			134		
Net current assets				2 345	3 117
Total net assets				26 535	26 217
Representing:					
Society fund at the beginning of the year			26 217		
Surplus arising during the year			318		
Total Society fund at end of the year				£26 535	£26 217

308

The question suggested a horizontal format for the revenue statement but many societies use the vertical, and the vertical will be used for the balance sheet.

Note: In the above example note that figures for both xx15 and xx14 are given. When producing published final accounts as a charity or in fact any type of business, it is normally required that you show the previous year's figures alongside the current year's figures, so the reader has a comparison to use to help them understand the accounts for this year.

Note: Publications by the Charity Commission which provide useful additional information on this topic are CC15b Charity reporting and accounting – the essentials, CC16 *Receipts and payments accounts pack* and CC17 *and CC39 Accruals accounting* (https://www.gov.uk/running-charity/money-accounts).

Focus points

You should now be able to

✷ prepare a Receipts and Payments Account
✷ prepare an Income and Expenditure Account and the related Balance Sheet.

1 The Broadway Needlecraft Society was formed on 1 September xx12. The Treasurer has recorded all receipts and payments in the Cash and Bank Book. At the end of the year, 31 August xx13, the summary of receipts and payments showed:

	£
Members' subscriptions	1425
Sundry expenses	480
Rent	390
Rates	300
Annual dance expenses	150
Sales of dance tickets	600
Equipment	225
Purchase of refreshments	705
Sales of refreshments	825

Additional information from the records showed that there was an unpaid bill for printing for the dance for £25, which is regarded as a 'sundry'. Note also that the amount paid for rates included £30 in respect of the next year.

You are required to:

a prepare a Receipts and Payments Account for the financial year
b prepare an Income and Expenditure Account for the financial year
c calculate the accumulated fund on 31 August xx13
d explain why the sundry expenses and rates amounts in the Income and Expenditure Account differ from the amounts shown in the Receipts and Payments Account.

2 The Borough Social Club presents you with the following Receipts and Payments Account for the year ended 31 July xx12.

You are required to compile an Income and Expenditure Account for that year. The profit or loss on each activity should be clearly shown. A Statement of Financial Position at 31 August xx12 should also be prepared.

The following information is to be taken into consideration:

Stocks held at the beginning of the year: Refreshments £60, Stationery £10. Both stocks were nil at the end of the year. Dance prizes to the value of £100 had not been awarded and would be used in the following year.

Receipts and Payments Account for the year ended 31 August xx12

Receipts	£	Payments	£
Balance at		Draw prizes	250
beginning	1000	Printing of draw	
Subscriptions	3500	tickets	50
Sales of draw tickets	1000	Hire of dance band	250
Sales of dance tickets	2500	Prizes for dances	500
Sales of flowers		Flower show	
after flower show	50	prizes	150
Flower show		Purchase of	
entry fees	50	refreshments	700
Sales of		Purchase of new	
refreshments	1750	tables and chairs	1500
		Purchase of	
		crockery	100
		Printing of dance	
		tickets	60
		Cleaning	1855
		Heating and lighting	700
		Rates	345
		Postage and	
		stationery	100
		Balance at	
		end of year	3290
	£9850		£9850

3 The Bumpy Pitch Cricket and Social Club produced the following Trial Balance on 31 December xx12.

	Dr £	Cr £
Capital at 1 January xx12		21 360
Clubhouse	20 000	
Club room equipment	4 200	
Sports equipment	2 700	
Sales of refreshments		2430
Purchase of refreshments	1 850	
Interest-free loan from a member		5 000
Subscriptions received for xx12		3 700
Subscription outstanding from xx11	50	
Receipts from club room games		1 820
Maintenance of games and sports equipment	975	
Postages	305	
Sundry expenses	685	
Printing and stationery	715	
Wages (50% refreshments, 50% cleaning)	2 080	
Cash at bank	620	
Cash in hand	130	
	£34 310	£34 310

You are required to prepare:

a an account to show the profit or loss on sales of refreshments
b the Income and Expenditure Account for the year ended 31 December xx12 and a Statement of Financial Position at that date.

The following information is to be taken into account:

a Sports equipment is to be depreciated at 20% per annum and club room equipment at 10% per annum.

b Subscriptions due for xx12 and not yet paid £150. Assume that all unpaid subscriptions will be paid eventually.

c There is an unrecorded account for refreshments amounting to £120.

d The stock of refreshments on hand at 31 December xx12 was £160.

4 The following particulars relate to the Riverside Social Club for the year ended 31 December xx12. From them prepare the club's Income and Expenditure Account and Statement of Financial Position for presentation to the members.

	£
Capital account (1 January xx12)	3 370
Book value of Games and Drama Equipment (1 January xx12)	1 050
Book value of Furniture and Fittings (1 January xx12)	970
Cash at bank (31 December xx12)	1 180
Petty cash in hand	50
Payments during the year	
Rent of premises	2 500
Rates	580
Printing and stationery	170
Postages	100
Sundry expenses	60
Purchase of new games equipment	280
Expenses of dramatic performances	290
Repairs and cleaning	330
Lighting and heating	200
Receipts during the year	
Subscriptions for xx12	3920
Sales of tickets for dramatic performances	430
Catering officer – profit from refreshments	40

The following matters must also be taken into account:

a   Subscriptions due but unpaid for xx12 amount to £180
b   Rates paid in respect of next year, £120
c   Expenses still unpaid for the last Dramatic Performance, £10
d   Electricity account unpaid, £80
e   The old Games and Drama equipment is to be depreciated by
    20%, that purchased in the year by 10% and the Furniture and
    Fittings by £100.

Information technology and bookkeeping

In this chapter you will learn:

▶ *About computers' basic functions*
▶ *How computers can assist bookkeeping*
▶ *About their advantages over manual methods*

Although this *Teach Yourself* text has referred to the use of information technology in various places it largely assumes you will be doing bookkeeping work by hand. For a small business, or for keeping your personal accounts using double entry methods, this may be the case in reality. However, as a business grows, producing accounts by hand can become very difficult and time consuming, and a computer can often be used to reduce the workload and improve the usefulness of accounting information to you in managing the business.

As the bookkeeper it is *very* important that you understand what the computer is doing in order to give it the right information and to enable you to understand what it produces as its output. A certain amount of the routine work, however, such as posting entries, doing arithmetic, balancing accounts and producing draft final accounts can be taken over by the machine. This chapter introduces you to the use of the computer in this way.

Basic functions of the computer

A computer typically performs four basic functions in a business setting.

▶ *Handling inputting of data* – using the parts of the computer system, such as the keyboard and the mouse, a computer user can input data into the computer. Data can also be input to your computer from online sources, such as a website, be delivered by email or by a USB device of some sort.

▶ *Storing data* – once the information has been input into the computer it will often be stored to prevent the need for it to be input again next time. The computer will have its own internal 'hard drive' for this purpose. The computer will also use various external devices that can store information electronically for this purpose, such as writeable CD-ROMs, DVDs or external hard drives.

▶ *Manipulating data* – having got the data into the computer it will be possible to manipulate the data in whatever way is appropriate for the job you need to perform. For example, to perform arithmetic on the data or creating charts from it.

▶ *Outputting data* – the results of the computer's manipulation of data will need to be shown to the computer user for it to be of further use to them. This may be performed via a computer screen, on paper via a printer or stored back onto an external storage device (or *Cloud*) to be used as input to future manipulations.

The parts of a computer system can be separated into two groups – hardware and software. Hardware refers to the pieces of the computer that you can touch and see, such as the keyboard, the mouse and the computer screen. The software refers to the instructions that are given to the computer to describe what it should do with the data you have given it.

People who write software for computers will often put together sets of instructions to perform standard tasks that can then be reused by other people. These sets of software instructions are referred to as computer packages. Packages can be designed to fulfil very general functions such as spreadsheets (e.g. Microsoft Excel or Open Office Calc) and databases (e.g. Microsoft Access or Open Office Base), or to perform more specific functions. Packages designed to help with bookkeeping functions are examples of this latter kind of package.

Role of information technology in business

Information technology in the form of the computer has been applied to a wide range of business activities. It is used to perform tasks including wordprocessing (such as typing and storing client correspondence), for statistical analysis (such as performance data analysis), and to help in planning future activities. Computers are also useful in supporting electronic communications and information handling, using ways of linking different computers together, such as local area networks or the Internet. This includes email and websites these days which have become important business tools. Social media (like Facebook or Twitter) can also play a useful role in interacting with customers and helping your business grow its customer base.

Computers and bookkeeping

Computers are very good at manipulating numbers and can be effective in supporting many of the tasks that make up the bookkeeping function. Computer packages are available to help with a number of these functions, or just to take over the role of one of the functions. In either case the computer will need to be integrated with the normal manual bookkeeping system that will supply the input data and then use the computer output. The computer will become part of the bookkeeping role.

Modern basic bookkeeping packages are often Cloud based – so the package's software and your data doesn't only reside on your computer but enables you to access it via various devices connected to the internet. This can add useful flexibility to your accounting function, both to how and when input accounting information and also for accessing this data to help you manage your business.

In terms of bookkeeping functions most commonly taken over by a computer, either as standalone functions or in an integrated form. These most typically are:

▶ managing the Books of Prime Entry

▶ managing the Sales Ledger

▶ managing the Purchase Ledger

▶ managing the General Ledger

▶ production of a Trial Balance and the Final Accounts.

Where the computer package performs all of these tasks the user will be required to enter the data from the source documents into the computer, which will then complete the Books of Prime Entry and post the correct totals to the Ledgers they hold automatically. The user will be able to view what the computer has done at any stage of the operation in the same way as a user is able to view the manual process. They will also be able to correct errors that occur due to changes in circumstances or incorrect information given to the computer at the start of the process.

The computer will store the information input to it by the user over a period of time and will output the accounts information on request. This may be useful, for example, in performing credit management when needing to check on debtor balances at any point in time. At the end of the bookkeeping period the computer package will produce a Trial Balance or Final Accounts using the data it has stored during the period.

In some cases it may be desirable not to use a totally integrated package of the nature just described. It is possible, if required, to just use a computer to perform one of the functions and continue to keep the rest of the accounts manually in the way described in the rest of this text.

Advantages of using a computer in bookkeeping

The use of a computer as part of a bookkeeping function offers the user a number of benefits over an entirely manual system.

▶ *Accuracy is improved* – as a computer is not prone to arithmetic and procedure errors like humans, once the correct data has been entered, correct bookkeeping principles will be applied throughout the computer's operation and all the arithmetic will be performed correctly. This greatly reduces the likelihood of errors occurring in the bookkeeping process.

▶ *Storage of data is better* – as the computer must store information between its data manipulation stages, the need to keep manual records is reduced. The computer can also reuse data entered for one purpose for other reasons so information only needs to be kept in one place for all the uses to which the business may wish to put it. For example, for accounts production, and for credit control or marketing analysis.

▶ *Flexible access to data* – the computer offers the user more flexible access to the data by helping them to look at it in different ways, to output it in different forms and formats and to use it as input to other packages.

▶ *Traceable history* – the computer will keep an accurate listing of all the actions it has performed so that they can be retraced if it is necessary. This is useful when looking to correct errors or to check the accounts are accurate. If your business needs to be reviewed, or audited, this trace will be very important as evidence of how the bookkeeping has been performed.

▶ *Data can be analysed* – once the data is available in the computer then different and additional analysis can be performed in efficient ways. This can lead to insights into business activity and opportunities not necessarily easily spotted by accident or as a result of manual analysis (that is likely to be more time consuming to do).

Management of information technology in bookkeeping

Although the computer may take over a number of the routine functions of bookkeeping, it will be very rare that the knowledgeable bookkeeper can be done away with when a computer is introduced. There is still the need for someone who is experienced in the recording function to assess what the computer has generated and to ensure the correctness of the accounts it has produced. There is also still a data preparation role that needs to be performed when taking data from the source documents and preparing it for entry into the computer.

It is also likely that the output from the computer will not appear in an identical format to the old manual system. For example, the format of accounts produced by the computer may appear differently. This is noticeable, for example, when comparing the 'T' form of accounts with the account statement received from the bank which will have been produced by a computer. It is important that the bookkeeper is aware of the different formats in which this data can appear.

Remember this

The computer will not replace the role of the bookkeeper in its entirety in any business; however, the use of the computer is likely to affect the functions performed by the bookkeeper. It will remove much of the routine work they conventionally have performed and replace it with more specialist roles that continue to require good knowledge of the practice of bookkeeping.

Further information

The 'Taking it further' section of this book provides details of specific bookkeeping packages, and other business computing tools, that may be of use to you in supporting bookkeeping in your business, or in managing your private accounts.

Focus points

On completion of this chapter you should:

✳ Understand the basic functions of a computer
✳ Appreciate the general business uses of computers
✳ Understand how computers can be useful to undertake bookkeeping tasks
✳ Know the advantages of switching to a computer from a paper-based system
✳ Appreciate how the role of a bookkeeper will change if a computer is introduced into your accounting system.

Partnership

In this chapter you will learn:

- ▶ *About the differences between sole traders and partnerships*
- ▶ *About the legal position of a partnership*
- ▶ *About goodwill and separate accounts for partners*

Objective

This chapter introduces you to the meaning of 'partnership' and how the profit earned is divided between partners. It also illustrates the accounting between partners when the partnership is formed, when a new partner is admitted and when one leaves.

In the previous chapters we have assumed the business we are performing the bookkeeping for is owned by a sole proprietor, or alternatively referred to as a sole trader. This was the earliest form of proprietorship, and it still exists as the most common business type particularly in smaller businesses involved in selling and distribution activities.

With the growth in the size of the business, the Capital required to provide the necessary equipment and to finance ordinary trading is usually found to be larger than the resources of any one individual. A further handicap faced by a sole trader is that, in the event of the business failing, the proprietor is liable, to the last penny, for the payment of the business creditors. The liability is said to be **unlimited**. This contrasts to that of the shareholders in a Limited Company, which is restricted to the amounts, if any remain, unpaid on their shares (their parts of the business) they have contracted to take (hence the term *limited liability* that applies to companies; see Chapter 19 for further details).

Between these two extremes we sometimes encounter the situation where two, or more, individuals agree to work together, sharing their resources and any profits earned. This situation is referred to as a **partnership**. Just as in the case of the Sole Trader, *each* partner usually has unlimited liability for the whole of the debts of the partnership firm.

A partnership is a particularly suitable form of business proprietorship where:

▶ a large amount of Capital is not required

▶ liabilities to suppliers and others are unlikely to be considerable

- the business is of a size in which each partner can take part in the general supervision.

For these reasons, partnerships are often found in the professions and in the smaller merchanting and manufacturing businesses.

UK Partnership Act 1890

In the UK some, albeit limited, statutory (i.e. legally enforceable) control over the organization of a partnership was imposed by this Act. It defines partnership *as the relation which subsists between persons carrying on business in common with a view to profit.*

The Act of 1890 provides certain rules which, in the absence of other written or verbal arrangement between the partners, can be applied in defining the duties of the partners to each other, and their responsibility to persons outside the firm with whom either has business dealings.

As it is usually desirable to make special arrangements in each individual case, and to have a permanent record of what is agreed upon, a **Deed**, or **Articles of Partnership,** is often drawn up by which each of the partners agrees to be bound. These also provide for such modifications of the Act of 1890 as may be thought necessary by the partners.

The Deed may state:

a the period for which the partnership is entered into

b the nature of the business to be carried on

c the amount of Capital to be introduced and in what circumstances it may be withdrawn

d the ratio in which Profits and Losses shall be shared

e how much each partner shall be entitled to draw on account of accruing profits

f whether Interest shall be allowed on Partners' Capitals

g the salaries, if any, to be paid to individual partners.

As regards **a**, if no period is stated, or the partnership is continued without any fresh agreement after the original period has expired, it is said to be a Partnership at Will.

Of the above, items **c, d, e, f** and **g** have special bearing on the *accounts*, and will therefore be considered separately.

CAPITAL

The Capital brought into a partnership by each of the partners may take the form of cash, or property in kind, such as machinery, buildings, stock, etc.

In any event, the agreed value of the total capital introduced must be credited to the Partner's Capital Account, and the proper Asset Account debited.

If the introduced Capital totals are to be considered to be **fixed**, the profit shares and drawings on them by the partners that would normally be applied to these Capital accounts will be dealt with instead through separate Current Accounts instead of treating them as directly part of Capital, as we saw in the case of a sole owner. We will illustrate how this works in Example 18.2 but this simply implies that the total the partnership owes to each partner is the total of their Capital account plus (or minus) any total in their Current account.

PROFITS AND LOSSES

Partners may share any profits and losses on any agreed basis. In the last resort (if no specific agreement to the contrary has been made) the Partnership Act provides that they are to share these equally. Sometimes profits and losses may be divided in the ratio of the Fixed Capitals introduced by the partners; in other cases, where one partner takes a more active part than another, this may be rewarded with a bigger proportionate share.

DRAWINGS

It is better to agree at the outset on a limit for each partner's drawings. As cash withdrawn by partners depletes the circulating Capital of the business, interest may be charged on drawings from the date it is withdrawn to the end of the firm's financial year. To avoid this calculation the agreement may stipulate that drawings on account of profit throughout the year will be in the profit-sharing proportion. Drawings may be in the form of goods or the use of business services for private purposes, as well as cash. With any non-cash drawings event the purchase or expense account will be credited and the partner's Current Account debited with the value of the drawings taken.

INTEREST ON CAPITALS

Prior to the division of the Net Profit, the Partnership Deed may provide for charging Interest on the Capital of each partner. If this were not done in a case where, for example, Capital Accounts were unequal, but Profits and Losses were divided equally, the partner having the larger (or largest) Capital would lose out proportionally to the others.

Remember this

Such Interest on Capital is not a business expense, and would be debited in the Appropriation or Net Profit and Loss Account when dealing with distributions of profit or sharing out of losses.

PARTNERSHIP SALARIES

A management salary may be paid to one or more of the partners if they devote more time to the business than their co-partners, or if they are *active*, as distinct from *sleeping* (or *dormant*, non-active) partners. The latter are those who have contributed Capital, but take no part in the daily supervision of business affairs.

Salaries paid or payable to the partners will, like interest on Capital, be debited in the Appropriation Account. They are, in effect, a part of the determined profit due to the proprietor.

PARTNERS' ADVANCES

If a partner, to assist the firm, advances (gives) it cash as a *loan*, it is usually treated in the books in a different way from the Capital invested. The amount should instead be credited to a separate Loan Account in the partner's name.

GOODWILL

Goodwill is a business Asset, which may be defined as 'the worth inherent in an established business producing a normal and reasonable profit on the Capital employed in it'.

It is *worth* or *value* over and above that represented by the *Tangible* Assets, such as buildings, plant, stock and book debts, and can so be termed an *Intangible* Asset.

If the business were sold, it would clearly be normal for a purchaser to be required to pay something for the right to enjoy a continuity of the profits arising from an established business, and this is well brought out in the case of changes to a partnership.

An incoming partner can be expected to pay the existing partners for the goodwill represented by a share of profit, and an outgoing partner is entitled to have goodwill taken into account in determining the sum due to them from the business as they leave it. The Deed of Partnership will often indicate how the value of the goodwill is to be determined, for example, by reference to past profits or as an estimate of future maintainable profits.

The best way to illustrate the various similarities and differences between accounting for a sole trader or for a partnership is by way of examples.

▶ Example 18.1

A joins B in partnership on 1 January xx10. The Capital is provided as £15 000 by A, who is a dormant partner, and £5 000 by B, who works full-time for the business and is wholly dependent on it.

Assuming the gross receipts for xx10 are £60 000, and the working expenses £19 000, prepare a Profit and Loss Account incorporating these items, and also the distribution of profit, allowing 10% Interest on Capital, and dividing the balance equally.

A. AND B.
Profit and Loss Account
Year ended 31 December xx10

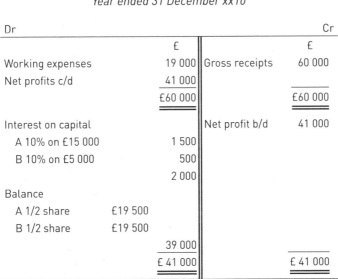

Dr		£		Cr £
Working expenses		19 000	Gross receipts	60 000
Net profits c/d		41 000		
		£60 000		£60 000
Interest on capital			Net profit b/d	41 000
A 10% on £15 000		1 500		
B 10% on £5 000		500		
		2 000		
Balance				
A 1/2 share	£19 500			
B 1/2 share	£19 500			
		39 000		
		£ 41 000		£ 41 000

We can see the benefit to A of charging interest on Capital. B would perhaps think it appropriate that a salary should be paid, but if the agreement does not include a reference to it, none will be due.

The interest due to each partner and the amount of the profit share can be carried direct to Capital Account, but is more usually credited to a Current Account. The following example illustrates the use of Current Accounts in this way.

▶ Example 18.2

Rogers and Shaw enter into partnership on 1 January xx11, and agree to divide Profits and Losses equally, after charging Interest on Capital at 10% per annum.

On 31 December xx11, the following Balances are extracted from their Books:

		Dr	Cr
		£	£
Rogers:	Capital		13 000.00
	Drawings	1 156.00	
Shaw:	Capital		12 000.00
	Drawings	1 156.00	
Sales			34 257.00
Discounts received			81.00
Purchases		5 413.00	
Discounts allowed		187.00	
Salaries		11 497.00	
Wages		12 500.00	
Accounts receivable		4 200.00	
Rates		1 075.00	
Printing and stationery		292.00	
Travelling expenses		596.00	
Bad debts		24.00	
Repairs and renewals		133.00	
Cash in hand		11.00	
Bank overdraft			34.00
Subscriptions		8.00	
Bank charges		46.00	
Accounts payable			662.00
Factory and warehouse premises		19 234.00	
Plant and machinery		2 506.00	
		£60 034.00	£60 034.00

The inventory at 31 December xx11 was valued by the partners at £1125.

You are required:

▶ to prepare Trading, Profit and Loss Account for the year to 31 December xx11, and a Statement of Financial Position at that date

▶ to show the Partners' Current Accounts.

The following adjustments are necessary:

▶ Provide £150 for wages accrued due.

▶ Provide 1% on the amount of the Accounts receivable for Bad and Doubtful Debts.

▶ Provide £500 depreciation in respect of Plant and Machinery.

In this example you should be careful to note how the provisions for **wages, doubtful debts** and **depreciation** are dealt with in the Statement of Financial Position.

ROGERS AND SHAW
Trading, Profit and Loss Account
Year ended 31 December xx11

	£		£
Purchases	5 413.00	Sales	34 257.00
Wages	£12 500.00	Inventory, 31 December xx11	1 125.00
Add Provision	150.00		
	12 650.00		
Gross profit c/d (50% to turnover)	17 319.00		
	35 382.00		35 382.00
Salaries	11 497.00	Gross profit b/d	17 319.00
Travelling expenses	596.00	Discount received	81.00

(Continued)

		£		£
Printing and stationery		292.00		
Discounts allowed		187.00		
Repairs and renewals		133.00		
Rates		1 075.00		
Bad debts	£24.00			
Add Provision	42.00	66.00		
Bank charges		46.00		
Subscriptions		8.00		
Depreciation of plant and machinery		500.00		
		14 400.00		
Net profit c/d		3 000.00		
		17 400.00		17 400.00
Interest on capitals:			Net profit b/d	3 000.00
Rogers 10% on £13 000		1 300.00		
Shaw 10% on £12 000		1 200.00		
		2 500.00		
Rogers, ½ share	250.00			
Shaw, ½ share	250.00			
		500.00		
		£3 000.00		£3 000.00

Note: In practice, the Provisions are seldom shown separately in the Profit and Loss Account, e.g. Wages would be shown in the one sum of £12 650.00 only.

ROGERS AND SHAW
Statement of Financial Position
As at 31 December xx11

Non-current Assets	£	£	£	£
Factory and warehouse premises				19 234.00
Plant and machinery			2 506.00	
less depreciation			500.00	
				2 006.00
TOTAL FIXED ASSETS				21 240.00
Current Assets				
Inventory		1 125.00		
Accounts receivable	4 200.00			
less provision	42.00			
		4 158.00		
Cash in hand		11.00		
			5 294.00	
deduct Current Liabilities				
Accounts payable		662.00		
Wages accrued		150.00		
Bank overdraft		34.00		
			846.00	
NET CURRENT ASSETS				4 448.00
TOTAL ASSETS minus CURRENT LIABILITIES				£25 688.00

(*Continued*)

Non-current Assets	£	£
Financed by:		
Current Accounts		
Rogers		
Interest on capital	1 300.00	
Profit share	250.00	
	1 550.00	
less drawings	1 156.00	
		394.00
Shaw		
Interest on capital	1 200.00	
Profit share	250.00	
	1 450.00	
less drawings	1 156.00	
		294.00
Capital Accounts		
Rogers	13 000.00	
Shaw	12 000.00	
		25 000.00
		£25 688.00

Private Ledger
ROGERS – CURRENT ACCOUNT

Dr				Cr	
xx11		£	xxx11		£
Dec 31	Drawings	1 156.00	Dec 31	Interest on capital 10% on £13 000	1 300.00
31	Balance c/d	394.00	31	One half Profit, year to date	250.00
		£1 550.00			£1 550.00
			xx12		
			Jan 1	Balance b/d	394.00

SHAW – CURRENT ACCOUNT

Dr				Cr	
xx11		£	xx11		£
Dec 31	Drawings	1 156.00	Dec 31	Interest on capital 10% on £12 000	1 200.00
31	Balance c/d	294.00	31	One half Profit, year to date	250.00
		£1 450.00			£1 450.00
			xx12		
			Jan 1	Balance b/d	294.00

Creating or changing a partnership

When two sole traders amalgamate to form a partnership it is usually necessary to value the assets that each is contributing to the new business. They may agree the values themselves or employ a professional valuer, and goodwill (as described earlier in this chapter) should be taken into account.

Similarly when a new partner is joining the firm, or an old one is leaving, a revaluation of assets will usually be necessary so that the correct amount can be attributed to each partner.

▶ **Example 18.3**

A and B are partners who share equally in the profits and each has contributed £10 000 capital. The net assets therefore total £20 000. When they decided to accept C as an equal partner it was agreed that Goodwill should be recognized with a value of £12 000. This extra asset will be balanced by crediting the capital accounts of A and B with their share, i.e. equally, £6000 each. If the partnership agrees to retain this Goodwill in the accounts then interest, if payable, would be payable on the increased capitals of A and B, and on the £16 000 capital introduced by C. If it is agreed that Goodwill should not be shown on the Statement of Financial Position it will be written off in the new profit-sharing ratio. This is done equally and so £4000 will be deducted from each partner's capital.

Summarized balance sheets:

		£	£
► Originally	Sundry net assets		20 000
	Capital accounts		
	A	10 000	
	B	10 000	£20 000

► *After valuing goodwill at £12 000*			
	Sundry net assets		20 000
	Goodwill		12 000
			32 000
	Capital accounts		
	A	16 000	
	B	16 000	£32 000

► *C joins, paying £16 000 into the business for an equal share in the profits*

Sundry net assets		20 000
Goodwill		12 000
Cash		16 000
		£48 000
Capital accounts		
	A	16 000
	B	16 000
	C	16 000
		£48 000

▶ *Goodwill is written off*

Sundry net assets		20 000
Cash		16 000
		£36 000
Capital accounts		
	A	12 000
	B	12 000
	C	12 000
		£36 000

Focus points

On completion of this chapter you should:
* have a brief understanding of the legal position of a partnership
* appreciate the importance of a legal agreement governing the division of profit in a partnership, in particular the rules for salary, interest on capital and loan interest and their application
* know the basis of valuation of the business when there is a change in the partners, in particular goodwill and its allocation between the partners
* be able to produce the separate capital and current accounts for each of the partners.

1 Explain why interest may be credited to a partner.
2 Define goodwill and explain its importance in partnership accounting.
3 Earle and Yeoman are considering establishing a dairy to be run by them in partnership. Earle is to provide nine-tenths of the capital required, but, having no practical knowledge of the work, is not expected to take much active part in its operation. Yeoman is experienced in running a dairy and she will manage the business.

 You have been asked by them for your advice on the financial provisions to be included in the Partnership Deed. What would you suggest, and why?

4 In the absence of agreement, to what extent are partners entitled to interest on capital in and loans to the firm?

 Illustrate your answer by reference to the following:

	£
A Capital	10 000.00
B Capital	5 000.00
A Loan	3 000.00

 Profits of the firm (before charging any interest), £2500.

5 On 1 January xx12, A and B entered into partnership but without any formal deed of partnership. A provided £10 000 as capital, and B provided £500. On 1 July xx12, A advanced £2000 on loan to the firm.

 Accounts were prepared and disclosed a profit of £6000 for the year to 31 December xx12, but the partners could not agree as to how this sum should be divided between them. A contended that the partners should receive 5% interest on capital and that A should receive 6% interest on the loan to the firm, and the balance then available should be divided equally. B contended that, as B did most of the work, B should be paid a salary before any division of profit was made.

 Show how the profits of the firm should be divided and state what different division, if any, would be made if A had written a letter to B agreeing that a partnership salary of £1500 should be paid to B.

6 A, a sole trader, prepared accounts as on 31 March xx10, when the Capital Account showed a balance of £9000. On 1 April B joined A as a partner on the terms that before B's entry a Goodwill Account of £4000 should be raised, that B should bring in £3000 in cash as capital, interest at 5% per annum should be allowed on Capital Accounts and the balance of profit be divided between A and B, in the proportion of 3 to 1.

The profit for the year to 31 March xx11, before charging interest, was £4050. Show the division of this between A and B. Show also what the division would have been had no provision been made as to goodwill, the other arrangements being as stated above.

7 X and Y are partners, and they admit Z as a partner, profits to be shared as follows: X four-ninths, Y three-ninths, Z two-ninths.

Y is credited with a partnership salary of £4500 per annum, and X and Y guarantee that Z's share of profits shall not be less than £8000 in any year.

The profits for the year ended 31 December xx13, prior to providing for Y's salary, amounted to £38 214.

Prepare the Appropriation section of the firm's Profit and Loss Account.

8 A, a sole trader owning an established business, took B into partnership on 1 January xx12, at which date the goodwill of the business was agreed to be worth £6000. A's capital (exclusive of goodwill) was £10 000, and B brought in £3000 as his capital. Interest on Capital Accounts was to be allowed at 5%, and A and B were to divide the remaining profit in the ratio of 2 to 1.

The profit for xx12 before charging interest, was £35 600.

Calculate the division of this sum between A and B on the alternative assumptions that:

a goodwill was ignored on B's entering the business
b goodwill was taken into account at its correct value.

9 Bright and Smart carry on business in partnership, sharing profits in the proportion of three-fifths and two-fifths respectively.

On 1 January xx13, the Capital Accounts showed the following credit balances: Bright, £8000; Smart, £6000.

The Partnership Agreement provides that the partners shall be allowed interest on capital at 5% per annum and that Bright shall be entitled to a salary of £6000 per annum and Smart to one of £4000 per annum. During the year ended 31 December xx13, the partners' drawings were: Bright, £3550; Smart, £2425.

The profit for the year, prior to making any of the above adjustments, was £23 500.

Write up the Profit and Loss Appropriation Account and show how the Capital Accounts of the partners would appear on the Statement of Financial Position at 31 December xx13.

10 A and B entered into partnership on 1 January xx12, sharing profits and losses equally.

A contributed £5000 as capital, comprising £2000 in cash and fixtures and plant valued at £3000.

B could only introduce £1000 in cash, but it was agreed he should be given credit in the sum of £1500 for his sales connections, and also receive a salary at the rate of £4800 per annum.

On 30 June xx12, B paid in an additional £500, and at the same date C entered the firm, paying £1600 for a quarter share of the profits and goodwill and bringing in £1000 cash as his capital, all of which it was agreed should be left in the business.

A and B continued to share the profits in the same relative proportions as before, and it was arranged that as from the date of C's entry, B's salary should cease, but 10% per annum interest on capitals should be allowed.

The profits for the year to 31 December xx12, prior to charging such interest and B's salary, were £16 800. Draw up a Statement showing the division of this amount between the partners, making any necessary apportionments on a time basis, and open Ledger Accounts to record the whole of the above.

11 Joan and John entered into partnership as merchants on 1 January xx11. Joan brought in cash £500 and inventory £1000; John brought in cash £2300 and a lorry £8700. The agreement provided that John was to have a salary from the firm of £2250 per annum and that each partner might draw (on account of salary and profit)

£100 per month plus £5000 each on 15 December; otherwise the terms of the Partnership Act, 1890, were to apply.

At the end of xx11 the following Trial Balance was extracted from the books:

Trial Balance
31 December xx11

	Dr £	Cr £
Capital Accounts		12 500.00
Accounts receivable	950.00	
Cash	25.00	
Carriage inwards	500.00	
Bank		135.00
Inventory	1 000.00	
Rent paid	1 550.00	
Sales		36 000.00
Lorry	8 700.00	
Carriage outwards	130.00	
Discounts received		575.00
Petty cash expenditure	52.00	
Purchases	11 500.00	
Drawings	12 400.00	
Accounts payable		697.00
Discounts allowed	50.00	
Rates paid	1 200.00	
Salaries (not Partners)	10 850.00	
Fixtures and fittings (cost)	1 000.00	
	£49 907.00	£49 907.00

Notes:

1 Inventory 31 December xx11, valued at £1800.
2 Rent accrued but not paid, £150.
3 Rates paid in advance, £140.
4 Depreciate the lorry at 10% per half-year on the diminishing balance system, and the Fixtures and Fittings at 5% per half-year on original cost.
5 Bank charges not yet entered in books, £50.

   Prepare Trading, Profit and Loss Accounts for xx11 and a Statement of Financial Position at the end of the year.

12 The following Trial Balance has been extracted as at 31 March xx13, from the books of C Spargo and W Penna – partners sharing profits and losses in the proportion of 2 to 1 respectively.

	Dr £	Cr £
Inventory, 1 April xx12	3 690.00	
Purchases and sales	36 892.75	89 469.97
Bad Debts written off	291.67	
Plant and machinery (cost £7000)	6 650.00	
Furniture and fittings (cost £1200)	1 164.00	
Returns	371.56	297.54
Discounts	351.71	403.69
Drawings: C Spargo	3 560.00	
W Penna	2 380.00	
Accounts receivable and payable	5 620.00	4 872.68
Light and heat	1 397.80	
Rent and rates	3 650.63	
Insurances	1 131.50	
Salaries	11 215.68	
Wages	26 394.93	
General expenses	445.62	
Bad Debts reserve		200.00
Commissions		363.97
Capital: C Spargo		5 800.00
W Penna		3 800.00
	£105 207.85	£105 207.85

Value of inventory on 31 March xx13, £1793.

You are asked to draw up Trading, Profit and Loss Accounts for the year, using the following data for making necessary adjustments:

1 Depreciate plant and machinery 10% on cost.
2 Depreciate furniture and fittings 5% on cost.
3 Amount of insurance pre-paid, £131.75
4 Amount of wages due but unpaid, £511.65.
5 The Bad Debts Reserve is to be increased to an amount equal to 5% of debtors' balances.
6 Amount of commissions due but not received, £34.94.
7 Capital Accounts to be credited with interest at 5% per annum.

(No interest to be charged on drawings.)

No Statement of Financial Position is to be drawn up. Instead, you are to show the following accounts in full for the year ended 31 March xx13:

1 Plant and Machinery Account.
2 Insurance Account.
3 Bad Debts Reserve Account.
4 Commission Account.

13 The firm of John Smith & Sons, makers of engineering equipment, consists of John and Magnus Smith. They share profits equally, after each has been credited with interest at 5% on his capital at the beginning of the year.

At 31 January xx14, the end of the firm's financial year, the following are the balances in the Ledger:

	£	£
Purchases: Raw materials	18 562.00	
Finished goods	860.00	
General office expenses	934.00	
Returns inwards	413.00	
Accounts payable, including an unsecured loan of £500, maturing in xx16		2 617.00
Bad Debts provision		205.00
Inventory: Raw materials	3 906.00	
Finished goods	101.00	
Wages (factory)	48 687.00	
Salaries (factory)	11 252.00	
Rent, insurance, etc. (factory)	1 246.00	
Rent, insurance, etc. (factory), prepaid	25.00	
Net rents from workmen's cottages		97.00
Fire expense	750.00	
Carriage outwards	909.00	
Factory equipment and machinery	14 315.00	
Factory equipment and machinery depreciation provision		2 000.00
Cash	14.00	
Sales		85 200.00
Interest paid on overdraft, etc.	61.00	
Accounts receivable	4 135.00	
Capital: John Smith		12 420.00
Magnus Smith		3 740.00
Drawings: John Smith	837.00	
Magnus Smith	371.00	
Bank		1 099.00
	£107 378.00	£107 378.00

The inventory of raw materials at 31 January xx14 was valued at £4310. There were then no finished goods on hand.

The 'Fire Expense' Account shows the balance of a heavy loss from fire in xx10. £150 of this amount is now to be written off.

£22 of bank overdraft interest is accrued and has not been allowed for.

The Equipment Depreciation Provision is to be increased by £315.

Prepare suitable Final Accounts and a Statement of Financial Position.

14 On 1 January xx13, A and B go into business as advertising consultants, on the footing that each contributes £1000 cash as capital, profits and losses to be shared equally.

The £1000 provided by A is borrowed by him privately from his bankers at 8% p.a. interest.

It is agreed that B, who devotes his whole time to the business, shall receive prior to the ascertainment of profit a management salary of £1250 p.a.

Office accommodation is acquired on 1 February xx13, at a rent of £300 p.a., payable quarterly, the first payment is to be made on 31 March xx13.

Furniture and fittings are purchased on the latter date from OF Ltd, for a sum of £72 cash, and B introduces other similar equipment of a value of £36 to be credited to his Capital Account.

Apart from the above items, at 31 December xx13, there has been received in cash by A and B as consultants' fees the sum of £6150, and at that date fees totalling £340 are outstanding and due to them.

Heating, lighting, etc., amounted to £900 during the period, and A and B incurred travelling and entertaining expenses of £763 in connection with visits to clients, all of which has been paid.

Prepare an Income Statement for the business of A and B for the year ended 31 December xx13, and a Statement of Financial Position at that date.

Limited companies

In this chapter you will learn:

▶ *About limited liability*
▶ *About the differences between public and private limited companies*
▶ *About different types of shares*

Objective

This chapter contains a brief introduction to Limited Liability companies and the legal requirements for their annual accounts. It also briefly illustrates the basic accounting considerations when changing from a partnership to a company.

The limited company, as an artificial 'person' in UK Law, comes into existence through registration under the provisions of the various Companies Acts (the latest being the 2006 Act which came into full force on 1 October 2009), and is distinct as a legal entity from changing generations of its owners (referred to as shareholders). The latter, when buying shares, are able to limit their liability to the nominal ('face') value of the shares taken by them. An applicant for 100 shares of £1 each originally offered for sale by the company at £1 each has, once their offer is accepted by the company, a liability to pay £100 *and no more*, even if the company should in future be unable to meet the claims of its creditors. The creditors have contracted with the company as a separate legal 'person'. They can only look for payment to the company therefore – not its individual shareholders (normally).

Remember this

The possibility for limited personal liability that companies create provided an immense stimulus to the development of business because:

* the company, unlike the Sole Trader, or Partnership firm, can obtain capital funds from a very large number of persons
* the individual shareholder can take as many, or as few shares as they desire, and, having paid for them in full, are normally protected from any further liability.

Public and private companies

All Companies incorporated under the Companies Acts are bound by its provisions and comprise two main classes: Public Companies and Private Companies.

A **Public Company** is one whose name ends with the words 'public limited company' or 'plc'. It must have a minimum allotted share capital of £50 000. Its shares will be on the London Stock Exchange where anyone can buy them (hence the term 'public').

A **Private Company** is any company which is not a Public Company, and it is prohibited from offering its shares or debentures for sale directly to the public. Instead, it can only obtain its funding by private arrangements.

The bookkeeping and accounting requirements are the same for all companies but the disclosure requirements are greater for Public Companies and reduced for small- or medium-sized Private Companies.

A broad distinction is that a Public Company is one in which the public are substantially involved only as providers of capital, whereas in a Private Company management and proprietorship are often identical, companies often being formed chiefly to obtain the benefit of limited liability rather than the provision of new capital.

Restrictions on the transfer of shares in a Private Company may mean that a would-be seller must first offer their shares to an existing shareholder, or accept a price determined in accordance with the Articles, and other operational documents of the company.

Remember this

Companies House is the Government department responsible for managing the registration process for companies, and all their subsequent annual or irregular filings. Check out their website for more details on the differences between company types and all the information you may need about how to register different types of companies and the subsequent paperwork you will have to manage for your company – they have some good resources there to help you – http://www.gov.uk/government/organisations/companies-house.

The Memorandum and Articles of Association

Until the new Companies Act 2006 came into force in 2009, any one or more people could form an incorporated Company by subscribing their names to a document called the **Memorandum of Association** and otherwise complying with the requirements of the Companies Act. This document was, in effect, the Charter of the Company, and stated various key bits of information about the business needed to create it. For example, it included:

► the name of the company (with 'Limited' as the last word of the name)

► the location of the Registered Office of the company

► the objects of the company (the range of activities the company was set up to perform)

► that the liability of the members was limited

► the amount of the Share Capital with which the company was proposed to be registered, and its division into shares of a fixed amount.

This document only now (for new businesses formed after 1 October 2009) needs to say the signatures to the registration want to create a company and that they agree to be its members and to take at least one share each (each member of a company must have at least one share to be allowed to be a member – although some may have more than one of course). It no longer has to detail how those shares are divided between members, for example. All of the other content that used to be on this document is transferred to the details of a second document – called the **Articles of Association** – which is now the key operating document of the new company and the one to which you should refer if you want to find out about the operation of a company. This document did exist before the new rules came into effect but had a more specific operation in conjunction with the Memorandum.

The Articles are like the rules of a club or society, and provide for the general conduct of the company's affairs.

All members of the company are bound by the Articles in force, even if they buy their shares subsequently and were not original subscribers when the business was created and the 'rules' drawn up. If you don't create your own set of Articles, or the specific details of those you write don't cover a particular issue, there is a 'model' set that in effect become your set of operating rules generally, or for that specific issue, whether you like it or not (i.e. a similar idea to the Partnership Agreement default rules we discussed in the previous chapter). Therefore it is usually wise to work through these model rules carefully to ensure you are happy with what they impose on you, or write new rules for your own business if you want to change them.

So what do the Articles cover? They describe (amongst other things if relevant):

► The basic framework of decision making of the company directors (their appointment, removals, remuneration, etc.).

► Questions related to shares and share transfers (e.g. initial allocation of shares to the initial members, how sales of further shares are to operate, how the company can buy back existing shares if it wanted to and details on the various voting rights of shares if more than one type of share is issued).

► Distributions made (e.g. how and when dividends might be paid).

When thinking about forming a company remember that the name chosen for the new company must not so closely resemble that of an existing company as to deceive or cause confusion in the mind of the public. You therefore have to pick a name that makes you unique or the registration process will be rejected.

The Articles you create when you form a business don't have to remain fixed for ever. They may be altered or added to by passing what is called a 'special resolution' of members at a general meeting. A three-quarters (75%) majority of those who have voting rights in the company is required to alter the articles and not less than 21 days' notice of the intention to propose the resolution as a special resolution must have been given to all current shareholders to make sure they know this is about to happen.

For the company to come into existence these registration documents must be lodged with Companies House as the Government department responsible for corporate registrations. On approval this department will issue a company number, the formal registration number of the new company. This number must be used on letterheads and other formal documentation of the business so those you trade with will be able to see you are a registered company.

Share capital

Shares, as units of ownership, may be generally classified as Ordinary and Preference Shares. All shareholders are entitled to receive payouts of the company's profits if any are earned. These payouts to shareholders are called **dividends**. Preference shares carry a fixed rate of dividend.

Some preference shares may also have the right to be converted into ordinary shares, at stated times and in a stated ratio. These rights will be recorded in the issuing documents for these shares. Such shares are referred to as *Convertible Preference Shares*. Preference Shareholders have a priority for dividends if there are profits available.

Ordinary Shares take what profit remains, and may earn much larger dividends therefore in prosperous years, but conversely earn no dividend at all in poor years. The shareholders also have the opportunity of capital appreciation through an increase in the market price of their shares. This appreciation is referred to as a **capital gain**.

Other forms of shares include Cumulative Preference Shares where any arrears of the agreed fixed dividend are carried forward to the following period and Redeemable Preference Shares are those whose value are to be redeemed at some agreed point in time either out of *profits*, or from the proceeds of a fresh issue of *capital*: otherwise the shareholder of any class may only realize their investment by sale of the shares in the market.

The two latter classes represent variations of the simple Preference Share, and are usually of importance in the case of a Public Company, which will try to appeal to the investor to place funds with the company.

Voting rights are commonly restricted to the Ordinary Shareholders, though Preference Shareholders often get voting rights during any period when their dividend is unpaid for some reason as a feature of the terms of the shares.

It must be observed that with both Public and Private Companies the bonus of limited liability is conferred only on the understanding that the capital fund of the company is maintained intact. This means that capital must not be returned to shareholders as dividend. Dividends should only be paid out of profits periodically determined by preparing accounts, as recommended by the directors and as approved by the voting shareholders in general meeting.

The Articles may give the directors power to pay *interim* dividends which would be paid to shareholders during the year. Other dividends are usually paid after the end of the business year.

Debentures

In addition to issuing shares, a company may issue debentures, which are acknowledgements of *loans* made to the company. The debenture-holder, unlike the shareholder, is a *creditor*, with all a creditor's remedies that enable them to collect on their debt.

Debentures issued by companies incorporated under the Companies Acts are usually redeemable at a future date. Meantime, the debenture-holder is entitled to receive interest at a fixed rate per cent whether or not profits exist in a particular year out of which to pay it.

A further feature of debentures is that the holders are almost always *secured* creditors. This means that the company pledges or charges some part of its property (e.g. its factory premises) in favour of such creditors specifically. They may therefore, on default by the company, appoint a Receiver (called a Receiver for debenture-holders) and realize the security to obtain the best value for it and repay themselves out of the proceeds.

Therefore an issue of debentures, because of the minimum risk of loss to the holder, may enable money to be *borrowed* at a rate of interest relatively low in comparison with the rate of dividend paid on Preference and Ordinary *Shares*.

Unsecured loan stock

Many companies, particularly well-known public companies, are able to borrow without the necessity of providing any security. There will be negotiated rates of interest and repayment terms but the liability is sufficiently different from that associated with debentures for a separate classification to be justified.

Books of Account

STATUTORY BOOKS

The Companies Acts require every company to keep proper Books of Account to record its:

- cash receipts and payments
- trading purchases and sales
- assets and liabilities.

Proper Books of Account are necessary to give a true and fair view of the state of the company's affairs and to explain its transactions. They may be kept in bound books, loose cards, or in computer readable form so long as they provide an accurate, accessible record of the transactions.

The *Statutory Books* of the company similarly required to be kept include:

- the Register of Members
- the Register of Charges (e.g. Debentures)
- the Register of Directors and Secretaries
- separate Minute Book for meetings of directors, and of shareholders.

The **Register of Members** is the principal statutory book in which particulars are to be kept of members, their shareholdings, transfers, etc.

Access to the **Register of Charges** is clearly a help to an unsecured creditor or other person giving credit to the company, enabling them to see what part of the company's property is already charged.

Accounts and audit

The Directors of both Public and Private Companies must once in each year present to the company in a **General Meeting** an Income Statement.

A Statement of Financial Position made up to the same date must also be presented, together with a report of the directors as to their dividend recommendations and the general state of the company's affairs.

The Statement of Financial Position must contain a summary of the Authorized and Issued Share Capital of the company, and particulars of the general nature of its Assets and Liabilities. The Companies Acts lay down detailed requirements as to the contents of Statement of Financial Position and Income Statement.

Every company must at each annual general meeting appoint an Auditor, or Auditors, who must in general belong to a professional body of accountants recognized by the appropriate government department to be qualified to perform audits. If the company fits the definition of a small company (this varies from time to time but currently is – meeting two of the following three criteria: turnover of the company is less than £6.5 million, balance sheet total not more than £3.26 million and not more than 50 employees on average) then the company can usually opt for a review by an auditor rather than a full audit of the accounts. It will do this because it is usually cheaper to have a review undertaken rather than a full audit. The Auditors report to the members on the accounts examined by them, and have a right of access at all times to the books, accounts and vouchers of the company.

Remember this

In practice there are occasions where even small companies have to have an audit or shareholders (owning at least 10% of the shares) can demand one if they wish. Check these details out on the www.gov.uk website if they apply to you (see https://www.gov.uk/audit-exemptions-for-private-companies).

Let's illustrate these requirements with an example.

Example 19.1

From the following particulars, prepare a Statement of Financial Position of Wick Plc at 30 November xx12, grouping the Assets and Liabilities in the form required by the Companies Acts:

	£
12% Debentures, repayable xx26	20 000.00
Cash at bank	4 911.00
Inventory, 30 November xx12	34 009.00
Goodwill, at cost	30 800.00
40 000 5.6% Preference shares	40 000.00
80 000 Ordinary shares	80 000.00
Doubtful Debts provision	500.00
Contingent liability on bills discounted	250.00
Accounts receivable	12 350.00
Freeholds, at cost	32 750.00
Accounts payable	6 692.00
Profit and Loss Account, 1 December xx11 (Cr)	14 900.00
Plant and machinery, at cost, less depreciation, provided to date (£20 000) 1 December xx11	54 600.00
Deposit with Local Authority	9 800.00
Additions to plant and machinery, at cost	742.00
Profit for the year, *less* Dividends on Preference shares	7 600.00
Depreciation for the year	10 000.00

The Authorized Capital of the company is 50 000 5.6% Preference Shares of £1, and 100 000 Ordinary Shares of £1.

Remember that the presentation of tangible Non-current Assets should include the cost and aggregate depreciation provided to the date of the Statement of Financial Position.

There is also the requirement to distinguish between Current Liabilities, those due to be paid within one year from the Statement of Financial Position date and those not due to be paid until one year or longer after the Statement of Financial Position date.

You should obtain a copy of the published accounts of a public company for a more detailed example of modern presentation. These can readily be found on the websites of most large companies.

WICK PLC
Statement of Financial Position
at 30 November xx12

Non-current Assets	Cost	Depreciation	Net Book Value
	£	£	£
Intangible Asset Goodwill	30 800.00	–	30 800.00
Tangible Assets Freehold land	32 750.00	–	32 750.00
Plant and machinery	75 342.00	30 000.00	45 342.00
Total Fixed Assets	£138 892.00	£30 000.00	108 892.00

Current Assets		
Inventory	34 009.00	
Accounts receivable, less doubtful debts		
provision (£500.00)	11 850.00	
Local Authority Deposit	9 800.00	
Cash and Bank Balance	4 911.00	
	60 570.00	
deduct Accounts payable – amounts due within one year	6 962.00	
Net Current Assets		53 608.00
Total assets less current liabilities		162 500.00
deduct Accounts payable – amounts due after one year. 10% Debentures repayable xx26		20 000.00
Net Assets		£142 500.00

Represented by
Capital and Reserves

Share Capital	Authorized	Issued and Fully Paid
	£	£
5.6% Preference Shares of £1.00	50 000.00	40 000.00
Ordinary Shares of £1.00	100 000.00	80 000.00
	£150 000.00	£120 000.00

Reserves	
Profit and Loss Account	22 500.00
	£142 500.00

Notes: There is a contingent liability of £250.00 in respect of Bills discounted. There should also be presented the corresponding amounts at the end of the immediately preceding financial year for all items shown in the Statement of Financial Position. In practice it is unlikely that the pence columns would be shown.

▶ **Example 19.2**

The following is the Statement of Financial Position at 30 June xx10, of Bleak House & Co:

	£	£		£	£
Non-current Assets			*Capital accounts*		
Goodwill	63 000		B Bleak	74 000	
Plant & machinery	4 000		H House	29 000	
		67 000			103 000
Current Assets			*Current liabilities*		
Inventory	42 140		Accounts payable	8 440	
Accounts receivable	20 780		Bankers	18 600	
Cash	120	63 040			27 040
		£130 040			£130 040

The partners shared profits and losses three-fifths to B Bleak and two-fifths to H House.

A private limited company, Bleak House Ltd, was formed to buy the business as from 1 July xx10, the purchase price being £106 000. All the Assets and Liabilities were taken over at book values, except the Goodwill and the Plant and Machinery. Plant and Machinery were valued for the purpose of the Sale and Purchase Agreement at £58 000.

For the amount due to him, B Bleak received 20 000 5.6% Preference Shares of £1 each, valued at £1 each, in the new company, and the balance in cash.

H House received the whole of his share in £1 Ordinary Shares, allotted at par, except for £3200 paid to him in cash.

In addition to the above, 30 000 Preference Shares were issued to the public at par for cash, and 60 000 Ordinary Shares at a premium of £0.10 per share; these issues were subscribed and paid up in full (see below).

You are required to record the above in the books of Bleak House Ltd and to give the commencing Statement of Financial Position of the new company.

This is an example of the sale of a partnership to a company. A value will have been agreed for the Tangible Assets and Liabilities to give an agreed Net Asset amount. This is less than the amount of the purchase consideration so the excess must represent the payment made for goodwill. The example also uses the vertical format for the Statement of Financial Position.

▲ Solution to Example 19.2
Books of Bleak House Ltd

B. BLEAK AND H. HOUSE – VENDORS

Dr		£	£			£	£	Cr
xx10				xx10				
July 1	Accounts payable		8 440.00	July 1	Sundry Assets:			
	Bankers		18 600.00		Cash	120.00		
	Balance c/d		94 000.00		Accounts receivable	20 780.00		
					Inventory	42 140.00		
					Fixed assets	58 000.00		
							121 040.00	
			£121 040.00				£121 040.00	
				July 1	Balance b/d		94 000.00	
					Goodwill		12 000.00	
July 1	*B Bleak:*							
	5.6% Preference shares	20 000.00						
	Cash	55 800.00	75 800.00					
	H House:							
	Ordinary shares	27 000.00						
	Cash	3 200.00	30 200.00					
			£106 000.00				£106 000.00	
								[Continued]

GOODWILL

Dr		£	Cr
xx10			xx10
B Bleak and H House		12 000.00	

5.6% PREFERENCE SHARES

Dr		Cr
		£
	xx10	
	July 1 B Bleak	20 000.00
	1 Applications and allotments	30 000.00
		£50 000.00

ORDINARY SHARES

Dr		Cr
		£
	xx10	
	July 1 H House	27 000.00
	1 Applications and allotments	60 000.00
		£87 000.00

APPLICATIONS AND ALLOTMENTS

Dr		Ordinary	Preference			Cr Ordinary	Preference
xx10		£	£	xx10		£	£
July 1	Share capital A/cs	60 000.00	30 000.00	July 1	Cash	66 000.00	30 000.00
July 1	Share premium A/c	6 000.00	–				
		£66 000.00	£30 000.00			£66 000.00	£30 000.00

SHARE PREMIUM ACCOUNT

Dr		Cr
		£
	xx10	
	July 1 Applications and allotments	£6 000.00

CASH BOOK

Dr		£	£			Cr	£
xx10				xx10			
July 1	B Bleak and H House		120.00	July 1	B Bleak and H House		18 600.00
1	Applications and Allotments			1	B Bleak		55 800.00
	Ordinary shares	66 000.00		1	H House		3 200.00
	Preference shares	30 000.00		1	Balance c/d		18 520.00
			96 000.00				
			£96 120.00				£96 120.00
	Balance b/d		18 520.00				

There would also be accounts for accounts payable, accounts receivable, inventory.

BLEAK HOUSE LTD

Statement of Financial Position

at 1 July xx10

	£	£
Non-current Assets		
Intangible asset Goodwill		12 000.00
Tangible assets Plant and machinery at cost		58 000.00
		70 000.00
Current Assets		
Inventory	42 140.00	
Accounts receivable	20 780.00	
Cash	18 520.00	
	81 440.00	
Deduct Accounts payable – amounts due within one year	8 440.00	
Net Current Assets		73 000.00
Total Assets less Liabilities		143 000.00
Representing		
Share Capital and Reserves		

Share Capital	*Authorized*	*Issued and Fully Paid*	
	£	£	
5% Preference shares of £1.00	50 000.00	50 000.00	
Ordinary shares of £1.00	100 000.00	87 000.00	
	£150 000.00		137 000.00
Share premium account			6 000.00
			143 000.00

Note: in future years comparative figures will also be shown, usually consisting of at least the previous year's figures. This is the case for all companies normally.

	B Bleak	H House
	£	£
Prior to sale the partners' Capitals are	74 000.00	29 000.00
They share profits and losses as 3:2.		
They *lose* £9000.00 on revaluation of		
Plant and machinery	5 400.00	3 600.00
	68 600.00	25 400.00
The net worth of their business is thus reduced to £94 000.00		
But the Purchase Price is £106 000.00, a *profit* (in effect, Goodwill) of £12 000, shared in the profit-sharing ratio	7 200.00	4 800.00
	£75 800.00	£30 200.00

Alternatively: the partners were paid £106 000 in respect of capital of £103 000, a net gain of £3000, being a loss of £5000 on plant and gain of £8000 to £12 000 on goodwill. This gain of £3000 will be shared in the original profit-sharing ratio. The issue of shares to the public follows the normal debit to cash book, credit to liability accounts. The share premium, £0.10 per share, is credited to a separate account and the nominal amount, £1.00 per share, to the ordinary and preference share accounts.

Focus points

On completion of this chapter you should be aware:

✳ of the nature of limited liability status of companies and how a company is established

✳ of the differences between Public and Private Limited Companies

✳ of the major types of shares a company can issue

✳ of the statutory requirement to keep certain records and books

✳ that the principles of presentation for company accounts usually provide the 'best practice' for any accounts, subject to the extra information which must be provided when the public have a legitimate interest

✳ that the bookkeeping entries to record the change to a limited company are related to the capital structure only. All the earlier chapters are relevant to companies, sole traders and partnerships.

Testing Yourself

1   AB & Co Ltd has an authorized Capital of £8000, divided into 8000 Ordinary Shares of £1 each. On 31 December xx13, 6000 shares had been issued and fully paid, and there were also balances on the books of the Company in respect of the following:

	£
Sales	40 350.00
Purchases	14 128.00
Wages	13 084.00
Inventory (1 January xx13)	746.00
Salaries	6 525.00
Rent	2 135.00
Rates	1 348.00
Insurance	729.00
Repairs	37.00
Debenture interest	75.00
Bank charges	14.00
Travelling expenses	197.00
Sundries	188.00
Goodwill, at cost	3 000.00
Patents, at cost	2 506.00
Plant and machinery, at cost	1 240.00
Experimental account (asset)	1 777.00
Accounts receivable	2 316.00
Accounts payable	846.00
Bank overdraft	187.00
5% Debenture	2 000.00
Preliminary expenses	142.00
Profit and Loss Account (liability) at 1 January xx13	804.00

Inventory, as taken on 31 December xx13, amounted to £911, but includes an item of £65 for catalogues, the invoice for which has not yet been passed through the books.

The charges for Carriage Inwards, amounting to £102, have been debited to Sundries Account.

You are requested to prepare a Trading, Profit and Loss Account for the year ended 31 December xx13, providing 5% depreciation on Plant and Machinery, and £84 for Bad Debts. It is required to provide 2½% for discounts to be allowed to Accounts receivable, ignoring any provision of a similar kind for Accounts payable.

2 Tompkins, the accountant of Gloria Tubes Ltd, submits to you the following Revenue Account of the Company for the year ended 28 February xx15.

Dr			Cr
	£		£
Wages	28 200.00	Balance of Profit, 1 March xx14	1 250.00
Purchases	12 500.00	Inventory, 28 February xx15	2 350.00
Salaries	13 468.00	Rates, prepaid	21.00
Commission	2 803.00	Sales	61 550.00
Rates	3 105.00	Discounts received	125.00
Carriage inwards	180.00		
Repairs and maintenance	217.00		
Inventory, 1 March xx14	2 120.00		
Depreciation: £			
Plant, 10% 710.00			
Fixtures, 5% 195.00			
Lorries, 20% 280.00	1 185.00		
Directors' fees	105.00		
Packing and carriage	486.00		
Insurance	87.00		
Debenture interest	60.00		
Bank interest	22.00		
Sundry expenses	308.00		
Profit	450.00		
	£65 296.00		£65 296.00

The authorized capital of the Company is £15 000, in shares of £1 each. Of these, 14 951 have been issued as fully paid to the vendor, who is the managing director, and his wife.

A 6% Debenture for £1000 is outstanding in favour of the managing director's wife.

£1452 is owing to suppliers, and £2500 by customers. In respect of the latter 2% is to be providedfor as bad debt provision. At 28 February xx15, the Company had £1767 in the Bank, while at 1 March xx14, the book values and original cost of the Fixed Assets were:

	£	£
Plant	7100.00	7500.00
Fixtures	3900.00	4200.00
Lorry	1400.00	2000.00

Prepare in proper form Trading, Profit and Loss Account for the year ended 28 February xx15, and a Statement of Financial Position at that date.

3 The authorized capital of the Waterloo Engineering Co Ltd is £80 000 in £1 shares. The Trial Balance was extracted from the Company's books as on 31 March xx14.

You are required to prepare the Manufacturing Account, Profit and Loss Account and Statement of Financial Position of the Company after taking into consideration the following items:

a The item 'Delivery Expenses' includes £175 in respect of the subsequent trading period.
b Wages £515 and Directors' Fees £100 are outstanding.
c No provision has been made for the half-year's Debenture Interest due on 31 March xx14.
d The Machinery and Plant is to be depreciated at the rate of 10% of the original cost of £36 450 and the Lorry is to be written down to £3000 being half of the original cost.
e The Bank Statement shows on 31 March xx14 a credit of £15 for Interest on Deposit, but this item has not been entered in the Company's books.

f The General Reserve is to be increased by £2000.

g The Inventory held on 31 March xx14 was valued at £8765. Ignore income tax.

	Dr	Cr
	£	£
Issued capital (60 000 shares)		60 000.00
Sales		138 980.00
Land and buildings	30 000.00	
Machinery and plant	29 530.00	
Accounts receivable and payable	30 059.00	8 131.00
Purchases	46 150.00	
Interim dividend	3 000.00	
Delivery expenses	3 910.00	
Inventory, 31 March xxx3	5 782.00	
Discounts	1 537.00	729.00
Returns inwards	1 100.00	
Salaries	2 697.00	
Travellers' commission and expenses	3 740.00	
Profit and Loss Account, 31 March xxx3		2 530.00
Lorries	3 987.00	
5% Debentures 2000/04		20 000.00
Rent and rates (factory £1650, office £224)	1 874.00	
Wages	61 846.00	
General expenses	892.00	
Factory power and light	2 839.00	
Debenture interest	500.00	
General reserve		6 000.00
Repairs to machinery	1 421.00	
Directors' fees	300.00	
Bank deposit account	3 500.00	
Bank current account	1 696.00	
	£236 370.00	£236 370.00

The analysis and interpretation of accounts

In this chapter you will learn:

▶ *About ratio analysis*

▶ *How to calculate and interpret ratios*

▶ *That ratios must be interpreted in the context of each business*

Objective

This chapter explains the importance of the accounts to the proprietor and manager of a business. It describes how to obtain additional information from the accounts by the calculation and use of ratios.

Much of what you have read so far concerns the recording of business transactions from the earliest stage in the Books of Prime Entry to the preparation of the Final Accounts.

It is important, however, that we don't lose sight of the fact that a key role for accounts is that they may assist the proprietor and/or manager of the business to make decisions about its operation, and their involvement in the business. We should try to regard the records made as telling a story of what has happened in a business and telling it in a clear and intelligible manner.

A very simple instance of this is seen in the ordinary Ledger Account. Having taken note of the account's heading we should be able to describe to anyone interested not only the nature of the entries appearing in it, but also the final result of the transactions, both from the personal and the impersonal aspect.

▶ **Example 20.1**

Here is a customer's account as shown in the Sales Ledger. By looking at this account you should be able to describe what activities have occurred relating to this customer in this period. At the beginning of the year £50 was owed by him, and a month later he returned goods to the value of £10, further goods being supplied to him on 28 February.

On 10 March, he remits a sum of £20, which is stated to be 'on account' – in itself often a sign of weakness. Despite this, goods are again invoiced to him on 3 May, and on 4 June a cheque is received for the balance of what was due as far back as 1 January.

The bank subsequently reports that the cheque has not been met, and Brown is accordingly debited with the amount of the cheque *and* discount.

Between then and 8 August, he either settles with his creditors as a whole, or is made bankrupt. A first and final dividend of £0.25 in the £ is received, and £0.75 in the £ has to be written off as a Bad Debt.

H. BROWN

Dr								Cr
Date	Details	Fo	Amount	Date	Details	Fo	Amount	
xx11			£	xx11			£	
Jan 1	Balance		50.00	Feb 1	Returns		10.00	
Feb 28	Goods		25.00	March 10	Cash on A/c		20.00	
May 3	Goods		15.00	June 4	Bank		19.50	
June 7	Bank, cheque returned		19.50		Discount		0.50	
7	Discount		0.50	Aug 8	Bank, First and Final Dividend of £0.25 in the £		15.00	
				31	Bad Debts		45.00	
			£110.00				£110.00	

The analysis of individual accounts in this way is therefore useful to a business in performing its regular activities.

Analysis of the Final Accounts

The Income Statement (otherwise called the Trading, Profit and Loss Account) and Statement of Financial Position, representing the logical conclusion of a complete cycle of the bookkeeping work, provide principal documents for analysis.

To deal firstly with the Trading Account part of the Income Statement, the following may have to be considered:

▶ How does the sales figure compare with that of the previous year, or other period, and how far have alterations in selling prices contributed to any difference noted?

- Similarly as regards purchases and the cost of materials bought.

- Is the closing inventory much in excess of that held at the beginning of the year, and if so, in a manufacturing business, to what extent do they consist of raw material or the finished product? In the former case, have purchases been made in anticipation of a rise in the price of materials? In the latter case, is the turnover partly seasonal so that a large part of the stock is sold early in the following trading period? What is the average stock carried, and what is its relation to the turnover?

- Does the business earn a fairly consistent rate of Gross Profit, expressed as a percentage to turnover? If less than the usual Gross Profit is earned, is it because selling prices have declined or because the closing stock is valued at the then market price which is below the original cost?

- Should the Gross Profit percentage rise, is the cause to be found in more favourable selling prices, or in an improper inflation of closing stock values?

The Profit and Loss Account

This section of the Income Statement includes, as we have seen, the indirect or 'overhead' expenses of the business.

To a large extent these do not vary in proportion to the sales or turnover figure, and therefore it is always necessary to watch carefully the individual items, and the total to which they amount. These figures must be covered each trading period irrespective of the performance of the business.

Broadly speaking, the Profit and Loss Account part of the Income Statement is concerned with the reconciliation of **Gross** and **Net Profit**. Stated in another way, Gross Profit may be said to consist of the indirect expenses and Net Profit.

INDIRECT EXPENSES

To assist scrutiny, some suitable arrangement of these expenses is most desirable. Subheadings may be inserted, such as:

1 *Production Expenses*
  Factory Rent, Rates, etc.
  Repairs to Plant
  Depreciation of Plant, etc.

2 *Selling and Distribution Expenses*
  Travellers' Salaries and Commission
  Travelling Expenses
  Rent of Show Rooms, etc.

3 *General or Administrative Expenses*
  Office Salaries
  Bank Interest
  Depreciation of Office Furniture, etc.

A classification of the Profit and Loss Debits in this way is much more helpful than a mere haphazard listing of the balances on the various Ledger Accounts.

NET PROFIT
This is of importance because it represents:

▷ the amount which the proprietor may withdraw in the form of cash, and still leave their Capital intact

▷ the net yield on the Capital invested, which may conveniently be stated as a percentage return on that Capital.

The net earnings of the business can only be determined after including all expenses, and all forms of income, as we saw in Chapter 14, and clearly the proprietor will expect to receive something in excess of the rate of interest obtainable from the investment of an equivalent amount of capital in, say, gilt-edged securities or a building society. How much more should be expected will largely depend on the degree of risk to which his business Capital is exposed in each particular case.

The Statement of Financial Position
A point to be borne in mind is that the Income Statement and the Statement of Financial Position should be read together. Each serves to explain and interpret the other. As an example, if a profit is disclosed at the end of the period, it must be reflected in an increase of the Net Assets. If a loss has been sustained,

these Assets will be less at the end of the period than they were at the beginning. Further, when depreciation is charged in the Income statement, not only will the profit figure be reduced, but the book value of the Non-current Asset in question will similarly be reduced in the Statement of Financial Position.

The Statement of Financial Position is concerned with showing the position of the business *at a particular date*. That position may substantially alter on the day after its preparation, or it may be materially different on the day before it was prepared. The most informative Balance Sheet is that which gives the typical or average state of affairs but this may not always be the one produced and published by a business operating in the commercial world.

When analysing a Statement of Financial Position we may well begin with the Liabilities: Who is interested in the business as a provider of Capital? Apart from the liability to the proprietor on Capital Account, there may be amounts due to trade creditors, and to bankers. The latter liabilities rank ahead of the former, and the proprietor will usually have to wait until all other claims are met before he can recover any part of his original investment.

The proportion of the Proprietor's Capital to other liabilities should also be noted. If relatively large sums are due to suppliers and others, the position must be further investigated by reference to the total Assets available, and their division between Non-current and Current Assets.

Just as liabilities may be divided between Non-current or Deferred Liabilities (those in favour of the proprietors) and Current Liabilities (those owed to creditors), so it is from the Current or Floating Assets that the creditors primarily look for payment.

We have already considered the distinction between Non-current and Current Assets and the following example introduces other points.

▶ Example 20.2

The Statement of Financial Position of T, a haulage contractor, at 28 February xx14, is set out here.

Non-current Assets

	£	£
Leasehold warehouse, offices, sheds, etc., at cost, 1 March xxx0		3 511.00
Motor vehicles, at cost		
less Depreciation, at cost		
1 March xx13	£5 700.00	
Less Depreciation	2 037.00	3 663.00
Total fixed assets		7 174.00

Current Assets

	£	£
Inventory of fuel, oil, waste, etc., as estimated by T	495.00	
Accounts receivable, gross	2 606.00	
Insurance prepaid	15.00	
Cash in hand	29.00	3 145.00
		£10 319.00

T Capital

	£	£
Balance forward	£7 350.00	
Add Profit for year	1 750.00	
	9 100.00	
Less Drawings	1 600.00	7 500.00

Current Liabilities

	£	£
Accounts payable	2 118.00	
Accrued expenses	432.00	
Western Bank Ltd	269.00	2 819.00
		£10 319.00

You are required:

- ▶ to comment carefully upon the position disclosed
- ▶ to draw up a statement showing the amount of the Net Current Assets.

1 ANALYSIS AND COMMENT

The **Profit** for the year is more than 20% of the Capital. Before accepting this as good news, we should look at the **Assets** of the business and the basis of their valuation to ensure this 'headline' figure provides us with a true picture of the activity of the company over the period reported upon.

The first item, Leasehold Warehouse, Office, etc., is stated at cost six years ago. No provision for depreciation has been made by reference to the term of the lease.

By contrast, Motor Vehicles has been depreciated, but we do not know the rate. A proper figure for depreciation would probably be from 15% to 20% of the original cost, i.e. on the straight-line method (see Chapter 15).

The inventory is shown 'as estimated'. Estimates may be good or bad, and information should be sought as to whether the quantities or values, or both, have been estimated, and whether the values are in line with cost or market price, whichever was the lower at the date of the Statement of Financial Position.

As the Book Debts are described 'gross', their full face value has clearly been taken, and there is no provision made for Doubtful Debts. The amount of this provision should be estimated as described in Chapter 14. It would then be a charge in the Income Statement, and would reduce the value of Book Debts.

It would seem that the profit for the year may be over-stated because of possible over-valuations of the Assets mentioned above. You should obtain answers to each question posed before being comfortable with the headline profit figure.

Lastly, there is a pressing need for the collection of the Book Debts to provide money out of which to pay the trade creditors and accrued expenses. The extent of this urgency will in part depend on the limit set to the Overdraft facilities the company receives from its bank.

2 STATEMENT OF NET CURRENT ASSETS

This may be drawn up as follows:

Net Current Assets (or net working capital)		£
Inventory of Fuel, oil, etc., as estimated		495.00
Accounts receivable (gross)		2606.00
Insurance prepaid		15.00
Cash in hand		29.00
		£3145.00
Deduct:		
	£	
Accounts payable	2118.00	
Accrued expenses	432.00	
Western Bank Ltd	269.00	
		2819.00
Total net current assets		£326.00

The insurance prepaid is an asset at the date of the Statement of Financial Position. If the business was discontinued it could be recovered from the insurance company and if the business carries on then the following period will receive the benefit of it.

It will usually be useful to calculate other ratios or percentages in addition to the Profit Margin. Current Assets as a multiple of Current Liabilities (i.e. 3145/2819 = 1.12 times), which implies that virtually all the inventory and accounts receivable would need to be turned into cash to enable the creditors (short term) to be paid. This is a lower value for the ratio than would be ideal in most businesses and might cause concern to the creditors.

Similarly, Permanent capital as a multiple of Fixed Assets 7500/7174 = 1.05 times which means that the permanent capital is nearly all used to finance the Non-current Assets, with virtually the whole of the Current Assets being financed by the short term creditors.

RATIO ANALYSIS

The extent of analysis that can be performed on a business's accounts is virtually unlimited. There are many ratios which can be calculated to quantify the relationships between items in the Income Statement and the Statement of Financial Position. In practice, a limited set of ratios are usually used to provide most analysis you may need. We will illustrate the main ratios, and their interpretation, in this section.

Gross profit margin and return on capital employed have been mentioned earlier (also see Chapters 3 and 12). They are related by the net asset turnover (the same as the capital turnover as net assets equal capital employed).

GP margin = Gross Profit/Sales

Return (Gross) on capital = Gross Profit/Capital employed

Asset turnover = Sales/Capital empoyed (same as Net Assets)

Example 20.3

P James produces the following Income Statement and Statement of Financial Position:

INCOME STATEMENT
for the year ended 31 December xx12

	£		£
Opening inventory	10 000	Sales (all credit)	177 000
Purchases (all credit)	120 000		
	130 000		
Less closing inventory	12 000		
Cost of Sales	118 000		
Gross Profit c/d	59 000		
	177 000		177 000
Wages	35 000	Gross Profit b/d	59 000
Administrative Expenses	1 800		
Light and Heat	400		
Telephone	250		
Rates	1 200		
Repairs and Renewals	800		
Motor Vehicle Expenses	1 100		
Depreciation M/Vehicles	3 000		
Fixtures/Fittings	1 450		
Net Profit	14 000		
	59 000		59 000

STATEMENT OF FINANCIAL POSITION
as at 31 December xx12

	£		£
Non-current Assets		**Capital**	
Freehold Premises	49 900	as at 1.1.12	86 000
Motor Vehicles 15 000–6000	9 000	Add Profit for year	14 000
Fixtures/Fittings 7250–2900	4 350		100 000
	63 250	Less Drawings	9 250
			90 750
Current Assets	£	**Current Liabilities**	
Inventory	12 000	Accounts payable	10 000
Accounts receivable	22 125		
Bank	3 375 37 500		
	£100 750		£100 750

The basic ratios can be calculated:

Gross Profit margin	*59/177 = 0.3333, or 33.33%*
Net Profit margin	*14/177 = 0.0791, or 7.91%*

Gross return on capital employed. Which capital figure should be used? That at the beginning of the year, the end or an average? Technically an average would be appropriate but usually the opening amount is used as the capital account is not normally adjusted until the year end. In this example this would be £86 000.

	59/86 = 0.6860, or 68.60%
or for **Net returns**	*14/86 = 0.1628, or 16.28%*

The **net asset turnover**, which indicates how often the capital employed in the business is 'turned over' or sold, during the year is

177/86 = 0.0206, or 2.06 times

Using the gross figures we can now see that the gross margin to sales of 33.33% was earned 2.06 times during the year to give a return on capital employed of 2.06 × 33.33 which equals 68.6% approx. Similarly with the net basis, 2.06 × 7.91% = 16.3%, approx.

Profit margin	times	Asset turnover	equals	Return
$\dfrac{Profit}{Sales}$	×	$\dfrac{Sales}{Capital}$	=	$\dfrac{Profit}{Capital}$

This relationship explains how some businesses, for example, food retailing, may only earn a small profit margin to sales but have a very rapid turnover, and so earn this small margin several times a year to give a good annual return on Capital employed. A manufacturer with a much longer payment cycle from credit customers requires a much higher profit margin to obtain the same overall return on Capital employed.

Other ratios that may be calculated include:

Inventory turnover

Cost of sales / average stock which is (10 + 12)/2 = 11
118   / 11 = 10.7 times, or nearly once a month.

This may be good, as it means that the stock is turning over very quickly meaning we do not have the cash resources of the business tied up in unsold inventory for long, so it is unlikely that there will be any obsolete inventory, or it could mean that there is often not enough choice for prospective customers to choose from so that sales are being lost.

Non-current asset turnover

Sales / Non-current assets
177   / 632.5 = 2.8 times, a much lower rate than for the inventory.

We may wish to ask ourselves if we have excess capacity. Could we sublet or sell surplus premises?

Current ratio, sometimes called **working capital ratio**

Current assets / Current liabilities
37.5   / 10 = 3.75 times or 3.75:1

An ideal value should be around 2:1 (although this will vary, based on products produced and industry operating within) so this value may be high. A high value suggests that you will be able to pay the creditors on time and that will encourage them to give you good service. A low value suggests you may struggle to pay your short-term debts from your current assets. This can be fatal for any business.

Liquid ratio, similar to the current ratio but excludes stock.

Debtors and cash / Current liabilities
25.5   / 10 = 2.5 times or 2.5:1

Two other useful ratios from the many that are available relate to the amount of credit allowed to debtors and received from creditors.

Debtors at 31.12. xx12 £22 125.

Sales during the year £177 000, per month £177 000/12 = 14 750

Average credit allowed is 22 125/14 750 = 1.5 months. Most businesses would be very pleased with this ratio if, as is the case with James, all sales are made on a credit basis. The longer this period, the longer James's cash is tied up in debts not available for other ones.

Before calculating the comparable figure for accounts payable we should consider what purchases are supplied by the accounts payable. Is it merely the goods for resale, £120 000 in the year, or should some of the expenses be included. If only the purchases (and this is the only item that the data tells us is purchased on credit) then *monthly purchases on credit are 120 000/12 = 10 000, and*

Average credit received is

Accounts payable at 31.12. xx12/Average monthly purchases on credit 10 000/10 000 = 1 month, which seems reasonable.

All these ratios use figures from the accounts. Those from the Income Statement are those for the whole year, and there may have been seasonal factors or expansion during the year. The Statement of Financial Position values are those on one specific date and may not necessarily be representative of each figure throughout the year. We must consider this when using any figures in our ratios from the Statement of Financial Position.

What is 'normal', or more importantly, what should the value be in order to calculate truly representative ratios from final accounts? Several figures in the accounts will reflect particular policies adopted by the management, or be different in different industries, and the basic comparison should be with the value that was expected rather than necessarily with other companies in different industries unless care is taken to ensure comparability of the figures used. If there is a significant difference from expected results then a more detailed analysis must be made of the components making up the ratio.

What is a good ratio, what is a bad ratio? Again it largely depends on what was expected based on your understanding of the business and its environment. A high liquidity ratio means that your creditors can be paid promptly but would it be better to have more stock to sell? A manufacturer with spare capacity can accept an order for quick delivery, but what if no customer places that order?

It is important to bear in mind that no two businesses are the same. Although ratios from one business can be compared with another, they should not be taken out of the context of the other ratios and information available about the business if you are to avoid misunderstanding what the accounts are telling you.

Testing yourself

1 A trader's Capital appears on the 'liabilities' side of the Statement of Financial Position. In what sense is it true that the Capital is a liability of the business?

   What would you infer if the trader's Statement of Financial Position (assumed correctly drawn up) showed the Capital on the 'Assets' side?

2 Give an example of one of each of the following:

   a Non-current Asset
   b Current Asset

   Explain the difference (if any) in the purposes for which such Assets are held by a trader or manufacturer.

3 Suppose that you have been newly appointed to an administrative position in a wholesale merchanting business. What data would you call for, and what tests would you apply to this, in order to find out if the general financial position of the business is sound and healthy?

4 The following is an account taken from the Sales Ledger of Herbert Charleston. Explain clearly what information this account gives you.

LILIAN BRYAN

Dr		£			Cr £
xx 14		£	xx 14		£
Jan 1	Balance	102.00	Feb 3	Returns	21.00
March 3	Goods	336.00	April 4	Cheque	401.00
				Balance carried forward	16.00
		£438.00			£438.00
April 4	Balance forward	16.00	Sept 22	Cheque	164.00
June 23	Goods	141.00			
Aug 3	Interest charged	7.00			
		£164.00			£164.00
Sept 26	Cheque dishonoured	164.00	Nov 15	Bad Debts A/c 164.00	
		£164.00			£164.00

5 Briefly explain the meaning of the items shown in the following Ledger Account

E. SIMPSON – CAPITAL ACCOUNT

Dr					Cr
xx12		£	xx12		£
June 30	Cash drawings	2 200.00	Jan 1	Balance	3 636.00
Sept 30	Purchases, motor car for self	9 060.00	June 30	Cash	500.00
			Sept 30	Freehold property	11 225.00
Nov 30	Balance	4 116.00	Nov 30	A Graham	15.00
		£15 376.00			£15 376.00

Note: On 20 November, A Graham, a creditor, for goods supplied had agreed to accept a cash payment of £0.50 in the £ in full discharge of his account of £30.

6 Each year a firm calculates the following percentages:

a Gross profit per cent on sales

b Net profit on gross profit

c Net profit per cent on capital.

What information do you think is obtained from these calculations?

7 From the following figures which were extracted from the books of a manufacturer you are asked to prepare an account or statement in a form which will give the proprietor the maximum information as to his trading results, including the percentages of the various items to turnover, and to state what conclusions can be drawn from the figures:

Year end 30 September

	xx14	xx15
	£	£
Purchases of material	45 823.00	56 494.00
Wages: Productive	25 064.00	36 768.00
Non-productive	10 620.00	10 984.00
Returns inwards	472.00	1 903.00
Discount received	180.00	36.00
Salaries	11 560.00	15 584.00
Selling expenses	1 720.00	2 784.00
Discount allowed	420.00	492.00
Works expenses	3 176.00	3 456.00
Office expenses	6 370.00	8 420.00
Inventory at commencement of year	2 189.00	2 876.00
Sales	120 472.00	165 903.00

The Inventory of material at 30 September xx15 was valued at £1882.

8 Criticize, under the appropriate headings, any five of the items of the Balance Sheet of B M Downfield. In your opinion, is the financial position satisfactory? Give reasons for your answers.

Statement of Financial Position of BM Downfield
for xx15–xx16

Liabilities		£	Assets		£
Accounts payable	12 500.00		Cash		1 300.00
Bank	3 200.00		Bills receivable		2 680.00
Capital	1 040.00		Accounts receivable		3 200.00
			Inventory		6 860.00
			Plant	£2 000.00	
			and cost of repairs	200.00	2 200.00
			Fittings, cost price in xxx0		500.00
	£16 740.00				£16 740.00

9 The following accounts showing the result of a year's trading, with comparative figures for the preceding year, have been submitted to the proprietor of a manufacturing business, who has forwarded them to you for criticism. Rearrange the accounts in the form you consider will give the maximum information (showing also the percentages of the various expenses to turnover), and state any conclusions which can be drawn from the figures.

Income Statement

Year ended 31 Dec

	xx10 £	xx11 £		xx10 £	xx11 £
Inventory	2 105.00	2 001.00	Sales	50 000.00	48 000.00
Purchases	5 576.00	5 524.00	Inventory	2 001.00	1 495.00
Wages (productive)	15 500.00	15 400.00			
Works expenses	960.00	909.00			
Gross profit c/d	27 860.00	25 661.00			
	£52 001.00	£49 495.00		£52 001.00	£49 495.00
Rent and rates	3 700.00	3 720.00	Balance b/d	27 860.00	25 661.00
Wages (non-productive)	7 800.00	7 990.00			
Salaries	11 808.00	11 818.00			
Travellers' commission and expenses	920.00	900.00			
Office expenses	272.00	270.00			
Bad debts	200.00	414.00			
Net profit	3 160.00	549.00			
	£27 860.00	£25 661.00		£27 860.00	£25 661.00

Taking it further

General bookkeeping help

▶ *Basic Accounting* and *Small Business Accounting* – if, having completed this book, you are looking for other books that will extend your knowledge of the context of bookkeeping practice you may like to obtain copies of one or both of these related books in the *Teach Yourself* series. They look at other aspects of using accounts and operating the financial parts of a business as well as providing a revision of the key principles of bookkeeping.

▶ *Business Accounting* by Alan Sangster and Frank Wood (Pearson Education) – there are many textbooks that you can refer to that will extend your knowledge of bookkeeping practice. This is a particularly good one.

Other business advice and help

▶ HM Revenue and Customs – all manner of advice and assistance in all aspects of personal and business tax (http://www.hmrc.gov.uk).

▶ Accountants – a good accountant or other business adviser can be a useful asset for a small business. A good directory of accountants can be found on the Accountingweb website (http://www.accountingweb.co.uk).

▶ Banks – each UK bank, both High Street banks and now online banks, welcome small businesses and provide a range of advice and support from forming a business through issues of how to manage a successful business. You should visit the websites of each bank to see what they have to offer.

▶ Charity Commission – if you are operating a charity you will find much helpful advice on its financial management aspects from this body via its website (https://www.gov.uk/government/organisations/charity-commission).

- Federation of Small Businesses – a group for small businesses in the UK with more than 170,000 members providing a variety of advice and support (http://www.fsb.org.uk).

- Accountingeducation.com – an online community for those interested in studying or teaching accounting. All its services are free (http://www.accountingeducation.com).

Courses and qualifications

- LearnDirect – an excellent source of information about courses in bookkeeping available around the UK (http://www.learndirect.co.uk).

- Association of Accounting Technicians – established in 1980 to provide a recognized professional qualification and membership body for accounting technicians; the AAT now has more than 120 000 student, affiliate, full and fellow members worldwide (https://www.aat.org.uk/).

- Professional Accounting Qualifications – a number of professional bodies exist in the UK of which accountants can become members having completed various entry requirements which usually consist of passing a series of examinations in accounting, and related fields, and obtaining professional experience. These include:

  ▷ Institute of Chartered Accountants in England and Wales (ICAEW): http://www.icaew.co.uk

  ▷ Chartered Association of Management Accountants (CIMA): http://www.cimaglobal.com

  ▷ Association of Chartered Certified Accountants (ACCA): http://www.accaglobal.com

  ▷ Chartered Institute of Public Finance Accountants (CIPFA): www.cipfa.org

  ▷ Institute of Chartered Accountants of Scotland (ICAS): http://www.icas.org.uk

  ▷ Institute of Chartered Accountants of Ireland (ICAI): http://www.icai.ie

  ▷ Chartered Institute of Tax: http://www.tax.org.uk

- International Association of BookKeepers – IAB offers an internationally recognized qualification in bookkeeping: http://www.iab.org.uk.

- University qualifications – many universities offer degrees or diplomas in accounting areas. These can be obtained through a variety of study methods including part-time and evening study. For example, see the undergraduate and postgraduate degrees offered by the University of Birmingham (http://www.bham.ac.uk/business) or the various courses offered by the Open University (e.g. the 12-week course Introduction to Bookkeeping and Accounting or the one-year Professional Certificate in Accounting) (http://oubs.open.ac.uk).

Bookkeeping software

There are many bookkeeping and accounting software packages on the market from the very cheap (even free) software that may be given to you by your bank on opening an account with them, particularly a business account, to the very complex and very expensive systems operated by the largest, multinational businesses. The following represent the two main UK package suppliers for general purpose accounting software that provide useful basic services, which are widely used by individuals and businesses in the UK:

- Sage Accounting Packages – this company is the leading supplier of accounting packages in the UK. They offer a range of packages from the very small and straightforward to the complex. Some are offered on a modular basis so that you can buy only the services you wish to use. Other services can then be integrated into your accounting system later as your needs develop (http://www.sage.co.uk). A particularly good introductory guide to this is 'Get Started in Sage Line 50' by Mac Bride (*Teach Yourself*).

- QuickBooks – provided by Intuit UK this software claims more than 4 million global users for this suite of programs that covers all the basic needs you would have as a business for a basic accounting package (http://www.quickbooks.intuit.co.uk).

As an alternative to the packages that are hosted (in part at least) on your own computer, you may now opt for one of a number of good Cloud-based computing packages. These give you the advantage of being able to access your accounts across a range of devices, and when away from your office base. Common Cloud-based accounting packages include:

- Clearbooks (http://www.clearbooks.co.uk)

- Quicken Online (QBO: http://www.intuit.co.uk/quickbooks)

- Xero (http://www.xero.com)

- Freeagent/Iris openbooks (http://freeagent.com)

- Sage/One Accounts (http://www.sage.co.uk)

Other options also exist, and new products come to this new market regularly. Different products will fit different needs better. Most have trial or demo capability so you can try them out a bit first before you commit to using them.

NOTES

In all cases the latest price and other details for each of the above suggestions should be found by accessing their respective websites, as product ranges and specifications can change over time.

All website addresses are correct at the time of producing this book. If you find addresses no longer seem to operate try using a web search engine (e.g. http://www.google.com) with the title given above to find other possible information.

Neither the authors nor publishers of this book in any way recommend any of the above services or products. The above is provided only for information purposes and no responsibility will be accepted for the outcomes of any actions taken by users of this book based on this list.

Answers to questions

For reasons of space, the answers provided here are limited to double-entry and numerical answers only. Answers to other questions can be found in the text and in the sample solutions to examination papers (see next section).

Questions on Chapter 2

1. a Cash total £288.70, Cheques total £523.33, Total paid in £812.03
   b see Example 2.2

2. a Cash columns total £7988.16, Discount allowed £25, Bank cash book balance £4658.16
   b Lodgement not in bank £1325, unpresented cheques £1065

3. a £10,45; £5,4; £1,16: 50p,2; 20p,4; 5p,2; 1p,1
   b Total £487.91

4. (Note that the opening stock is valued at £12 per unit and all purchases are at £12 per unit; therefore ALL value amounts will be units multiplied by £12.)

   a see 'Inventory records'
   b Balance 10 units and £120
   c Adjustment –2 units, –£24. Inventory was perhaps stolen. If this is suspected a business may wish to explore this further!

Questions on Chapter 3

8. Total invoice value £48 + VAT 9.60 = £57.60

9. Total purchases £4719, goods £925

10. Total credit note value £323.75 goods plus VAT £64.75 = £388.50

11	a	A	£1200	B	£300
	b	A	20%	B	25%
	c	A	25%	B	33⅓%

12 Purchases

	Total	£14 541.25
	Goods	£13 791.25
	Sundries	£750.00

Purchase	Returns	Total £1008,	all goods
Sales	Total	£7598.00	
	Goods	£7580.00	
	Sundries	£18.00	
Sales	Returns	Total £10,	all sundries

Questions on Chapter 4

3 a Debit

  b Debit

  c Credit

  d Credit, normally, as Sales larger than Purchases

  e Credit

4 Debit balance of £829.00

5 a

	Goods	VAT
Purchases	£545.00	£109
Purchase returns	38.50	7.70
Sales	370.00	74.00
Sales returns	56.00	11.20

  b Due from Customs and Excise   £38.50

6 Sales £780Cr VAT £156Cr Customers £936Dr

7	a	Purchases	£950	Creditors	£950	Sales	£830	Debtors	£830
	b		950		1140		830		966

VAT £54Dr

8   £7623

Questions on Chapter 5

2   a   Credit landlord   b   Credit cash
        Debit rent   Debit rent
        Credit cash
        Debit landlord

3   Balance is £40.75 Dr being £48.50 minus £7.75 but all
    transactions should appear on the statement.

4   Dr Balances   Cash £63.50   Remember the Cash Book
                  Bank £94.85   is also the ledger account
                                but ledger accounts will be
                                needed for Abbott, stamps,
                                etc.

    Discount Dr £1.00 Cr £2.35

5   Dr Balances Cash £35.00 Bank £612.00
    Discount Dr £6.75 Cr £2.00

6   Cheque payment £354.90

7   Cash Dr Balance £8.75
    Bank Cr Balance £11.75

8   a   Dr side   Personal
                                    Impersonal
                                    Private

        Cr side   Impersonal
                                    Personal
                                    Personal
                                    Impersonal

9 Dr Balance £124.60
  Cr Balance Bank £267.15
  Discount Dr £1.25 Cr £2.50

10 a Plant A/c Debit
   b Robinson's personal A/c Credit
     Cash £170.00 and Discount allowed £2.60
   c Fire Loss A/c Credit
   d Motor Van A/c Credit
   e Fitter's personal A/c Debit
     Cash £250.00 and Discount received £10.75

Questions on Chapter 6

4 Extra expense £8.36 to give overdraft of £66.05

6 Cashbook £160 o/d

7 a Favourable Balance £65.82
  b Unfavourable Balance £233.96

8 Favourable Balance £80.39

Questions on Chapter 7

2 Nov 1 Cash from bank £195
  Total expenditure for month £330
  Dec 1 Cash from bank £330

3 Bank Balance £1646.38. Petty Cash Balance £100
  Total PC expenditure £66.72, Analysis £22.40, 12.65,
  20.72, 10.95
  Discount allowed £17.00, Discount received £15.00

Questions on Chapter 9

1 Balances in TB:

Capital Cr	£6 350.00
Cash Dr	£347.00
Bank Cr	£2 332.00
TB Totals	£20 155.00

2 Balances in TB:

Capital Cr	£10 000.00
Cash Dr	£50.00
Bank Dr	£3 165.95
TB Totals	£11 159.00

3 Balances in TB:

Capital Cr	£6 050.00
Cash Dr	£50.00
Bank Dr	£3 464.50
Discount Cr	£2.50
Discount Dr	£17.50
TB Totals	£7 974.40

4 Balances in TB:

Capital Cr	£4 510.80
Cash Dr	£250.00
Bank Dr	£117.95
Discount Cr	£19.50
Discount Dr	£1.75
TB Totals	£5 666.90

5 Balances in TB:

Capital Cr	£2 500.00
Cash Dr	£162.10
Bank Dr	£255.05
Discount Dr	£5.75
TB Totals	£6 131.30

(including opening and closing stock)

6 Balances in TB:

Capital Cr   £10 650.00
Cash Dr   £100.00
Bank Dr   £4 556.70
Discount Dr   £9.20
Discount Cr   £98.50
TB Totals   £13 474.00

7 Balances in TB:

Capital Cr   £2 000.00
Cash Dr   £23.50
Bank Dr   £5 853.50
Discount Dr   £2.45
Discount Cr   £6.25
TB Totals   £7 543.75

Questions on Chapter 10

4 £2 555.40

5 Short Credit £103.20

7 a Short Dr £12.25
  b Short Dr £5.35
  c None
  d Short Dr £0.50
  e Short Cr £40.00

8 TB Totals £49 546.00

9 TB Totals £27 952.00

10 Original Balance short Dr £122.25

Questions on Chapter 12

5 b £40.00 profit

6 Net Profit. Dept A   £72.00

                  B   £710.00

                  C   £226.00

Dr P/L A/c £8.00 Balance of general expenses

Questions on Chapter 13

1 **a** Short Debit £100.00: None: Short Debit £30.00

  b Debtors understated £100.00; Fixtures understated £212.00: Profit understated £242.00: Bank balance understated £30.00

3 Statement of Financial Position Totals £83 350.00

5 Capital £23 264.00
Net Profit £1994.00
Statement of Financial Position Totals £24 054.00

6 Gross Profit £15 700.00. Net Profit £5250.00
Statement of Financial Position Totals £12 750.00

7 Gross Profit £11 550.00. Net Profit £1100.00
Statement of Financial Position Totals £58 200.00

8 Gross Profit £10 108. Net Loss £1769
Statement of Financial Position Totals £12 557

9 Gross Profit £10 250.00 (33%)
Net Profit £1000.00 (3¼%)
Statement of Financial Position Totals £13 269.00

10 TB Totals £2717.00
Gross Profit £13.00. Net Loss £100.00
Statement of Financial Position Totals £2184.00

11 Gross Profit £14 349.00. Net Profit £2586.00
Statement of Financial Position Totals £8205.00

Questions on Chapter 14

3 Profits xx11 £22 517.00. xx12 £22 638.00

4 P/L Debit £2941.00

5 P/L Debit £214.50

6 P/L Debit £1461.75

7 Bad Debts £314.09. Reserve £234.83

9 P/L Dr xx11 £122 951.40
  xx12 £141 434.38
Omission overstates xx11 Profits and understates
Liabilities £3441.18

10 P/L Dr Rent £2360.00. Rates £1903.36

11 P/L Dr Rates £2580.00. Wages £48 562.00
Stationery, etc. £747.00
Bad Debts and Reserve £409.00
Discounts £107.54

12 P/L Dr £90.00

13 P/L Dr £1151.00. Payments in advance etc. £147.00
Accrued expenses £45.00

14 Profit £7580

Questions on Chapter 15

3 **a** Depreciation £1760 each year NBV after xx11 £1760
  b Depreciation £1760, 1408, 1126, 901 NBV after xx11
  £3605

4 P/L Dr xx12 £62.00

  xx13 £59.00

  xx14 £56.00

  xx15 £532.00

  xx16 £516.00 (net)

5 P/L Dr £1500.00 p.a. BS net £8500, £7000

6 Depreciation £3432.00 (calculating depreciation for a
half-year where appropriate). On new £81, on sold £9, on
Balance £3342
Profit on sale £9.00

7 Depreciation (nearest £) £2890.00
Loss on sale £2305.00

8 Depreciation £5000.00 p.a.

Interest   xx15 £1650.00

                xx16 £1100.00

                xx17 £550.00

9 Depreciation (opening Balances): xx11 £120.00

                                         xx12 £133.00

10 Gross Profit £35 545.00. Net Profit £10 013.00
139% on Capital
Statement of Financial Position Totals £17 816.00

11 Dr fixtures and fittings. Cr S Maxton and Sons
Dr Brampton Bros. Cr Perkins Ltd
Dr Cash £520.
    Typewriters £600. Cr Motor car £1120
Dr Profit and Loss. Cr Plant and machinery
Dr Cash £11. Cr O Carfax £11
    Bad Debt £44. O Carfax £44

12 Dr Lease £18 000. Cr Cash £18 000
Dr Cash £12 000. Cr Loan A/c £12 000
Dr Loan £250. Cr Cash (4 times) £250
Dr Interest payable £1175. Cr Cash £1175
Dr Profit and Loss Account £720. Cr Lease
Depreciation £720

13 £986.00 less £20.00 depreciation: £966.00

14 Profit £1306.00. Statement of Financial Position
Totals £3499.00

15 Gross Profit £2261.00. Net Profit £326.00
Statement of Financial Position Totals £37 918.00

Questions on Chapter 16

1 **a** £600, **b** £605, **c** £605

2 Draw £700, Dance £1790, Flower show £50, Refreshments
£990. Surplus £3820 after writing off crockery £100 and
capitalizing £1500. Club capital £4890

3　a　£420, **b**　£570 after depreciation of £(540 + 420).
Club capital £21 930

4　Surplus £32, after depreciation of £338
Club capital £3402

Questions on Chapter 18

4　Interest on Loan £150.00
Profit Shares £1175.00

5　a　Interest on Loan £50.00
Profit Shares £2975.00

　　b　Salary £1500.00
Interest on Loan £50.00
Profit Shares £2225.00

6　a　Profit A £2437.50. B £812.50. Interest A £650 B £150
　　b　Profit A £2587.50. B £862.50. Interest A £450 B £150

7　X £14 694.00. Y £11 020.00. Z. £4500.00 + 8000.00 =
12 500.00

8　a　A £23 800.00. B £11 800.00
　　b　A £23 900.00. B £11 700.00

9　Profit Shares, after deducting drawings
Bright £11 530.00. Smart £6995.00

10　A　Profit £5951.25. Interest £290.00
　　B　Profit £5951.25. Interest £190.00. Salary £2400.00
　　C　Profit £1967.50. Interest £50.00

11　Gross Profit £24 800.00. Net Profit £9730.00
Statement of Financial Position Totals £10 862.00

12　Gross Profit £23 699.62
Net Profit (before Interest) £5308.36
Balances carried forward:
Plant A/c £5950.00 Dr. Insurance A/c £131.75 Dr
Bad Debts Reserve £281.00 Cr
Commission A/c £34.94 Dr

13 Manufacturing A/c £80 071.00
Gross Profit £4265.00
Net Profit (before Interest) £2189.00
Statement of Financial Position Totals £20 879.00

14 Profit £3627.00
Statement of Financial Position Totals £5663.00

Questions on Chapter 19

1 Gross Profit £13 136.00. Net Profit £1788.20
Statement of Financial Position Totals £11 690.20

2 Gross Profit £20 900.00. Net Loss £850.00
Statement of Financial Position Totals £17 803.00

3 Gross Profit
(Manufacturing A/c) £22 787.00
Net Profit £8319.00
Statement of Financial Position Totals £103 095.00

Examination papers and sample solutions

THE ROYAL SOCIETY OF ARTS EXAMINATIONS BOARD
BOOK-KEEPING (107)
UPDATED
Stage I
(TIME ALLOWED – TWO HOURS)

You have TEN minutes to read through this question paper before the start of the examination.

Questions 1–4 are compulsory. You are advised to complete these questions before attempting Question 5.

You should attempt Question 5 if you wish to be considered for the award of a Credit.

Calculators may be used; however, a proportion of marks will be awarded for method and you should therefore ensure that workings are shown clearly throughout the examination.

Marks will be lost for untidy work.

Answers should be written in ink pen or ballpoint pen.

QUESTION 1

a John Jennings is the owner of a small engineering firm. During October the following transactions took place:

3 Oct   New office equipment was purchased from Mega Systems, consisting of 2 computers at £1950 each, 2 printers at £395 each and a photocopier at £2470 all less 12½ per cent trade discount. Twenty-five per cent was paid by cheque, the remainder on credit.

10 Oct   I Hardrup who owes the firm £603.50 has been declared bankrupt. A cheque for 20p in the pound of the amount owed has been received in full and final settlement of the debt. The remainder is to be written off as a bad debt.

15 Oct   A delivery van has been sold for book value of £1950 to R Groves on credit. A cheque for one-third has been received, the balance is to be paid on 15 December.

You are required to show journal entries, with narrations to record the above transactions.

b His accounts were reviewed on 31 October and the following errors were discovered:

i A cash payment of £143 to M Dyson had been entered in the cash book and also posted to the ledger as £341.

ii Goods bought on credit from T Clark costing £390 had been entered in J Clarkson's account.

You are required to show journal entries, with narrations, to record items i and ii.

c John Jennings' financial year ends on 31 October. From the balances given below prepare the closing journal entries to transfer the figures to the final accounts.

General expenses £2074
Carriage inwards £652
Discount allowed £890

(26 marks)

QUESTION 2

Helen Gibson runs a small business selling a wide range of garden furniture. On 1 October her sales ledger contained the following debtors:

	£
C Burrell	956.28
J Coates	639.74
M Kennedy	808.36

During the month of October the following transactions took place:

Sales on credit

October		Goods £	VAT £	Total £
3	J Coates	519.32	103.86	623.18
8	M Kennedy	384.94	76.99	461.93
14	C Burrell	625.18	125.04	750.22

Returns Inward

October		Goods £	VAT £	Total £
20	C Burrell	52.73	10.55	63.28
23	M Kennedy	48.60	9.72	58.32

Payments received by cheque

October		Discount Allowed £	Cheque value £
17	J Coates	16.99	322.75
24	M Kennedy	40.42	767.94
29	C Burrell	11.95	466.05

You are required to:

a Open ledger accounts for all accounts receivable and enter the balances as at 1 October.

b Enter the transactions which have taken place during the month of October to the appropriate ledger accounts and balance the accounts at the end of the month.

c Show the entries which would appear in the sales, returns inward and VAT accounts in the general ledger.

d Prepare a sales ledger control account for the month of October and reconcile the balance with the total debtors balances in the sales ledger.

(26 marks)

QUESTION 3

D King works in the assembly unit of a local factory, his clock number is 17. The firm operates a piece work system, piece rates are paid at a rate of £17.25 for every 25 items produced. During week 28, ending 31 October, D King assembled 450 items.

Deductions are to be calculated as follows:

Company pension scheme	6% of gross pay
National Insurance	12.8% of gross pay
PAYE	£60.23
Social club	£2.50

The company's national insurance contribution to be paid on behalf D King is £42.84.

You are required to complete the following pay slip.

(12 marks)

Clock No				Week No						Week ending		
							Deductions					
Name	Numbers produced	Rate	Gross pay	Tax	National Insurance	Pensions	Others	Total	Net Pay	Employers' National Insurance Contribution		

QUESTION 4

Excel Products are one of your suppliers. Their account in your ledger is as follows:

xxxx		£	xxxx		£
14 Oct	Purchases returns	95	1 Oct	Balance b/d	1350
			6	Purchases	1850
29	Bank	1330			
29	Discount	20	20	Purchases	1050
30	Purchases returns	75			
31	Balance c/d	2730			£4250
		£4250	1 Nov	Balance b/d	£2730

On 2 November the following statement of account is received from Excel Products.

xxxx			Debit £	Credit £	Balance £
Oct	1	Balance			2775
	3	Bank		1400	1375
	3	Discount		25	1350
	6	Sales	1850		3200
xxxx			£	£	£
Oct	14	Returns inwards		95	3105
	20	Sales	1050		4155
	28	Sales	1550		5705

You are required to:

a Prepare a reconciliation statement, starting with the balance in your books of £2730 to explain the difference between the balance in your ledger and the closing balance on the statement of account.

b Briefly explain why a supplier may disallow a cash discount.

(12 marks)

QUESTION 5

On 1 November the Lawnswood Tennis Club had the following assets and liabilities: Club Premises £45 500, Equipment £12 750, Bar stock £980, Bank balance £5220, Cash £326, Accounts payable for bar supplies £450.

The following receipts and payments were made during the year ended 31 October.

		£
Subscriptions:	98 full-time members, each paying	250
	45 part-time members, each paying	125
Travelling expenses to away matches		1454
Payments to suppliers for bar purchases		8428
Lighting and heating		2962
Payment of league entry fees		545
Rent received from private functions		1485
General expenses		3835
Rates		3180
Insurance premium		2472
Bar staff wages		5950
Purchase of new equipment		5790
Stationery and postage		508
Bar takings		16 592

On 31 October the following information was available:

i Rent of £395 was owing to the club for private functions.

ii Insurance prepaid was £1854.

iii There was an inventory of stationery valued at £96 and a stock of drinks valued at £1080. There were no bar creditors.

You are required to:

a Prepare a bar trading account for the year ended 31 October.

b Prepare a receipts and payments account for the year ended 31 October.

c Prepare an income and expenditure account for the year ended 31 October.

Note: A Statement of Financial Position is NOT required. Clearly show how you have dealt with the adjustments. Full and part-time members are listed and accounted for separately.

(24 marks)

POSSIBLE SOLUTIONS

1 a	John Jennings	General Journal	Dr	Cr
xxxx			£	£
Oct 3	Office equipment			
	2 computers @ 1950	3900		
	2 printers @ 395	790		
	1 photocopier	2470		
		7160		
	Less 12½% trade discount	895		
	Bank 25%		6265.00	1566.25
	Mega Systems 75% Creditor			4698.75
			£6265.00	£6265.00

Being purchase of office equipment from Mega Systems of which 25% was paid in cash and 75% on credit

Oct 10	Bank	120.70	
	I Hardrup Debtor £603.50 @ 20p in the pound		120.70
	Being receipt of cheque for 20p in the pound received in full settlement of debt of £603.50 owing from I Hardrup		
	Bad Debts	482.80	
	I Hardrup Debtor		482.80
	Being transfer of remaining debt due from I Hardrup now written off as a Bad Debt following his bankruptcy		
Oct 15	Bank one-third of £1950	650.00	
	R Groves two-thirds of £1950	1300.00	
	Delivery Van Disposal Being sale of Delivery van to R Groves, who paid one-third by cheque with the balance to be paid on 15 December 1997		1950.00

b		£	£
xxxx	M Dyson (Creditor)	198.00	
Oct 3	Bank (Cash Book) Being correction of error in Cash Book when a payment of £143 had been entered as £341, £198 too much		198.00

xxxx	J Clarkson	390.00	
Oct 31	T Clark		390.00

Being correction of error in
posting when goods bought
from T Clark had been
posted to the account of
J Clarkson

c

Oct 31	Sundries		
	Trading Account	652.00	
	Carriage inwards		652.00
	Profit and Loss Account	2074.00	
	General expenses		2074.00
	Profit and Loss Account	890.00	
	Discount Allowed		890.00

Being the transfer of these
expense accounts to the final
accounts at the end of the year

2 a and b

Having read the question you should add up all the columns of
figures, and check the cross-casts.

HELEN GIBSON
Sales Ledger
C. BURRELL

Dr						Cr
xxxx		£	xxxx			£
Oct 1	Balance b/d	956.28	Oct 20	Returns		63.28
14	Sales		29	Bank		466.05
	plus VAT	750.22		Discount		11.95
			31	Balance c/d		1165.22
		£1706.50				£1706.50
Nov 1	Balance b/d	1165.22				

J. COATES

Dr		£	Cr		£
XXXX			XXXX		
Oct 1	Balance b/d	639.74	Oct 20	Bank	322.75
3	Sales			Discount	16.99
	plus VAT	623.18	31	Balance c/d	923.18
		£1262.92			£1262.92
Nov 1	Balance b/d	923.18			

M. KENNEDY

Dr		£	Cr		£
XXXX			XXXX		
Oct 1	Balance b/d	808.36	Oct 23	Returns	58.32
3	Sales		24	Bank	767.94
	plus VAT	461.93		Discount	40.42
			31	Balance c/d	403.61
		£1270.29			£1270.29
Nov 1	Balance b/d	403.61			

A reference column would be included if references had been given.

c

General (or Nominal) Ledger
SALES

Dr	XXXX	£	XXXX		Cr £
			Oct 31	Total for the month	1529.44

RETURNS INWARDS (OR SALES RETURNS)

Dr		£	XXXX	Cr £
XXXX				
Oct 31	Total for the month	101.33		

VAT

Dr		£	Cr		£
xxxx			xxxx		
Oct 31	Total for the month	20.27	Oct 31	Total for the month	305.89
	Balance c/d	285.62			
		£305.89			£305.89
			Nov 1	Balance b/d	285.62

d SALES LEDGER CONTROL ACCOUNT

Dr		£	Cr		£
xxxx			xxxx		
Oct 1	Balance b/d	2404.38	Oct 31	Bank	1556.74
31	Sales plus VAT	1835.33		Discount	69.36
				Returns plus VAT	121.60
			31	Balance c/d	2492.01
		£4239.71			£4239.71
Nov 1	Balance b/d	2492.01			

A reference column would be included if references had been given.

Accounts receivable balances at 31 October	£
C Burrell	1165.02
J Coates	923.18
M Kennedy	403.61
Total per Control Account	£2492.01

3 Calculate the necessary figures and then complete the pay slip.

			£
For 25 items the gross pay is £17.25 or 69p each			
For 450 items the gross pay will be 450 × 69p =			310.50
deductions	Company pension 6%	18.63	
	National Insurance 12.8%	39.74	
	PAYE given	60.23	
	Social Club given	2.50	
	total deductions		121.10
	Net pay		£189.40

Insert here:

Centre Number: 23
Candidate's Name A. N. OTHER

Clock No 17					Week No 28					Week ending 31 October		
						Deductions						
Name	Numbers produced	Rate	Gross Pay	Tax	National Insurance	Pensions	Others (Social Club)	Total	Net Pay	Employers' National Insurance Contribution		
		£	£	£	£	£	£	£	£	£		
D. KING	450	17.25/25 or 69p. ea.	310.50	60.23	39.74	18.63	2.50	121.10	189.40	42.84		

424

Remember the Employers' National Insurance, given, £42.84

Now enter ALL the data into the pay slip.

4 a RECONCILIATION STATEMENT WITH EXCEL PRODUCTS

	£
Balance in Purchase Ledger 31 October	2730
add Purchase in transit from Excel (29 Oct)	1550
Purchase returns (30 Oct) not yet credited by Excel	75
Payment made (29 Oct) not yet credited by Excel	1330
and related discount	20
Balance on Excel's statement dated 28 October	£5705

b Cash discounts are allowed because a payment has been received in accordance with the previously agreed terms of payment. If these terms have not been met then the discount may be disallowed. A common reason would be that the payment was late, or had not been calculated correctly. Often the later receipt by the supplier is said to be due to delay in the post or the banking system.

5 a Lawnswood Tennis Club

Bar Trading Account for the year ended 31 October xx1x

	£	£	£
Sales (Bar takings)			16 592
Opening inventory		980	
Payments to suppliers	8 428		
Accounts payable at 1 Nov xx1x	450		
purchases for year		7 978	
		8 958	
deduct closing inventory		1 080	

	£
Cost of goods sold during the year	7 878
Gross profit	8 714
Wages of bar staff	5 950
Net profit from bar during the year	£2 764

b It would be possible to use the profit from the Bar Trading Account, which incorporates adjustments for stock and creditors in the Receipts and Payment account, but it is not usual. When trading activities are significant an Income and Expenditure account is usually presented.

Lawnswood Tennis Club

Receipts and Payments Account for the year ended 31 October xx1x

			£	£
Receipts	Subscriptions	full-time	24 500	
		part-time	5 625	
				30 125
	Rent from private functions			1 485
	Bar takings			16 592
	Total Receipts			48 202
Payments	Bar purchases		8 428	
	Bar staff wages		5 950	
	League entry fees		545	
	Travelling expenses		1 454	
	Lighting and heating		2 962	
	General expenses		3 835	
	Rates		3 180	
	Insurance premium		2 472	

Stationery and postage	508	
New equipment	5 790	
		35 124
Surplus for year		35 124
Cash and bank balance		
at 1 November xxx9 (326 + 5220)		5 546
at 31 October xx1x		£18 624

Lawnswood Tennis Club

Income and Expenditure Account for the year ended 31 *October*
*xx*1*x*

			£	£
Income	Subscriptions	Full-time	24 500	
		part-time	5 625	
	Net profit from bar		2 764	
	Rent from private functions		1 880	
	(note 1)			
				34 769
Expenditure				
	Payment of League fees		545	
	Travelling expenses		1 454	
	Lighting and Heating		2 962	
	General expenses		3 835	
	Rates		3 180	
	Insurance premium (note 2)		618	
	Stationery and postage (note 3)		412	
Surplus of income over expenditure				13 006
				£21 763

Notes: 1 Rent received £1485 plus rent owing = £395 = £1880

2 Insurance paid £2472 minus prepaid £1854 = £618

3 Stationery purchased £508 minus inventory £96 = £412

Learning note. The Statement of Financial Position was **not** required. However, if you have time in an examination, or as a practical exercise now, it is worth while to produce the outline of one as a check on the accuracy of your work.

		1.11.x9	31.10.1x
		£	£
Accumulated fund	Premises	45 500	45 500
	Equipment	12 750	18 540
	Bar stock	980	1 080
	Bank	5 220	18 624
	Cash	326	
	Creditor	450	
	Stationery inventory		96
	Insurance prepaid		1 854
	Accounts receivable		395
		64 326	
	add surplus of year	21 763	
		£86 089	£86 089

THE ROYAL SOCIETY OF ARTS EXAMINATIONS BOARD

BOOK-KEEPING (104) UPDATED

Stage I

(time allowed – two hours)

You have TEN minutes to read through this question paper before the start of the examination.

Marks will be lost for untidy work.

Answers should be written in ink pen or ballpoint pen.

Calculators may be used.

You should answer only those elements for which you require certification.

ELEMENT 1

You are an employee of James W Lamb Limited which sells musical instruments, music books and sheet music. You have been asked to perform the following tasks:

a Record all the documents given here into the correct books of original entry (as printed in the answer book).

b Enter the correct date and name into the correct columns within these books.

Use the following analysis columns in the purchases and purchases returns day books: Instrument Purchases; Books and Music; Sundry Expenses; VAT; Total.

Use the following analysis columns in the sales and sales returns day books: Net; VAT; Total.

c Enter the figures into the correct columns within these books.

d Total the day books.

e Cross-cast the day books.

ELEMENT 2

James W Lamb Limited operates an imprest system for petty cash with a float of £250.00. The imprest was restored on 2 May so there was an opening balance of £250.00. You are required to enter the opening balance into the petty cash book and to perform the following tasks:

a Enter the petty cash vouchers into the petty cash book (as printed in the answer book). Use the following analysis columns: VAT; Postage/Carriage; Cleaning; Staff Refreshments; Sundry; Purchase Ledger.

b Total all the columns of the petty cash book. (You are not required to balance the petty cash book.)

c Enter the amount and sign the petty cash reimbursement request in the answer book with the amount required to restore the imprest after these payments have been made.

ELEMENT 3

You have been given a cash book with an opening balance overdrawn at the bank of £407.40 as at 2 May. You are required to enter the opening balance into the cash book and to perform the following tasks:

a Enter the receipts into the cash book in your answer book. All cash is banked immediately on receipt.

b Enter the payments into the cash book, in your answer book.

c Update the cash book from the bank statement for standing order payments; bank charges and credit transfers.

d Balance the cash book and bring down the balance to the following month.

e Complete the preprinted bank reconciliation statement in your answer book.

To be used when answering Element 1.

INVOICE						
H & B Publishing plc, Wentworth Road, New Malden						

James W Lamb Ltd Invoice No: 57/9529/105B
15 Sutherland Terrace Date: 2.5.1x
London WC1 2PS VAT Reg No: 559 733459

Qty	Description	Unit Price £	Total Net £	VAT Rate %	VAT Amount £	Total £
5	10 Classical pieces for violin & piano by Spencer Harvey	6.00	30.00	0.00	0.00	30.00
2	Learn as you play Clarinet J P Clifford	4.76	9.52	0.00	0.00	9.52
			39.52	0.00	0.00	39.52

TERMS: Net Monthly Account

INVOICE					
BULLET MUSICAL INSTRUMENTS PLC					
New End Industrial Estate, Birmingham, B14 1TS					
0121 942 7493					

James W Lamb Ltd15 Invoice No: 549127
Sutherland Terrace Date: 3 May xx1x
London WC1 2PS VAT Reg No: 549 2323 14

Qty	Description	Unit Price £	Total Net£	VAT Rate %	VAT Amount £	Total £
1	Bullet B12 Clarinet	215.00	215.00	20%	43.00	258.00
			215.00		43.00	258.00

TERMS:

To be used when answering Element 1.

INVOICE

SP Office Supplies   Invoice No
Unit 3 Crayfield Industrial   **14797**
Estate Crayfield Kent DA2 3DA

    James W Lamb Ltd   Date: 4.5.1x
    15 Sutherland Terrace   VAT Reg No: 922 923500
    London WC1 2PS

Your order: 5962   Despatch Date: 4.5.x1

Qty	Description	Unit Price £	Total Net £	VAT Rate %	VAT Amount £	Total £
6	Laser Printer Toner Cartridge Code Number: TONER6	13.00	78.00	20%	15.60	93.60
			78.00		15.60	93.60

TERMS: 30 Days Net

INVOICE

ACE COMPUTER MAINTENANCE

To

    James W Lamb Ltd   Invoice No: 5924/27
    15 Sutherland   Date: 4 May xx1x
    TerraceLondon WC1 2PS   VAT Reg No: 238 645842

Description	Total Net £	VAT Rate %	VAT Amount £	Total £
Call out visit to repair in-house computer	49.50	20%	9.90	59.40
Total	49.50	–	9.90	59.40

Units 10 & 11, Enterprise Park, London, W2 0BP

To be used when answering Element 1.

INVOICE

Shimco UK Ltd

Shimco House, 17 Cornhill, Nottingham

James W Lamb Ltd
15 Sutherland Terrace
London WC1 2PS

Invoice No: 5297
Date: 5 May xx1x
VAT Reg No: 121 3434 55

Qty	Description	Unit Price £	Total Net £	VAT Rate %	VAT Amount £	Total £
2	Shimco 501 Violins	140.00	280.00	20	56.00	336.00
			280.00		56.00	336.00

TERMS: By Return

INVOICE

Laker Envelopes Ltd
Laker House
HOLBORN WC1

Invoice No
01254

James W Lamb Ltd
15 Sutherland Terrace
London WC1 2PS

Date: 5.5.1x
VAT Reg No: 066 5725 96

Your order: Telephoned Despatch Date: 5.5.1x

Qty	Description	Unit Price £	Total Net £	VAT Rate %	VAT Amount £	Total £
200	A4 Envelopes LL 154	13.00 per 100	26.00	20%	5.20	31.20
400	A5 Window Envelopes LL 156	10.00 per 100	40.00	20%	8.00	48.00
			66.00		13.20	79.20

TERMS: 30 Days Net

To be used when answering Element 1.

	Invoice No: 2321
	VAT No: 479 9876 31
	Date 5 May xx1x

COUNTALOT & CO
Chartered Accountants
15 Uxbridge Road
Shepherds Bush
London W12 6XJ

In Account with James W Lamb Limited

	£
Auditing your books and records for the year ended 31 December xxx9	1500.00
Submitting a copy of the accounts together with supporting Income Tax computations to the Inspector of Taxes	250.00
Total excluding VAT	1750.00
VAT (20%)	350.00
TOTAL	2100.00

INVOICE
BULLET MUSICAL INSTRUMENTS PLC
New End Industrial Estate, Birmingham, B14 1TS
0121 942 7493

James W Lamb Ltd	Invoice No: 549139
15 Sutherland Terrace	Date: 5 May xx1x
London WC1 2PS	VAT Reg No: 549 2323 14

Qty	Description	Unit Price £	Total Net £	VAT Rate £	VAT Amount %	Total £
2	E11 Grenadilla Clarinets	370.00	740.00	20%	148.00	888.00
1	Bullet Top F# Alto Saxe	456.00	465.00	20%	93.00	558.00
			1205.00		241.00	1446.00

TERMS:

To be used when answering Element 1.

CREDIT NOTE			No: 7	
SHOSAKU VIOLAS (UK) LTD				
Date/Tax Point: 3 May xx1x				

James W Lamb Ltd
15 Sutherland Terrace
London WC1 2PS

VAT No: 542 3078 19

Quantity	Description	Catalogue number	Unit Price £	Total Amount £
1	15½" Viola	HA 200	132.00	132.00
		Total excluding VAT		132.00
		VAT (20%)		26.00
		Total credit		158.40

Reason for credit: Wrong model supplied to be replaced by HA300

CREDIT NOTE	No: 629
CENTRAL GASBOARD	
Date/Tax Point: 4 May xx1x	

James W Lamb Ltd
15 Sutherland Terrace
London WC1 2PS

Description	Total Amount £
Credit in respect of Invoice 5742	35.00
Total excluding VAT	35.00
VAT (20%)	7.00
Total credit	42.00

Reason for credit: Duplication of charges for repairs

To be used when answering Element 1.

CREDIT NOTE

Bullet Musical Instruments plc
New End Industrial Estate
Birmingham, B14 1TS
Tel 0121 942 7493

James W Lamb Ltd
15 Sutherland Terrace
London WC1 2PS

Credit Note No: 316
Date: 9 May xx1x
VAT Reg No: 549 2323 14

Qty	Description	Unit Price £	Total Net £	VAT Rate %	VAT Amount £	Total £
1	Bullet B12 Clarinet	215.00	215.00	20	43.00	258.00
Clarinet returned damaged			215.00		43.00	258.00
Ref: Invoice no 549127						

CREDIT NOTE   No: 17
LAKER ENVELOPES LTD
LAKER HOUSE, HOLBORN, WC1

Date/Tax Point: 12 May xx1x
James W Lamb Ltd
15 Sutherland Terrace
London WC1 2PS

Quantity	Description	Catalogue number	Unit Price £	Total Amount £
400	A5 Window envelopes	LL156	50p per 100	2.00
		Total excluding VAT		2.00
		VAT (20%)		0.40
		Total credit		2.40
Reason for credit: Wrong price charged invoice 01254				

To be used when answering Element 1.

INVOICE

JAMES W LAMB LIMITED, 15 SUNDERLAND TERRACE, LONDON, WC1 2PS

Tel 0171 692 5497

To

Miss L Collins	Invoice No: 1392
59 Chepstow Road	Date: 2 May 1995
Sutton	VAT Reg No: 526 8892 62

Description	Total Net £	VAT Rate %	VAT Amount £	Total £
Yamaha 26 Phenol Resin BbClarinet Outfit RR4	312.00	20	62.40	374.40
Learn as you pay Clarinet by J P Clifford	5.95	0.00	0.00	5.95
Total	317.95	–	62.40	380.35

Terms: Strictly 30 days net

INVOICE

JAMES W LAMB LIMITED, 15 SUNDERLAND TERRACE, LONDON, WC1 2PS

Tel 0171 692 5497

To

Mrs J Pledger	Invoice No: 1393
72 High	Date: 2 May xx1x
StreetWimbledon SW19	VAT Reg No: 526 8892 62

Description	Total Net £	VAT Rate%	VAT Amount £	Total £
"10 Classical pieces for violin and piano" by Spencer Harvey	7.50	0.00	0.00	7.50
Total	7.50	0.00	0.00	7.50

Terms: Strictly 30 days net

To be used when answering Element 1.

INVOICE				
JAMES W LAMB LIMITED, 15 SUNDERLAND TERRACE, LONDON, WC1 2PS Tel 0171 692 5497				

To

Goodwind Music Ltd		Invoice No 1394		
373 Broad Street		Date 2 May xx1x		
Hertford		VAT Reg No: 526 8892 62		
Herts				

Description	Total Net £	VAT Rate %	VAT Amount £	Total £
H & B 400 (Cash) 1/2 double				
Lacquer finish French horn	1075.00			
Shimco 501 (Korean) Violin	210.00			
	1285.00			
20% discount	(257.00)			
Total	1028.00	20	205.60	1233.60
Terms: Strictly 30 days net				

INVOICE

JAMES W LAMB LIMITED, 15 SUNDERLAND TERRACE,
LONDON, WC1 2PS
Tel 0171 692 5497

To

Rosewood Academy of Music	Invoice No 1395
Rosewood Road	Date 2 May xx1x
Chelmsford	VAT Reg No: 526 8892 62
Essex	

Description	Total Net £	VAT Rate %	VAT Amount £	Total £
2 Daug (Korean) Silver plated flutes at £195.00 each	390.00			
10% discount on flutes	(39.00)			
	351.00	20.00	70.20	421.20
10 copies of "First steps for the flute" by Rose Garney at £4.50 each	45.00	0.00	0.00	45.00
Total	396.00		70.20	466.20
Terms: Strictly 30 days net				

To be used when answering Element 1.

INVOICE

JAMES W LAMB LIMITED, 15 SUNDERLAND TERRACE
LONDON, WC1 2PS
Tel 0171 692 5497

To

Mr. H. J. Henkel	Invoice No: 1396
17 Tulip Grove	Date: 4 May xx1x
Ruislip	VAT Reg No: 526 8892 62
Middlesex	

Description	Total Net £	VAT Rate %	VAT Amount £	Total £
Sheffler 5013 short reach Bassoon	1850.00	20	370.00	2220.00
Total	1850.00	20	370.00	2220.00

Terms: Strictly 30 days net

INVOICE

JAMES W LAMB LIMITED, 15 SUNDERLAND TERRACE
LONDON, WC1 2PS
Tel 0171 692 5497

To

Sarah Linklater	Invoice No: 1397
278 Westmorland Road	Date: 5 May xx1x
Barnet Herts	VAT Reg No: 526 8892 62

Description	Total Net £	VAT Rate %	VAT Amount £	Total £
Bullet top F# lacquer finish Alto Sax	620.00	20	124.00	744.00
Total	620.00	20	124.00	744.00

Terms: Strictly 30 days net

To be used when answering Element 1.

CREDIT NOTE

JAMES W LAMB LIMITED, 15 SUNDERLAND TERRACE
LONDON, WC1 2PS
TEL 0171 692 5497

To

Mrs V Redbridge   Credit Note No: 12
16 Southport Road   Date: 5 May xx1x
Dover   VAT Reg No: 526 8892 62

Description	Total Net £	VAT Rate %	VAT Amount £	Total £
Bullet 862E Silver head flute	365.00	20	73.00	438.00
Total	365.00	20	73.00	438.00
Credit in respect of invoice 1350 – Goods returned damaged on arrival				

CREDIT NOTE

JAMES W LAMB LIMITED, 15 SUNDERLAND TERRACE
LONDON, WC1 2PS
TEL 0171 692 5497

To

Regis Music Ltd   Credit Note No: 13
Seaview Parade   Date: 5 May xx1x
Bognor   VAT Reg No: 526 8892 62

Description	Total Net£	VAT Rate %	VAT Amount £	Total £
"10 Classical pieces for violin and piano" by Spencer Harvey	7.50	0.00	0.00	7.50
Total	7.50	0	0.00	7.50
Credit in respect of invoice 1390, Goods returned ordered in error				

To be used when answering Element 2.

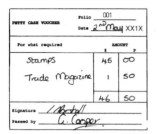

PETTY CASH VOUCHER

Folio _001_
Date _2nd May_ XX1X

For what required	AMOUNT £	P
Stamps	45	00
Trade Magazine	1	50
	46	50

Signature _/Marshall_
Passed by _G. Cooper_

PETTY CASH VOUCHER

Folio _002_
Date _2nd May_ XX1X

For what required	AMOUNT £	P
1 Roll Sello Tape		99
Post-it-notes	1	40
Paper clips	1	00
(includes 50p VAT)	3	39

Signature _Joan Daily_
Passed by _G. Cooper_

PETTY CASH VOUCHER

Folio _003_
Date _3rd May_ XX1X

For what required	AMOUNT £	P
New Mop head	1	60
VAT		32
Teabags		88
	2	80

Signature _Sarah Button_
Passed by _G. Cooper_

PETTY CASH VOUCHER

Folio _004_
Date _4th May_ XX1X

For what required	AMOUNT £	P
Sarah Button	15	00
Cleaner - wages		
	15	00

Signature _Sarah Button_
Passed by _G. Cooper_

PETTY CASH VOUCHER

Folio _005_
Date _4th May_ XX1X

For what required	AMOUNT £	P
F. Wright	25	00
Window Cleaner		
	25	00

Signature _F Wright_
Passed by _G. Cooper_

PETTY CASH VOUCHER

Folio _006_
Date _5th May_ XX1X

For what required	AMOUNT £	P
milkman	2	97
	2	97

Signature _Peter Monk_
Passed by _G. Cooper_

To be used when answering Element 2.

PETTY CASH VOUCHER	Folio 007		
	Date 10ᵗ May XX1X		
For what required		AMOUNT £	P
S + m News Purchase ledger account PL 516		19	57
		19	57
Signature SD Snall			
Passed by G. Cooper			

PETTY CASH VOUCHER	Folio 008		
	Date 12ᵗ May XX1X		
For what required		AMOUNT £	P
Joan Daily Reimbursement of Petrol Cost for Training course VAT		15 3	00 00
		18	00
Signature Joan Daily			
Passed by G. Cooper			

PETTY CASH VOUCHER	Folio 009		
	Date 17ᵗʰ May XX1X		
For what required		AMOUNT £	P
Stamps 10 × £1·00		10	00
		10	00
Signature / Marshall			
Passed by G. Cooper			

PETTY CASH VOUCHER	Folio 010		
	Date 19ᵗʰ May XX1X		
For what required		AMOUNT £	P
Milkman		2	97
		2	97
Signature Peter Monk			
Passed by G. Cooper			

PETTY CASH VOUCHER	Folio 011		
	Date 23ʳᵈ May XX1X		
For what required		AMOUNT £	P
Batteries for wall clock (Inc VAT 33p)		1	98
		1	98
Signature Joan Daily			
Passed by G. Cooper			

PETTY CASH VOUCHER	Folio 012		
	Date 24ᵗ May XX1X		
For what required		AMOUNT £	P
Sarah Butter Cleaners wages		15	00
		15	00
Signature Sarah Button			
Passed by G. Cooper			

To be used when answering Element 3.

Copies of cheques received

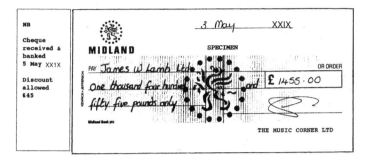

NB	
Cheque received & banked 5 May XX1X	
Discount allowed £45	

MIDLAND

3 May   XXIX

SPECIMEN

PAY James W Lamb Ltd   OR ORDER

£ 1455·00

One thousand four hundred and

fifty five pounds only

Midland Bank plc

THE MUSIC CORNER LTD

NB	
Cheque received & banked 12 May XX1X	

Lloyds Bank

8 May   XXIX

1-6   ACCRINGTON BRANCH   30-10-08
8A WHALLEY ROAD ACCRINGTON LANCS BB5 1AB

Pay James W Lamb Ltd   or order

Five hundred + seventy   £ 572 – 16

two pounds 16p

SPECIMEN

LJ Tebbit

Lloyds Bank Plc

GOODWIND MUSIC LTD

NB	
Cheque received & banked 17 May XX1X	

Girobank
Bootle Merseyside GIR 0AA

SPECIMEN   72-00-00

Pay James W Lamb Ltd   or order   14th May XXIX

Amount Three hundred + seventy two   £372 · 55

pounds 55p only

Signature

MISS L COLLINS
59 Chepstow Road
Sutton

L Collins

Please do not write in the space below

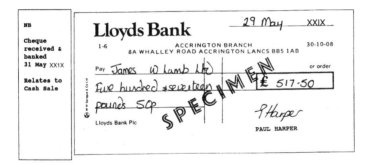

NB

Cheque
received &
banked
19 May XX1X

Relates to
Cash Sale

BARCLAYS

GOLDERS GREEN BRANCH,
883/885 FINCHLEY ROAD, LONDON, NW11 8RU

15 May XXIX

20-34-06

BARCLAYS BANK PLC

or order

Pay James W Lamb

Two thousand four hundred *
seventy pounds only

£2470.00

Cheque No.   Branch No.   Account No.

MS T P ROSALIA

NB

Cheque
received &
banked
30 May XX1X

BARCLAYS

GOLDERS GREEN BRANCH,
883/885 FINCHLEY ROAD, LONDON, NW11 8RU

26 May XXIX

20-34-06

BARCLAYS BANK PLC

or order

Pay James W Lamb Ltd

One hundred * two pounds 56p

£102.56

Cheque No.   Branch No.   Account No.

DEPENDABLE INSURANCE CO

NB

Cheque
received &
banked
31 May XX1X

Relates to
Cash Sale

Lloyds Bank

1-6   ACCRINGTON BRANCH   30-10-08
     8A WHALLEY ROAD ACCRINGTON LANCS BB5 1AB

29 May XXIX

or order

Pay James W Lamb Ltd

Five hundred *seventeen
pounds 50p

£ 517.50

Lloyds Bank Plc

PAUL HARPER

To be used when answering Element 3.

Copies of cheque receipts

...6..May............... XX1X   No...316......

Received
from......Mrs T Kirkby...............

The sum of...Thirty seven pounds 50.
..................Cash Sale..............

Cheque		
Cash	37	50
Discount		
	37	50

G. Cooper

WITH THANKS

...17..May............ XX1X   No...317......

Received
from......Miss L.M. Sharp..........

The sum of...Ninety three pounds 27p

....

Cheque		
Cash	93	27
Discount		
	93	27

G. Cooper

WITH THANKS

446

To be used when answering Element 3.

Copies of cheque counterfoils

3 May XX1X
TO
British Telecom
Old Balance
Deposits
Total
This Cheque £ 697.25
New Balance
003106

3 May XX1X
TO
H & B Publishing plc
Old Balance
Deposits
Total
This Cheque £ 215.00
New Balance
003107

4 May XX1X
TO
Bullet Musical Instruments plc
Old Balance
Deposits
Total
This Cheque £1497.20
New Balance
003108

12 May XX1X
TO
Yamaha Instruments (UK) Plc
Old Balance
Deposits Discount taken £24.80
Total
This Cheque £ 595.20
New Balance
003109

19 May XX1X
TO
Shimco UK Ltd
Old Balance Discount taken £23.50
Deposits
Total
This Cheque £727.50
New Balance
003110

28 May XX1X
TO HM Customs & Excise
Old Balance
Deposits
Total
This Cheque £2460.23
New Balance
003111

To be used when answering Element 3.

Statement of Account

Bank Statement				
			Barclays Bank plc	
			Holborn Branch	
James W Lamb Limited				
account No 32927797				
Sheet No 52 Date 2.6.1x				
Date xx1x	Description	Debit	Credit	Balance
2 May	Balance Forward			407.40 DR
3 May	Westminster City Council s.o.	242.00		649.40 DR
8 May	Cheque		1455.00	
	003106	697.25		108.35
9 May	003108	1497.20		
	Deposit		37.50	1351.35 DR
11 May	University of Guildford Credit Transfer		1597.23	245.88
17 May	Cheque		572.16	
	003109	595.20		
	003107	215.00		7.84
19 May	Deposit		93.27	101.11
22 May	Cheque		372.55	473.66
23 May	Cheque		2470.00	
	003110	727.50		2216.16
26 May	Overdraft Interest 20 Feb–19 May	14.62		
	Current Account Charge			
	20 Feb–19 May	107.98		2093.56

SAMPLE SOLUTIONS

1 Note: In the examination you would have some printed answer sheets.

James W Lamb Purchases Day Book

Date	Supplier	Instrument Purchases	Books & Music	Sundry Expenses	VAT	Total
		£	£	£	£	£
xx1x						
May 2	H&B Publishing plc		39.52		0.00	39.52
3	Bullet Musical Instruments PLC	215.00			43.00	258.00
4	SP Office Supplies			78.00	156.40	93.60
4	Ace Computer Maintenance			49.50	9.90	59.40
5	Shimco UK Ltd	280.00			56.00	336.00
5	Laker Envelopes Ltd			66.00	132.70	79.20
5	Countalot & Co			1750.00	350.00	2100.00
5	Bullet Musical Instruments PLC	1205.00			241.00	1446.00
	Totals	1700.00	39.52	1943.50	728.70	4411.72

Check 4411.72

James W Lamb Purchases Returns Day Book

Date	Supplier	Instrument Purchases	Books & Music	Sundry Expenses	VAT	Total	
		£	£	£	£	£	
xx1x							
May 3	Shosaku Violas (UK) Ltd	132.00			26.40	158.40	
4	Central Gasboard			35.00	7.00	42.00	
9	Bullet Musical Instruments plc	215.00			43.00	258.00	
12	Laker Envelopes Ltd			2.00	0.40	2.40	
	Totals	347.00	0.00	37.00	76.80	460.80	Check 460.80

James W Lamb Sales Day Book

Note that you are asked to use three analysis columns only. In practice separate columns for instruments and music might be appropriate.

Date	Customer	Invoice number	Net	VAT	Total
xx1x			£	£	£
May 2	Miss L Collins	1392	317.95	62.40	380.35
2	Mrs J Pledger	1393	7.50	0.00	7.50
3	Goodwind Music Ltd	1394	1028.00	205.60	1233.60
3	Rosewood Academy of Music	1395	396.00	70.00	466.20
4	Mr H J Henkel	1396	1850.00	370.00	2220.00
5	Sarah Linklater	1397	620.00	124.00	744.00
		Totals	4219.45	832.00	5244.15

Check 5244.15

James W Lamb Sales Returns Day Book

Note that you are asked to use three analysis columns only. In practice separate columns for instruments and music might be appropriate.

Date	Customer	Credit Note number	Net	VAT	Total
xx1x			£	£	£
May 5	Mrs V Redbridge	12	365.00	73.00	435.00
5	Regis Music Ltd	13	7.50	0.00	7.50
		Totals	372.50	73.00	445.50	Check 445.50

2 a

James W Lamb Petty Cash Book

Receipts Date xx1x	amount £	Description	Payments Voucher number	Total £	VAT £	Postage/ carriage £	Cleaning £	Staff refreshments £	Sundry £	Purchase Ledger £
May 2	250.00	Opening balance								
2		Stamps, magazine	1	46.50	0.00	45.00			1.50	
2		Stationery	2	3.39	0.50				2.89	
3		Mop head, teabags	3	2.80	0.32		1.60	0.88		
4		Wages, S Button	4	15.00	0.00		15.00			
4		Window cleaner	5	25.00	0.00		25.00			
5		Milkman	6	2.97	0.00			2.97		
10		S&M News PL 516	7	19.57	0.00					19.57

Receipts Date	amount	Description	Payments Voucher number	Total	VAT	Postage/ carriage	Cleaning	Staff refreshments	Sundry	Purchase Ledger
xx1x	£			£	£	£	£	£	£	£
12		Training course ex	8	18.00	3.00				15.00	
17		Stamps	9	10.00	0.00	10.00				
19		Milkman	10	2.97	0.00			2.97		
23		Clock batteries	11	1.98	0.33				1.65	
24		Wages, S Button	12	15.00			15.00			
b	250.00			163.18	3.69	55.00	56.60	6.82	21.04	19.57
									Check	163.18

c <u>Petty Cash Reimbursement Request.</u>   Date 24 May xx1x

Expenditure from 2 May xx1x to 24 May xx1x   £162.76

signed .... Petty cashier

approved by .... Authorized signatory

Date 25 May xx1x

3

James W Lamb Cash Book

Received Date	Detail	Discount Received £	Bank £	Paid Date	Detail	Discount Allowed £	Bank £
xx1x				xx1x			
May 5	The Music Corner L	45.00	1455.00	May 2	Opening overdraft		407.40
6	Mrs T Kirby, Cash sale		37.50	3	British Telecom		697.25
12	Goodwind Music Ltd		572.16	3	H & B Publishing		215.00
17	Miss L M Sharp		93.27	4	Bullet Musical In		1497.20
17	Miss L Collins		372.55	12	Yamaha Instr. (UK)	24.80	595.20
19	Ms T P Rosalia, Cash sale		2470.00	19	Shimco UK Ltd	23.50	727.50
30	Dependable Insurance Co		102.56	28	HM Revenue and Customs		2460.23
31	Paul Harper, Cash sale		517.50	3	Westminster CC S.O.		242.00
11	Uni of Guildford CT		1597.23	26	Interest 20.2–19.5		14.62
				26	Charges 20.2–19.5		107.98
				31	Balance, carried down		253.39
		45.00	7217.77			48.30	7217.77

d

| June 1 | Balance, brought down | | 253.39 | | | | |

e

Bank reconciliation statement at 31 May xx1x

	£	£
Balance as shown by bank statement		2093.56
add items paid in but not on statement		
Dependable Insurance	102.56	
Paul Harper	517.50	
		620.06
		2713.62
deduct cheques not yet presented to bank		
HM Revenue and Customs		2460.23
Balance as in cash book		£253.39

THE ROYAL SOCIETY OF ARTS EXAMINATIONS BOARD
BOOK-KEEPING (204)
Stage II
(TIME ALLOWED – TWO HOURS)

You have TEN minutes to read through this question paper before the start of the examination.

You are encouraged to show your working for each question as marks will be awarded for method.

Marks will be lost for untidy work.

Answers should be written in ink pen or ballpoint pen.

Calculators may be used.

You should answer only those elements for which you require certification.

ELEMENT 1

You are an employee of Vigilant Alarms Ltd and you have to perform the following tasks:

a Write up the appropriate personal accounts in the ledgers provided in your answer book from the day books and the cash book. (Date order is not important.)

All opening balances are as at 3 April.

You should use the following accounts:

Purchase Ledger

Adel Plastics	– opening balance	£470.30 Cr
Electronic Systems	– opening balance	£329.12 Cr
Spark Components	– opening balance	£586.75 Cr

Sales Ledger

Auto Services	– opening balance	£696.48 Dr
Gibsons Garages	– opening balance	£485.25 Dr
Qwikfit Security	– opening balance	£373.96 Dr

b Correct the running balance after each entry.

c Write up the accounts in the nominal ledger provided in your answer book from the day books and the cash book. (Date order is not important.)

All the opening balances are as at 3 April.

You should use the following accounts:

Capital	– opening balance	£14 700.00 Cr
Equipment	– opening balance	£14 500.00 Dr
Rent	– opening balance	£1 000.00 Dr
VAT	– opening balance	£269.80 Cr
Purchases	– opening balance	£8 520.00 Dr
Purchase Returns	– opening balance	£194.00 Cr
Sales	– opening balance	£12 670.00 Cr
Sales Returns	– opening balance	£76.30 Dr
Discount Received	– opening balance	£147.43 Cr
Discount Allowed	– opening balance	£62.37 Dr

d Reconcile the supplier's statement of account with the personal account in the purchases ledger as at 30 April by completing the supplier's reconciliation statement in the answer book.

e Complete the purchase ledger control account in your answer book as at 30 April.

f Complete the sales ledger control account in your answer book as at 30 April.

g Balance the control accounts as at 30 April.

h Write up an accounts payable list as at 30 April using the form in your answer book.

i Write up an accounts receivable list as at 30 April using the form provided in your answer book.

ELEMENT 2

You are an employee of Broadway Fencentre, a small firm which does not use day books, and you have to perform the following tasks:

a Draft a trial balance using the form in the answer book as at 30 April from the set of accounts given below.

b These accounts contain two obvious errors. A further two errors are noted on the memorandum. Find the errors in the accounts and correct all four making appropriate entries in the journal using the form provided in the answer book.

c Produce a revised trial balance using the form in the answer book.

To be used when answering Element 1(c).

VIGILANT ALARMS LTD
PURCHASES DAY BOOK

Date		DETAIL	GOODS	VAT	INVOICE TOTAL
			£ p	£ p	£ p
Apr	3	Adel Plastics	118.25	23.65	141.90
	5	Electronic Systems	81.28	16.25	97.53
	10	Adel Plastics	125.00	25.00	150.00
	12	Spark Components	575.96	115.19	691.15
	24	Electronic Systems	142.18	28.43	170.61
	26	Adel Plastics	298.12	59.62	357.74
			1340.79	268.14	1608.93

VIGILANT ALARMS LTD
PURCHASES RETURNS DAY BOOK

Date		DETAIL	GOODS	VAT	INVOICE TOTAL
			£ p	£ p	£ p
Apr	10	Electronic Systems	29.45	5.89	35.34
	14	Adel Plastics	24.00	4.80	28.80
	27	Electronic Systems	54.30	10.86	65.16
			107.75	21.55	129.30

To be used when answering Element 1(c).

VIGILANT ALARMS LTD
SALES DAY BOOK

Date		DETAIL	GOODS	VAT	INVOICE TOTAL
			£ p	£ p	£ p
Apr	4	Gibsons Garages	277.02	55.40	332.42
	12	Auto Services	78.47	15.69	94.16
	17	Gibsons Garages	109.45	21.89	131.34
	19	Qwikfit Security	318.98	63.79	382.77
	24	Auto Services	220.68	44.13	264.81
	27	Qwikfit Security	328.00	65.60	393.60
			1332.60	266.50	1599.10

VIGILANT ALARMS LTD
SALES RETURNS DAY BOOK

Date		DETAIL	GOODS	VAT	INVOICE TOTAL
			£ p	£ p	£ p
Apr	21	Gibsons Garages	24.17	4.83	29.00
	28	Qwikfit Security	53.45	10.69	64.14
			77.62	15.52	93.14

To be used when answering Element 1.

VIGILANT ALARMS LTD
CASH BOOK

Date		DETAILS	DISCOUNT ALLOWED £	CASH £	BANK £	Date		DETAILS	DISCOUNT RECEIVED £	CASH £	BANK £
Apr	3	Balances b/d		470.20	3182.84	Apr	3	Rent			250.00
	4	Sales		94.15			3	Adel Plastics	23.52		446.78
	4	VAT		18.83			5	Bank c		500.00	
	5	Cash c			500.00		14	Spark Components	29.34		557.41
	7	Gibsons Garages	12.13		473.12		19	Purchases		124.80	
	12	Sales		272.00			19	VAT		24.96	
	12	VAT		54.40			21	Electronic Systems			329.12

Date		DETAILS	DISCOUNT ALLOWED £	CASH £	BANK £	Date		DETAILS	DISCOUNT RECEIVED £	CASH £	BANK £
	19	Auto Services			696.48		28	Adel Plastics	6.95		131.99
	24	Qwikfit Security			373.96		30	Balances c/d		259.82	3820.32
	28	Gibsons Garages	16.28		309.22						
			28.41	909.58	5535.62				59.81	909.58	5535.62
May	1	Balances b/d		259.82	3820.32						

To be used when answering Element 1.

To be used when answering Element (d).

		ADEL PLASTICS			
		34 Towers Lane			
		Leeds			
		West Yorkshire			
		LS16 8ER			

Tel No 0532 16194   VAT No 987 101 62

Our Ref: Date 30 April

STATEMENT OF ACCOUNT

of: Vigilant Alarms Ltd
   Control Works, Long Causeway, Leeds

Date		DETAIL	DEBIT £	CREDIT £	BALANCE £
Apr	1	Balance			470.30
	3	Sales	141.90		612.20
	7	Receipt		446.78	165.42
		Discount		23.52	141.90
	10	Sales	150.00		291.90
	21	Sales returns		28.80	263.10

Terms of trading: net 30 days

To be used when answering Element 2(a).

BROADWAY FENCENTRE
NOMINAL LEDGER

Date		DETAIL	DEBIT £	CREDIT £	BALANCE £
		Bank			
Apr	3	Capital	10 500.00		10 500.00 (Dr)
	3	Cash		400.00	10 100.00 (Dr)
	5	Delivery Van		3 500.00	6 600.00 (Dr)
	12	C Lapwell	295.00		6 895.00 (Dr)
	14	Machinery		1 250.00	5 645.00 (Dr)
	17	Timberland		470.00	5 175.00 (Dr)
	19	Rent		280.00	4 895.00 (Dr)
	26	Manorcraft	429.00		5 324.00 (Dr)
	26	Drawings		250.00	5 074.00 (Dr)
	27	Cash	750.00		5 824.00 (Dr)
	28	Wages		1 090.00	4 734.00 (Dr)
		Capital			
Apr	3	Bank		10 500.00	10 500.00 (Cr)
		Cash			
Apr	3	Bank	400.00		400.00 (Dr)
	5	General expenses		55.00	345.00 (Dr)
	8	Sales	570.00		915.00 (Dr)
	12	Drawings		200.00	715.00 (Dr)
	17	Purchases		145.00	570.00 (Dr)
	26	Sales	490.00		1 060.00 (Dr)
	27	Bank		750.00	310.00 (Dr)

Date		DETAIL	DEBIT £	CREDIT £	BALANCE £
		BROADWAY FENCENTRE			
		NOMINAL LEDGER (*Continued*)			
	28	Golden Acres	143.00		453.00 (Dr)
	29	General expenses		69.00	384.00 (Dr)
		Delivery Van			
Apr	5	Bank	3 500.00		3 500.00 (Dr)
		Machinery			
Apr	14	Bank	1 250.00		1 250.00 (Dr)
		General Expenses			
Apr	5	Cash	55.00		55.00 (Dr)
	29	Cash	69.00		124.00 (Dr)
		Rent			
Apr	19	Bank	280.00		280.00 (Dr)
		Drawings			
Apr	26	Bank	250.00		250.00 (Dr)
		Purchases			
Apr	3	Timberland	470.00		470.00 (Dr)
	5	C Woodside	360.00		830.00 (Dr)
	11	T Woodstock	165.00		995.00 (Dr)
	17	Cash	145.00		1 140.00 (Dr)
	18	T Woodstock	258.00		1 398.00 (Dr)

| | | BROADWAY FENCENTRE | | | |
| | | NOMINAL LEDGER *(Continued)* | | | |
Date		DETAIL	DEBIT £	CREDIT £	BALANCE £
	24	C Woodside	242.00		1 640.00 (Dr)
	28	C Woodside	298.00		1 938.00 (Dr)
		Purchase Returns			
Apr	17	C Woodside		50.00	50.00 (Cr)
	26	T Woodstock		45.00	95.00 (Cr)
		Sales			
Apr	3	C Lapwell		295.00	295.00 (Cr)
	5	Manorcraft		290.00	585.00 (Cr)
	7	Ranchstyle		284.00	869.00 (Cr)
	8	Cash		570.00	1 439.00 (Cr)
	10	Golden Acres		185.00	1 624.00 (Cr)
	14	C Lapwell		324.00	1 948.00 (Cr)
	17	Ranchstyle		179.00	2 127.00 (Cr)
	18	Manorcraft		175.00	2 302.00 (Cr)
	26	Cash		490.00	2 792.00 (Cr)
		Sales Returns			
Apr	14	Golden Acres	42.00		42.00 (Dr)
	21	Manorcraft	36.00		78.00 (Dr)
		Wages			
Apr	28	Bank	1 090.00		1 090.00 (Dr)

To be used when answering Element 2(a).

BROADWAY FENCENTRE
PURCHASE LEDGER

Date		DETAIL	DEBIT £	CREDIT £	BALANCE £
		Timberland			
Apr	3	Purchases		470.00	470.00 (Cr)
	17	Bank	470.00		NIL
		C Woodside			
Apr	5	Purchases		360.00	360.00 (Cr)
	17	Purchase returns	50.00		310.00 (Cr)
	24	Purchases		242.00	552.00 (Cr)
	28	Purchases		298.00	850.00 (Cr)
		T Woodstock			
Apr	11	Purchases		165.00	165.00 (Cr)
	18	Purchases		258.00	423.00 (Cr)
	26	Purchase returns	45.00		378.00 (Cr)

To be used when answering Element 2(a).

BROADWAY FENCENTRE
SALES LEDGER

Date		DETAIL	DEBIT £	CREDIT £	BALANCE £
		Golden Acres			
Apr	10	Sales	185.00		185.00 (Dr)
	14	Sales returns		42.00	143.00 (Dr)
	28	Cash		143.00	NIL
		C Lapwell			
Apr	3	Sales	295.00		295.00 (Dr)
	12	Bank		295.00	NIL
	14	Sales	324.00		324.00 (Dr)
		Manorcraft			
Apr	5	Sales	290.00		290.00 (Dr)
	18	Sales	175.00		465.00 (Dr)
	21	Sales returns		63.00	402.00 (Dr)
	26	Bank		429.00	27.00 (Cr)
		Ranchstyle			
Apr	7	Sales	284.00		284.00 (Dr)
	17	Sales	179.00		463.00 (Dr)

To be used when answering Element 2(b).

BROADWAY FENCENTRE

Memorandum

To: Book-keeper   Copy to: Accountant

From: Chief Clerk   Date: 5 May

Subject: Further errors discovered in the Ledgers

Two further errors have been discovered in the Ledgers. These errors are detailed below:

Error 1

Purchases on credit from T Woodstock had been incorrectly posted to the account of C Woodside. These purchases amounted to £242.

Error 2

Sales on credit to Ranchstyle amounting to £185 had not been entered in the sales account or in an account for Ranchstyle in the sales ledger.

SAMPLE SOLUTIONS

1 Vigilant Alarms Ltd

a & b Personal Accounts in the Purchase Ledger

Adel Plastics

Date	Details	Debit	Credit	Balance
		£	£	£
April 3	Opening balance			470.30 cr
3	Goods & VAT		140.90	611.20 cr
10	Goods & VAT		150.00	761.20 cr
14	Goods & VAT return	28.20		732.40 cr
26	Goods & VAT		357.74	1090.14 cr
3	Cheque	446.78		643.16 cr
3	Discount	23.52		619.84 cr
28	Cheque	131.99		487.85 cr
28	Discount	6.95		481.90 cr

Electronic Systems

Date	Details	Debit £	Credit £	Balance £
April 3	Opening balance			329.12 cr
5	Goods & VAT		97.53	426.65 cr
10	Goods & VAT return	35.34		391.31 cr
24	Goods & VAT		170.61	561.92 cr
27	Goods & VAT return	65.16		496.76 cr
24	Cheque	329.12		167.64 cr

Spark Components

Date	Details	Debit £	Credit £	Balance £
April 3	Opening balance			586.75 cr
12	Goods & VAT		691.15	1277.40 cr
14	Cheque	557.41		720.49 cr
14	Discount	29.34		691.15 cr

Personal Accounts in the Sales Ledger

Auto Services

Date	Details	Debit £	Credit £	Balance £
April 3	Opening balance			696.48 dr
12	Goods & VAT	94.16		790.64 dr
24	Goods & VAT	264.81		1055.55 dr
19	Cheque		696.48	358.97 dr

Gibsons Garages

Date	Details	Debit £	Credit £	Balance £
April 3	Opening balance			485.25 dr
4	Goods & VAT	332.42		817.67 dr
17	Goods & VAT	131.34		949.01 dr
7	Cheque		473.12	475.89 dr
7	Discount		12.13	463.76 dr
21	Goods & VAT return		29.00	434.76 dr
28	Cheque		309.22	125.54 dr
28	Discount		16.28	109.26 dr

Qwikfit Security

Date	Details	Debit £	Credit £	Balance £
April 3	Opening balance			373.96 dr
19	Goods & VAT	382.77		756.73 dr
27	Goods & VAT	393.60		1150.33 dr
24	Cheque		373.96	776.37 dr
28	Goods & VAT return		64.14	712.23 dr

c Nominal Ledger

Capital

Date	Details	Debit £	Credit £	Balance £
April 3	Opening balance			14 700.00 cr

Equipment

Date	Details	Debit £	Credit £	Balance £
April 3	Opening balance			14 500.00 dr

Rent

Date	Details	Debit £	Credit £	Balance £
April 3	Opening balance			1 000.00 dr
3	Cheque	250.00		1 250.00 dr

VAT

Date	Details	Debit £	Credit £	Balance £
April 3	Opening balance			269.80 cr
4	VAT on cash sales		18.83	288.63 cr
19	VAT on cash purchase	24.96		263.67 cr
12	VAT on cash sales		54.40	318.07 cr
30	VAT on credit purchase	268.14		49.93 cr
30	VAT on credit purchase return		21.55	71.48 cr
30	VAT on credit sales		266.50	337.98 cr
30	VAT on credit sales return	15.52		322.46 cr

Purchases

Date	Details	Debit £	Credit £	Balance £
April 3	Opening balance			8 520.00 dr
19	Cash purchases	124.80	0	8 644.80 dr
30	Credit Purchases	1 340.79		9 985.59 dr

Sales returns

Date	Details	Debit £	Credit £	Balance £
April 3	Opening balance			76.30 dr
30	Credit sales return	77.62	0	153.92 dr

Discount Allowed

Date	Details	Debit £	Credit £	Balance £
April 3	Opening balance			62.37 dr
30	Allowed in month	28.41	0	90.78 dr

Purchases Returns

Date	Details	Debit £	Credit £	Balance £
April 3	Opening balance			194.00 cr
30	Credit purchase return		107.75	301.75 cr

Sales

Date	Details	Debit £	Credit £	Balance £
April 3	Opening balance			12 670.00 cr
4	Cash sales		94.15	12 764.15 cr
19	Cash sales		272.00	13 036.15 cr
30	Credit sales		1 332.60	14 368.75 cr

Discount Received

Date	Details	Debit £	Credit £	Balance £
April 3	Opening balance			147.43 cr
30	Received in month		59.81	207.24 cr

d Reconciliation of suppliers statement with ledger account

Adel Plastics at 30 April	£	£
Balance on suppliers statement		263.70 cr
add Goods received, and VAT		357.74 cr
		620.84 cr
deduct Cheque in transit	131.99	
Discount allowed on it	6.95	
		138.94 dr
Balance in our purchase ledger		£481.90 cr

e

Purchase Ledger control account

Date	Details	Debit £	Credit £	Balance £
April 3	Opening balance			1 386.17 cr
30	purchase returns	129.30		1256.87 cr
30	credit purchases		1608.93	2865.80 cr
30	cheques	1 465.30		1400.50 cr
30	discount received	59.81		140.69 cr

f

Sales Ledger control account

Date	Details	Debit £	Credit £	Balance £
April 3	Opening balance			1 555.69 dr
30	sales returns		93.14	1 462.55 dr
30	sales	1599.10		3 061.65 dr
30	cheques		1 852.78	1 208.87 dr
30	discount allowed		28.41	1 180.46 dr

g The format Debit Credit Balance automatically provides a balance which is confirmed by the lists in **h** and **i**.

h Creditors' list as at 30 April

	£
Adel Plastics	481.90 cr
Electronic Systems	167.64 cr
Spark Components	691.15 cr
	£ 1340.69

agrees with control account

i Debtors' list as at 30 April

	£
Auto Services	358.97 dr
Gibsons Garage	109.26 dr
Qwikfit Security	712.23 dr
	1180.46

agrees with control account

2 a Broadway Fencentre Trial balance at 30 April

		originally	(c) revised
Bank	4 734	4 734	
Capital		10 500	10 500
Cash	384	384	
Delivery Van	3 500	3 500	
Machinery	1 250	1 250	
General expenses	124	124	
Rent	280	280	
Drawings	250	450	
Purchases	1 938	1 938	
Purchase returns		95	95
Sales		2 792	2 977
Sales Returns	78	78	
Wages	1 090	1 090	
Purchase ledger			
C Woodside		850	608
T Woodstock		378	620
Sales ledger			
Golden Acres	0	0	
C Lapwell	324	324	
Manorcraft		27	0
Ranchstyle	463	648	
	14 415	14 642	14 800	14 800

(balances)

b Journal entries

Date				dr	cr
April 30	dr	Manorcraft		27	
		Sales returns of 36 posted as 63			
		(21 April)			
	30	dr	Drawings	200	
			Cash withdrawal not posted		
			(12 April)		

(Note there is no credit entry for either of these debits)

	30	dr	C Woodside	242	
			T Woodstock		242
			incorrectly posted to the credit of C Woodside (memo from Chief Clerk 5 May)		
	30	dr	Ranchstyle	185	
			Sales		185
			item no recorded in Sales day book and therefore not included in sales or the sale ledger (memo from Chief Clerk 5 May)		

Index